AMERICA'S
50 SAFEST CITIES

AMERICA'S 50 SAFEST CITIES

DAVID FRANKE

ARLINGTON HOUSE·PUBLISHERS

NEW ROCHELLE, N. Y.

Manufactured in the United States of America

Library of Congress Cataloging in Publication Data

Franke, David.
    America's 50 safest cities.

    1. Cities and towns—United States. 2. Crime
and criminals—United States. I. Title.
HT123.F72   301.36'3'0973   73-21890
ISBN 0-87000-242-2

Table of Contents

take other factors into consideration—depending on the reason for your move, such factors as employment opportunities, housing, cost of living, and climate. (That's why I provide that information for the 50 safest cities.) But a community's crime-rate is just as important a consideration today, and by using this book you can find a new home where you can take a walk at night without first reviewing your will.

The Federal Bureau of Investigation asks all local police agencies to submit an annual report listing the number of offenses recorded during the preceding year in various categories of crime. Most police and sheriffs' departments comply with this request, and from these massive collections of figures the FBI compiles its annual study, *Crime in the United States, Uniform Crime Reports.* Published in that study are the figures on the number of crimes in seven major categories in all communities of 25,000 or more population. From these statistics, and from the crime statistics of communities of under 25,000 population (too numerous to be listed in the report), the FBI arrives at a rate of crime *per 100,000 inhabitants* for the United States in general, for the nation's metropolitan areas, for the nation's other (smaller) cities, and for our rural areas. It cannot, of course, claim to be totally accurate, for the FBI must depend on the accuracy of the reports it receives from the local police agencies. Also, it is known that the rate of crime in the major cities is considerably higher than the police records show, for in these areas crime is so prevalent that many incidents are not even reported to the police—the attitude seems to be, "What's the use, it just results in a lot of red tape and the police can't catch them anyway." The FBI report is, however, as accurate a compilation as is possible under those circumstances, and as such it is an immensely valuable one.

The charts in this book give the number of offenses in each of the major crime categories, for each community with a population of 50,000 or more, in 1970 and 1971—the most recent years for which information is available as we go to press. Having listed the *number* of offenses in each crime category, I then determined the population of the city and fed this information into a computer. The computer was programmed to use this data to project the community's *crime-rate per 100,000 population.* For example, if a city of 50,000 population has two forcible rapes in a year, that is a rate of four forcible rapes per 100,000 population. By projecting all statistics into rates per 100,000 population you can compare the crime-*rate* in each town with the crime-rate of the nation at large, and with the crime-rates in the nation's largest metropolitan areas. It is the *rate* that is important in figuring out your odds of being hit by a major crime, and as the charts in this book show, the odds are much more in your favor in some cities than in others.

How, then, can you use *America's 50 Safest Cities?* As an example, let us assume you are living in New York City. Having been mugged and burglarized, you decide you have had it, and you begin your search for a safe city. You can obtain a transfer with your company to its Cleveland office, but you look in the charts and note that Cleveland has a crime-rate even worse than New York's. Your eye wanders to Lakewood, Ohio, a pleasant, stable community bordering Cleveland to the west. You compare Lakewood's crime rate in 1971 with that of New York, and this is what you see as their *rates per 100,000 population:*

	Murder	Forcible Rape	Robbery	Aggravated Assault	Burglary	Larceny $50 & Over	Auto Theft
New York	18.6	30.7	1,131.1	430.4	2,304.7	1,585.6	1,228.1
Lakewood	0	1.4	35.6	27.1	212.3	74.1	404.7

You discover, therefore, that New York's burglary rate is more than ten times as great as Lakewood's; its level of grand larceny, more than 21 times as great; and its number of robberies per 100,000 inhabitants, more than 30 times as numerous. You notice that in Lakewood there is one serious crime for every 136.2 people during the course of a year, while in New York City there is a serious *reported* crime (and no telling how many unreported ones) for each 15.0 people. In other words, your odds of being hit by a major crime are at least nine times as great in New York City.

So why haven't you moved yet?

The Crime Categories

The categories of crime we consider consist of four groupings of violent crime (murder and nonnegligent manslaughter, forcible rape, robbery, and aggravated assault) and three categories of property crime (burglary, larceny of $50 and over, and auto theft). Here is how the FBI defines these categories:

Murder and nonnegligent manslaughter: All willful felonious homicides as distinguished from deaths caused by negligence. Excludes attempts to kill, assaults to kill, suicides, accidental deaths, or justifiable homicides. Justifiable homicides are limited to: (1) the killing of a person by a peace officer in the line of duty; (2) the killing of a person in the act of committing a felony by a private citizen. (The FBI goes on to define manslaughter by *negligence* as "any death which the police investigation establishes was primarily attributed to gross negligence of some other individual than the victim.")

Forcible rape: Rape by force, assault to rape, and attempted rape. Excludes statutory offenses (no force used—victim under age of consent).

Robbery: Stealing or taking anything of value from the person by force or violence or by putting in fear, such as strong-arm robbery, stickups, armed robbery, assault to rob, and attempt to rob.

Aggravated assault: Assault with intent to kill or for the purpose of inflicting severe bodily injury by shooting, cutting, stabbing, maiming, poisoning, scalding, or by the use of acids, explosives, or other means. Excludes simple assault, assault and battery, fighting, etc.

Burglary—breaking or entering: Burglary, housebreaking, safe-cracking, or any unlawful entry to commit a felony or a theft, even though no force was used to gain entrance and attempts. Burglary followed by larceny is not counted again as larceny.

Larceny—theft (except auto theft): Thefts of bicycles, automobile accessories, shoplifting, pocketpicking, or any stealing of property or article of value that is not taken by force and violence or by fraud. Excludes embezzlement, "con" games, forgery, worthless checks, etc. (The FBI divides larcenies into those $50 and over in value, commonly known as grand larcenies, and those under $50 in value, commonly referred to as petty larcenies. We include statistics only on grand larcenies.)

Auto theft: Stealing or driving away and abandoning a motor vehicle. Excludes taking for temporary or unauthorized use by those having lawful access to the vehicle.

America's 50 Safest Cities

The charts at the back of this book provide the crime-rates for *all* U.S. cities with a population of 50,000 or more. But it is the safest of these cities that interest us here, and so here you will find basic information about each of them to help you decide if you want to consider moving there.

Because a personal trip to each of these cities was out of the question financially, these brief chapters on the 50 safest cities are based not on personal evaluation, but on information gathered by mail and over the telephone—from chambers of commerce, city officials, police chiefs, and other sources. Employment opportunities, medical facilities, housing costs, recreation and culture—these are just some of the factors you will want to consider in making a move, and that is the type of information I tried to obtain.

A few miscellaneous notes are in order.

In regard to climate, many localities—especially those in a harsh climate—will fudge on the statistics they present in their literature. "Average summer temperatures" or "average winter temperatures" are virtually devoid of meaning. You don't want an overall "average" of both day and night temperatures over a period of several months—you want to know how cold it is likely to get at night in January, or how hot during the day in July. Thus the two most interesting statistics are the *mean daily minimum temperature in January* (the coldest month almost everywhere) and the *mean daily maximum temperature in July* (the hottest month nearly everywhere). I provide you with whatever information is available in the city's literature, but if the climatic data is vague, and you are fussy about your climate, you can bet further investigation is in order. The most sensible solution is to pay a personal visit to your prospective new home—during its worst season.

In providing information on transportation, I do not, as a general rule, mention bus service or any highways other than Interstates. It is presumed that all cities in this population range will have a number of state and federal highways bisecting them (consult a road map or atlas) and that they all have interstate bus connections.

The statistical tables at the end of each community's chapter consist of information obtained from 1970 U.S. Census publications.

And at the end of each city's chapter, I have provided the names and addresses of sources of further information, usually chambers of commerce. I list the various pieces of literature available, but please don't be greedy—ask only for those items you really need.

Happy hunting!

1 LAKEWOOD, Ohio

Lakewood, America's safest city, is a next-door neighbor to Cleveland, the 351st safest city—and *that's* not very safe. The oldest suburb in the metropolitan area, and the closest to Cleveland's downtown, Lakewood's three miles of Lake Erie shorefront are lined by high-rise apartments and middle-class to plush homes of modern, Colonial, Cape Cod, Greek revival, Tudor, and Georgian designs.

Bright mercury-vapor lights, a 75-man police force, and criminal files claimed by the Lakewood Police Department to be the best in the area all help to keep the crime-rate down. But Lakewood is safe in other respects too. Its community-owned and operated hospital has been extensively modernized. Four ambulances are on duty day and night. Project Pride is the city's program of inspecting all Lakewood homes for electrical, plumbing, heating, and structural defects—a far cry from the usual municipal indifference to such potential hazards. And Lakewood has earned 13 national awards as the "fire-safest city" in the 50,000 to 100,000 population bracket—no other city comes close. Indeed, Lakewood is one of the few cities of its size with a class-3 fire insurance rating.

With its central location and excellent transportation facilities, most of Lakewood's breadwinners commute to jobs in Cleveland and the surrounding area. The biggest local employer is Lakewood Hospital, with over 900 employees and an annual payroll of $5 million. One of the main industrial residents is Union Carbide, whose Lakewood plant has been manufacturing electronic and carbon components since 1889. The largest locally owned business is Bonne Bell (cosmetics), whose "Georgetown Row" home office is a splendid example of the pride Lakewood's firms and residents take in their city. The five adjoining structures in Georgetown Row recall the architecture of Old London, Philadelphia, or Georgetown. The first is of American Federal design; the second represents Dolly Madison's home; the third town house resembles an old apothecary shop and houses the Liberty Bell Boutique; the fourth is a likeness of No. 10 Downing Street, official residence of English prime ministers; and the fifth is representative of Pennsylvania Dutch architecture.

Typical of firms that have made the move from downtown Cleveland to Lakewood is the northeast Ohio office of Liberty Mutual Insurance. Why did they move? "I'll give you six reasons why," says district manager Dave Jansen. "First, rents are lower. We have plenty of space, and room to expand. Second, it's easier to get female clerks and typists. Many of our ladies walk to work. Some of the best work part-time. Third, this office is easier to reach from the turnpike, the airport, almost anywhere. No traffic jams. Fourth, we have a municipal parking lot behind us—important because a lot of our men are in and out several times a day. Fifth, improved security. Lakewood police check our doors regularly. We've never been broken into. Sixth, restaurants, hotels and motels are nearby for sales meetings. Lakewood solved a lot of our problems."

Of the single-family homes in Lakewood, 95 percent are owner-occupied. Explaining how he and his wife decided which suburb to live in, Ray Biesmeyer, district manager for *House & Garden,* recalls: "We started out by disappointing a couple of real estate men in Shaker Heights. We looked south of town, in Brecksville, and even farther out, in exurbia. But Lakewood appealed to us the first time we drove through. Funny thing—we were impressed by the way Lakewood homes and yards are maintained; yet, at the same time, we felt a lack of pretension. It didn't look as if there were two cars in every garage and a second mortgage on every house."

Others prefer the high-rise apartment buildings along Lakewood's "Gold Coast." Mr. and Mrs. Norman Shaw, for example. "Convenience to downtown, for one thing," replies Mr. Shaw when asked why they chose Lakewood. "I've cut my travel time from 45 minutes to 15," explains the associate editor of the *Cleveland Press.* "The bus service is so good—right from the door—we were able to get rid of one of our cars. And it's easy for us to go back downtown after dinner." Not many suburbanites can make that statement.

A recent addition in Lakewood is the Westerly, an ultramodern retirement-apartment complex. A full program of senior citizens activities is available next-door at the Barton Center.

Lakewood's public school system enrolls over 10,000 students, and comprises ten elementary schools, three middle schools, and Lakewood High School. When the Committee for Education (Geneva, Ill.) rated public high schools across the nation, Lakewood High was on its list of 44 outstanding ones. Its many special features include a planetarium, two professionally equipped theaters, a computer terminal, a reading-improvement center, a foreign language laboratory, driver-education simulators and range, horticulture greenhouse, a swimming pool, and an art gallery. Approximately two-thirds of its graduates go on to attend a four-year college or university.

Lakewood also has a Lutheran school (kindergarten through eighth grade), a Seventh-Day Adventist school (grades one through eight), four Catholic schools providing education in the first eight grades, and two Catholic high schools—one for boys, the other for girls.

A Lakewood branch of Cleveland State University offers freshman and sophomore courses. Commuting is easy to the dozen or so colleges and universities in the Cleveland area—among them Case Western Reserve University and John Carroll University.

Lakewood Hospital has 339 rooms and 47 bassinets, and a staff of 22 resident doctors, four interns, and 350 registered nurses, which is augmented by some 300 visiting physicians. Its modern facilities include nine operating rooms, an intensive-care unit with cardiac monitoring, an emergency department that handles some 20,000 cases a year, an X-ray department providing both diagnostic and therapeutic treatment, and an outpatient clinic. Also located in the city are two nursing homes and the Lakewood School of Practical Nursing, whose students get their clinical experience at the hospital.

Lakewood's mean annual temperature is 48.8 degrees, and the average annual rainfall is 35.4 inches. The city's altitude is 582 feet above sea level.

Connecting with the Northwest Freeway (Interstate 90), you can drive from Lakewood to New York City or Chicago without ever encountering a red light. The Cleveland Rapid Transit System has a subway station in Lakewood, which offers fast and inexpensive transportation to any part of the Cleveland area, including the airport. Even if you drive, Cleveland's Hopkins International Airport is just 15 to 20 minutes away.

The *Lakewood Sun Post* is a weekly newspaper, and residents receive full media coverage with Cleveland newspapers, radio stations, and television channels.

Lakewood's 38 churches represent a wide variety of faiths and denominations, and 90 percent of the city's residents have a church affiliation. Its public library has a collection of almost 200,000 volumes. Highlights of the cultural calendar range from the annual Great Lakes Shakespeare Festival, with 70 or more performances in Lakewood's Civic Auditorium, to the West Shore Concerts series of the Cleveland Symphony Orchestra. Also performing in Lakewood are various concert artists, the West Shore Choral, and the Lakewood Little Theater. Pop concerts are popular in the summer. The Cleveland Museum of Art has a branch gallery in Lakewood High

School, and the Lakewood Historical Society operates a museum in "The Oldest Stone House," built in 1838.

Lakewood's recreational facilities include eight parks with a total of more than 69 acres, two public swimming pools, the largest ice rink in the county, seven baseball fields and 14 softball fields, 21 tennis courts, a bowling green, and seven bowling alleys. Men, women, and children will all find a complete recreational program offered by the city, and in addition to public courses there are private golf courses at Lakewood Country Club and Westwood Country Club. The Cleveland Yacht Club is adjacent to Lakewood. Picnics are popular at Lakewood Park, on a promontory along Lake Erie, and adjacent to the city is Rocky River Valley, offering a complete escape from the urban bustle on nature trails and bridle paths or on its three golf courses. And for spectator-sports fans, Cleveland offers major league play in baseball, football, and hockey.

FOR FURTHER INFORMATION Write to the Lakewood Chamber of Commerce, 12506 Edgewater Drive, Lakewood, Ohio 44107, and ask for its 28-page illustrated color booklet on the city.

CITY/STATE: _____Lakewood, Ohio_____

POPULATION: ___70,173___ 1960–70 change: ___+6.1___%
___0.6___% non-white. ___14.7___% over 65.

REAL ESTATE: Median value, $___21,700___. ___48___less than $10,000, ___6,081___$10,000 to $25,000, ___2,552___$25,000 and over. Median gross rent, $___114___. ___4,751___less than $100, ___6,757___. $100 to $150, ___2,946___$150 and over.

EDUCATION: Median school years completed, ___12.4___. ___65.5___% high school graduates.

INCOME: Median family income, $___11,579___. ___6,850___less than $10,000, ___9,659___$10,000 to $25,000, ___1,280___$25,000 and over.

EMPLOYMENT: ___30,702___in labor force, ___27.0___% in manufacturing, ___2.7___% unemployed.

2 ROME, New York

With a slight decrease in population since 1960, Rome is going nowhere fast. But it does offer a nice central location in New York State with the Adirondack Mountains and lakes directly to the north.

Rome's location is the lowest pass in the entire north and south sweep of the Appalachian mountain system. Wood Creek, which flows into Lake Ontario, is just half a mile from the Mohawk River, which empties into the Hudson and provides a waterway to the ocean at New York City. To the Indians, the portage between Wood Creek and the Mohawk River was De-O-Wain-Sta, the "great carrying place." It was used by them for countless generations before the coming of the white man.

The pass was of great military importance during the French and Indian and Revolutionary wars. It was at Fort Stanwix (built to guard the pass), on August 3, 1777, that the Stars and Stripes was first displayed to an enemy in battle; and over the same fort three days later that captured enemy flags were first flown under the Stars and Stripes.

The chamber of commerce calls Rome "the copper city"; that refers not to the police but to the wire, cable, and related products manufactured here. Among the largest employers are Revere Copper and Brass (copper tubing, Revereware); Rome Cable (wire cables), General Cable (electric wire and cables), Rome Strip Steel Company (cold rolled steel), and the Pettibone Corporation (heavy road equipment). The largest employer in the area, actually, is Uncle Sam— at nearby Griffiss Air Force Base, the largest military complex in the state and home to four major air commands.

In agriculture, Oneida County ranks first in milk production and seventh in vegetable production in the state. Flowers and nurseries, as well as fruit orchards (mainly apples), are also important to the economy.

A recent issue of the local newspaper listed homes for sale at prices ranging from $19,500 to $43,000. Most local housing falls into the middle-income range of $12,000 to $30,000, and full basements and at least three bedrooms are standard. Two-bedroom apartments usually rent for $135 to $180.

James C. Dunn, Police Chief since 1948, is the senior chief of New York State's cities. He has high praise for the local judges, and while the department has detective and other specialized bureaus, he abhors bureaucratic cop-outs for the men on his force. Any of the 64 men may be assigned to general police work—"I believe that every police officer should be in a productive police assignment." And he asserts proudly that "never a dollar's worth of corruption has occurred in the Rome Police Department."

Rome's public school system includes 19 elementary schools, two junior highs, and one high school. Less than 3 percent drop out of school before graduation, and 60 percent of Rome's graduates continue their education. Also in the community are three Catholic elementary schools, a coed Catholic high school, the New York State School for the Deaf, and the Rome State School for the Retarded.

Mohawk Valley Community College, located 15 miles east in Utica, operates an extension campus in Rome. Syracuse University is only 40 miles away, and it operates a campus in Utica. The Upper Division College of the State University of New York is building a campus at nearby Marcy, with its temporary classrooms in Utica; other SUNY campuses in the area are at Oswego and Potsdam. Other central New York State colleges include Hamilton College and Kirkland College (Clinton), Colgate University (Hamilton), and Cornell University (Ithaca). Vocational and adult instruction is available from the Rome public school system, the Rome Art and Community Center, the YMCA-Womens Community Center, and the Area Occupational Center in Verona.

Practicing in Rome are 37 medical doctors and 27 dentists. Rome and Murphy Memorial Hospital is a city-operated 200-bed facility, and Rose Hospital is a new, privately owned, 50-bed general hospital. Many professional nursing homes are in the area, and the Rome City Health Clinic provides outpatient care.

The mean January temperature is 20.8 degrees, the mean June temperature 80.1 degrees. Mean annual precipitation is 41.9 inches. The altitude is 450 feet.

Rome is about eight miles from the nearest exit on the New York State Thruway. Oneida County Airport is home-base to Mohawk Airlines, and passenger service is also available on the Penn-Central Railroad.

Media outlets include the *Rome Daily Sentinel,* several radio stations (with many more stations received from outside the community), and six television channels (all networks received). Cabletron TV provides additional New York City channels, plus an educational TV channel.

Rome's churches include 33 Protestant congregations as well as five Roman Catholic parishes, one parish each of the Polish National

Catholic, Greek Catholic, and Greek Orthodox Catholic churches, and one Jewish synagogue. There are numerous clubs and organizations, some reflecting the large Italian and Polish populations. Cultural centers and attractions include the Jervis Library, the Rome Art Association, the Rome Art and Community Center, the Rome Community Theater, the Community Concert Group, and the Rome Civic Band and Civic Chorus. The Rome Historical Society maintains Fort Stanwix Museum.

Recreational facilities in town include eight playgrounds, two swimming pools, four wading pools, and an indoor skating rink, with organized sports and crafts for both adults and children. Rome has eight public and private golf courses, plus three bowling alleys. You will want to visit Fort Stanwix National Monument, the grave of Francis Bellamy (author of the Pledge of Allegiance) in Rome Cemetery, and the factory-outlet stores of Revereware (in Rome) and Oneida Silversmiths (in Sherrill).

Lake Delta State Park provides picnic areas, camping grounds, and hiking trails minutes from your home. Also nearby are the Yacht Club (north on Route 26) and the Snow Ridge and Woods Valley ski areas. And to the north are the famed Adirondack Mountains and lakes region, its woods thick with deer, partridge, and pheasant, and its streams stocked with trout.

FOR FURTHER INFORMATION Write to the Rome Chamber of Commerce, 127 West Liberty Street, Rome, N.Y. 13440, and ask for its 52-page illustrated color booklet on the city, published by Windsor Publications, *Facts and Figures About Rome, New York;* also available are *Share in "Our Goodly Heritage"* (a brochure on the Fort Stanwix Museum), *Discovering Your American Heritage* (a brochure on Fort Stanwix National Monument), *Places to Visit and Things to Do in Rome, New York—City of American Traditions, Educational Opportunities in the Rome-Griffiss AFB Community, Capsule Summary of 1970 Census Data, Community Economic Profile,* and the *Industrial Directory.*

CITY/STATE: _____Rome, New York_____
POPULATION: ___50,148___ 1960–70 change: ___-2.9___%
___4.3___% non-white. ___8.4___% over 65.
REAL ESTATE: Median value, $__14,800__. ___944___less than $10,000, __4,381__$10,000 to $25,000, ___661___$25,000 and over. Median gross rent, $__80_____. __3,699__less than $100, __1,227__. $100 to $150, ___185___$150 and over.
EDUCATION: Median school years completed, ___12.0___.
___50.9___% high school graduates.
INCOME: Median family income, $__9,185__. __6,464__less than $10,000, __4,788__$10,000 to $25,000, __401__$25,000 and over.
EMPLOYMENT: __14,995__in labor force, __27.0__% in manufacturing, ___6.5___% unemployed.

3 WEYMOUTH, Massachusetts

A residential community on Boston's South Shore, Weymouth apparently doesn't have as much to interest the criminal class as Boston itself or Cape Cod, the second-home mecca farther south. Solidly middle class, almost all of Weymouth's homes are valued between $10,000 and $25,000. A majority of the families have incomes in that range too, though a substantial number earn less than $10,000.

Police Chief Joseph B. O'Kane reports that Weymouth's "citizens take pride in their town form of government. This civic interest does much to shape the actions of the citizenry, particularly the youth, toward keeping Weymouth a good town in which to reside."

He also says that "it is our department policy to vigorously pursue the investigation of any and all crimes, particularly those which show any pattern of multiple offenses." It is the "certainty of apprehension" projected in Weymouth, he suggests, that gives "notice to the criminally inclined that they would do well to go elsewhere."

Chief O'Kane does add, however, that "of major administrative concern is the fact that for the fifth consecutive year, Weymouth's Police Department has lost experienced police officers to other police departments because of low salary rates. Eighteen men, on whom thousands of dollars in equipment and training have been spent, have now left the department because of this issue. Objective consideration must be given to increasing police salaries to a more competitive level."

The present salary range is from $7,911.80 to $15,431.

The Fire Department, a force of 120 full-time men, has inspected all homes in the town for potential fire hazards. Another of its programs has identified all homes in which an invalid, deaf, dumb, or blind person resides, who would require special help in case of fire or other emergency.

Weymouth's public school system, attended by 13,840 pupils, consists of two high schools, a vocational-technical high school, four junior highs, and 18 elementary schools. One of the junior high facilities burned down in 1971, causing a temporary system of double shifts at another of the schools. Weymouth also has parochial schools, which enroll 1,843 students.

Tufts Library in Weymouth has more than 130,000 volumes and 2,000 records. The Weymouth Art Association, Weymouth Historical Society, and numerous other groups add to the cultural life of the community. The recreational program ranges from crafts, tennis, and archery to sailing instruction, swimming lessons, lifesaving classes, and ice skating. Special programs are available for the mentally retarded and physically handicapped, and a nature center has been established at one of the parks. Numerous leagues utilize the baseball and softball diamonds, one of which has lights for nighttime ball. Three beaches are open to the public in Weymouth.

CITY/STATE: _____Weymouth, Massachusetts_____

POPULATION: ___54,610___ 1960-70 change: ___+13.4___ %
___0.5___% non-white. ___8.4___% over 65.

REAL ESTATE: Median value, $___19,900___. ___212___ less than $10,000, ___8,359___ $10,000 to $25,000, ___2,000___ $25,000 and over. Median gross rent, $___136___. ___1,131___ less than $100, ___1,199___. $100 to $150, ___1,639___ $150 and over.

EDUCATION: Median school years completed, ___12.4___.
___67.5___% high school graduates.

INCOME: Median family income, $___11,631___. ___4,934___ less than $10,000, ___7,985___ $10,000 to $25,000, ___596___ $25,000 and over.

EMPLOYMENT: ___22,196___ in labor force, ___23.9___ % in manufacturing, ___2.8___ % unemployed.

4 UTICA, New York

Utica is 14 miles from Rome, our second-safest city, so they must be doing something right in central New York State. On the other hand, Utica's population is decreasing even faster than Rome's, so maybe both the bad guys and the good guys are trying to tell us something. There was a loss of 8.8 percent between 1960 and 1970, when the population rested at 91,611.

There is one good reason why crooks wouldn't be interested in Utica: there isn't that much to steal. A majority of the families have less than $10,000 annual income—a distinction shared only by Rome and Provo among the ten safest cities. Utica seems to have a generally blue-collar and ethnic coloration; Polish and Welsh foreign-language newspapers are published here, and less than half the population has a high school diploma.

While crime is low, it does exist, and Utica made the newspapers several times during 1973. A massive drug raid led to the arrest of 36 young persons, capping a four-month investigation by 90 policemen of the New York State, Utica, and Rome forces. Another headline-maker was the trial of four Utica men on charges of loan-sharking, with a grenade thrown in an FBI agent's home in New Hartford, a suburb described in chamber of commerce literature as "delightfully rural, quiet and peaceful."

Local industries range from appliances and beer to Sturdy Togs. General Electric plants produce radio receivers (enough to make this the radio capital of the world), tape recorders, and youth electronics equipment. The Univac Division of Sperry-Rand manufactures computer components. In aerospace accessories, there's the Bendix Corporation; in machine tools and heavy equipment, Chicago Pneumatic and Kelsey-Hayes. Other manufacturers include Dunlop (tire fabrics), Bossert Manufacturing (precision metals fabrication), Allegheny Ludlum (space-age metals), Horrocks-Ibbotson (fishing tackle), and Utica Duxbak (sporting attire). More well-known names are Utica Cutlery, Westinghouse, IBM, International Heater, Continental Baking, Sealtest (Dairylea), and Utica Club beer. Utica Mutual, Commercial Travelers, and other insurance firms make Utica their home too.

The Colonial motif prevails in both new and old housing. Prices range from $12,000 to $80,000, but a majority of homes are in the

$15,000 to $25,000 range. Especially attractive residential areas are found in the small suburban towns of New Hartford, Whitesboro, and the beautiful college-town of Clinton, where home prices range from $18,000 to $40,000 and up. Utica and its suburbs also have garden apartments featuring separate buildings, playgrounds, garages, and other amenities, with most two-bedroom units renting from $135 to $350.

The city's public school system comprises 21 elementary schools and three high schools. There are 13 parochial grade schools and three parochial high schools. Mohawk Valley Community College is in Utica, while Utica College (a branch of Syracuse University) is in New Hartford. Clinton is home to Hamilton College for men and Kirkland College for women. Many students commute to classes at Syracuse University, 50 miles west on the New York Thruway.

About 200 physicians, 130 registered nurses, and 120 dentists practice in Utica. Three hospitals—St. Luke's, St. Elizabeth, and Faxton—have a total bed capacity of 825, and two state mental hospitals are in the area. A Masonic home and hospital for the aged and infirm is located in East Utica, and a few miles west is an Eastern Star home and infirmary.

The January mean temperature is 20.8 degrees, with the highest mean monthly temperature being 80.1 degrees in June. Mean annual precipitation is 41.9 inches.

Utica lies directly on the New York Thruway. The Penn-Central Railroad has passenger service, and the world headquarters of Mohawk Airlines is at Oneida County Airport, which offers 30 passenger flights daily.

Two Gannet daily newspapers, the *Daily Press* (mornings) and the *Observer-Dispatch* (afternoons and Sundays), are published in Utica. The city has four AM and two FM radio stations, plus a television station affiliated with NBC and ABC. Schenectady and Syracuse television channels are also received, and 10 channels are available over cable TV.

The Munson-Williams-Proctor Institute is a Utica cultural center for all the visual arts. It sponsors a college-level school of the fine arts and a Victorian restoration, Fountain Elms, which serves as a museum and houses a school of the applied and decorative arts. Programs are sponsored by the 80-piece professional symphony orchestra and an opera guild, civic musical society, choral society, civic band, theater league, and community theater. Utica is a regular stop for the Boston "Pops" Orchestra, the Boston Symphony, the Metropolitan Opera, and Broadway road-shows. The library houses 142,000 volumes.

In the area are 16 Roman Catholic churches, 53 Protestant churches of many denominations, and seven synagogues—Orthodox, Conservative, and Reform.

The city has a wide range of recreational activities and facilities, including a week-long Winter Carnival in February. Utica is a world-renowned curling center, and international bonspiels are held here. Then there are the many attractions of the Adirondacks—a dozen ski areas within a 50-mile radius; fishing, swimming, and boating in the lakes that dot the area; deer, partridge, and pheasant country everywhere; and the famous Adirondack Trail for campers, hikers, and mountain climbers.

FOR FURTHER INFORMATION Write to the Greater Utica Chamber of Commerce, 1401–1410 First National Bank Building, Utica, N.Y. 13501, and ask for its 152-page color booklet, *An Adventure in Living;* also available are *Antique Country, Upper Mohawk Valley—A Place for All Seasons, Winter in Utica, Homes for Living,* and folders on the Munson-Williams-Proctor Institute and Utica Club brewery tours.

CITY/STATE: Utica, New York
POPULATION: 91,611   1960–70 change: -8.8 %
  5.9   % non-white. 15.0   % over 65.
REAL ESTATE: Median value, $ 16,300 . 1,233 less than $10,000, 6,963 $10,000 to $25,000, 1,184 $25,000 and over. Median gross rent, $ 71 . 12,792 less than $100, 1,774 . $100 to $150, 418 $150 and over.
EDUCATION: Median school years completed, 10.8 .
 42.1 % high school graduates.
INCOME: Median family income, $ 9,008 . 12,824 less than $10,000, 9,080 $10,000 to $25,000, 517 $25,000 and over.
EMPLOYMENT: 35,169 in labor force, 29.6 % in manufacturing, 6.6 % unemployed.

5 NASHUA, New Hampshire

There is nothing stagnant about Nashua: its population exploded 42.8 percent in the last decade, to 55,820. On the Massachusetts border, it is nicely situated for easy access to Boston (39 miles south), the White Mountains, and the Maine coast. Winter sports benefit from an annual snowfall of more than 70 inches.

Nashua is an industrial city, with half the work force engaged in manufacturing, and half of that unionized. There is very little unemployment. Electronics equipment is the largest industry, with shoes, paper goods, machinery, plastics, and wood and metal products also important. A Federal Air Traffic Control Center employs 760. Like most New England industrial towns, there is a varied ethnic mix—in this instance, French, Irish, Greek, Lithuanian, Polish.

Among the 128 manufacturers in the area, the largest are Sanders Associates (electronics), Nashua Corporation (copy paper and other products), J.F. McElwain Company (men's shoes), Improved Machinery (machinery), Sprague Electric Company (resistors), Doehla Greeting Cards (cards and stationery), and Hampshire Manufacturing Corporation (camping and beach toys).

Agricultural activities in the area include apple and peach orchards, truck gardening, and dairy farming. There is some granite production too.

Many of the homes in Nashua and its suburbs have been built in the last ten years. Building costs per square foot range from a low of $16 to a high of $20. The typical lot is 100 feet by 100 feet in size, costing $6,000. Approximately 7,500 rental units are also available.

Craig D. Sandler, Chief of Police, thinks the "biggest single factor" behind Nashua's low crime-rate is probably that "the Nashua police are free from local politics with regard to enforcement policy." Since 1913, he notes, "the department has been governed by a three-man Police Commission which is appointed by the governor of the state. They have powers to set compensation, hire and dismiss as the situation may dictate, and establish rules and regulations as necessary." The result? "This system has allowed the police to meet community needs on a constant basis. As the community has grown so has the quantity and quality of enforcement."

Chief Sandler adds that "the police have also enjoyed the position of being respected by the citizens, which has resulted in support of all law enforcement programs introduced in recent years. We are indeed fortunate in this respect."

The Nashua public schools include 11 elementary schools, two junior highs, and one high school, with another high school and two elementary schools being built. There are also a number of parochial elementary schools and two parochial high schools, one for boys and the other for girls. Institutions of higher learning in Nashua are Rivier College, a four-year liberal arts college for women; Daniel Webster Junior College; and the New Hampshire Vocational-Technical Institute. Within a 20-mile radius are the University of New Hampshire at Manchester; St. Anselm's College; Notre Dame College; the State College of Lowell, Mass.; Lowell Tech; and the Northeastern University extension at Burlington, Mass.

Medical facilities include Nashua Memorial Hospital and St. Joseph's Hospital, plus several nursing and convalescent homes.

January's average temperature is 17.2 degrees, July's 69.2 degrees. November is the wettest month, April the driest. The average annual snowfall is 70.25 inches, with an average annual precipitation of 37.94 inches.

Nashua is located nine miles off Interstate 93, and limousine service is available to Boston's Logan Airport. The *Nashua Telegraph* is a daily newspaper, with Boston and Manchester newspapers also circulated in town. The city has two radio stations and a television channel, which can be received by cable hookup; Boston television channels are also received.

The 29 churches in Nashua and the five in nearby Hudson represent Roman Catholic, Baptist, Methodist, Congregational, Greek Orthodox, Community, Advent Christian, Christian Science, Christ, Episcopal, Lutheran, Nazarene, Unitarian, and nonsectarian congregations. There is also a Jewish synagogue. More than 100 fraternal societies, clubs, and organizations are active. Cultural activities are presented by the Arts and Science Center, Community Concerts, the Nashua Symphony Orchestra, the Theater Guild, the Artists Association, the Nashua League of Arts and Crafts, the Nashua Historical Association, the Nashua Symphony Choral Group, and the Roode Gallery.

Recreational facilities include 22 parks and playgrounds, a municipal swimming pool, indoor and outdoor movie theaters, bowling alleys, a city-owned tennis court, a privately owned indoor tennis court, a sports arena, a YMCA-YWCA, and a country club with an

18-hole golf course, with three more golf courses nearby. Summer outdoor concerts and an outdoor art exhibit are popular, and many other attractions are within an easy drive from Nashua—to Boston, the Maine coast, or the beautiful White Mountains and lakes of New Hampshire.

FOR FURTHER INFORMATION Write to the Greater Nashua Chamber of Commerce, 78 Main Street, Nashua, N.H. 03060, and ask for its map of the city, *Nashua Facts and Figures* (a folder), the *Registered Community Audit*, a *Manufacturers Directory*, and fact-sheets on real estate firms, sales statistics, and miscellaneous information.

CITY/STATE: Nashua, New Hampshire
POPULATION: 55,820 1960-70 change: +42.8 % 0.8 % non-white. 8.5 % over 65.
REAL ESTATE: Median value, $19,300. 292 less than $10,000, 6,278 $10,000 to $25,000, 1,594 $25,000 and over. Median gross rent, $86. 3,928 less than $100, 1,674. $100 to $150, 1,005 $150 and over.
EDUCATION: Median school years completed, 12.2. 56.5 % high school graduates.
INCOME: Median family income, $10,866. 5,921 less than $10,000, 7,485 $10,000 to $25,000, 525 $25,000 and over.
EMPLOYMENT: 23,326 in labor force, 46.8 % in manufacturing, 2.7 % unemployed.

6 EUCLID, Ohio

Beware of calling Euclid a suburb of Cleveland. It may be just a few miles east of the big city, but Euclid has grown into an independent base. In fact, residents of many nearby suburbs come to Euclid rather than Cleveland for their jobs. Euclid does not depend on Cleveland for anything except its water supply.

On the shores of Lake Erie, without which the ecologists would have a crisis gap, Euclid is about as developed as it can get—only a couple of hundred undeveloped acres remain. That can be highly desirable from a standpoint of taxes and services, for it means that the city can concentrate on maintenance rather than building. Euclid's sewers, water lines, streets, and recreation facilities have been built and most will be paid for within the next ten years.

Nearly 150 manufacturing plants are located in Euclid, and they contribute 60 percent of the taxes received by the city. Among the major employers are the Addressograph Division of the Addressograph-Multigraph Corporation; Euclid, Inc., a subsidiary of White Motor Corporation (off-highway haulage equipment); the Euclid plant of General Motors' Fisher Body Division (automobile-trim fabrication and warehousing); General Electric's Refractory Metal Products Department; the Gould, Inc., Advanced Technology Group (anti-submarine-warfare systems and devices); Lincoln Electric Company (welders, electrodes, welding supplies); Motch & Merryweather Machinery Company (machine tools and saw blades); Reliance Electric Company (automation systems and equipment); and the headquarters of TRW, Inc. (jet aircraft-engine components).

A wide range of housing is available. A recent issue of the *Euclid News Journal* listed many properties, mostly in the $25,000 to $35,000 price range but with a good number costing $15,000 to $25,000 and a few ranging up to $90,000. For $33,900, for example, you could move into a four-bedroom Tudor with a 25-foot living room (with log fireplace), formal dining room, den, fenced lot, and convenient location near the main park. And $29,900 would get you a three-bedroom Colonial off Lake Shore Boulevard with 1 1/2 baths, living room with fireplace, basement, recreation room, and two-car garage.

The city has a rigid housing-inspection ordinance, requiring that every home be inspected before it can be sold. If not sold, it must be reinspected every 90 days.

Euclid has the largest police force in the county outside of Cleveland. Frank W. Payne, Chief of Police, sees the "omnipresence of uniformed police" as the most tangible factor in keeping the crime-rate low. "Our patrol cars are assigned to geographical beats with other cars overlapping into two or more beats," he explains. "Criminals observing a patrol car passing a particular area cannot assume that the time is ripe to commit a crime. Other police cars may be in the same area at any moment."

Similarly, "When a crime does occur our policy is to dispatch every available police car to the general area of the crime scene so that an apprehension can be made if at all possible. Again, this method discourages other persons who may be inclined to commit crimes when they witness this police show of strength."

The public school system consists of one senior high school, three junior high schools, and 11 elementary schools. About half of the faculty have master's degrees or above, and enrollment in the public system is 10,928. Parochial schools enroll another 2,818 students.

Medical facilities include Euclid General Hospital, with 375 beds; Euclid Clinic Foundation; and three medical clinics (two of them industrial clinics).

The city is at an altitude of 700 feet above sea level. Average annual precipitation is 33.5 inches.

As part of the Cleveland metropolitan area, Euclid is accessible to that city's major airport and to Interstates 90 (the Lakeland Freeway), I-71, I-77, and I-271. In addition to its own weekly newspaper, the *Euclid News Journal*, residents receive three Greater Cleveland dailies and all the radio and television stations of the area.

Euclid has more than 20 churches, representing Christian and Missionary Alliance, Assembly of God, Baptist, Catholic, Disciples of Christ, Christian Science, Episcopal, Lutheran, United Methodist, Presbyterian, and United Church of Christ congregations. A Jewish temple is also located in Euclid.

Cleveland offers many cultural advantages, but Euclid also has its Civic Chorus, Civic Orchestra, Cultural Council, Dance Association, Historical Society, Little Theater, Lyric Guild, Organ Society, Swing Era Band, Jadran Singing Society, Lincoln Players, and Three Arts Club. Among the many other organizations active in the city, ethnic ones include the Croatian Cultural Club, the Slovan Singing Society, and the Slovene Junior Chorus.

For $1.50 a year, a Euclid resident can obtain a pass that enables him to participate in most of the city's recreation programs at no extra fee. The parks and playgrounds include more than 30 acres of lakeshore property, and facilities range from 35 tennis courts (13 lighted) to 17 basketball courts (three indoors), an ice skating rink, ten swimming pools, six men's hardball diamonds (one lighted), and 14 softball diamonds (four lighted).

FOR FURTHER INFORMATION Write to the Euclid Chamber of Commerce, 22578 Lake Shore Boulevard, Euclid, Ohio 44123, and ask for its *Statistical Analysis, Apartments in Euclid, Euclid Ohio Schools, Churches, Euclid Clubs*, and the *Commercial and Industrial Directory*.

CITY/STATE: Euclid, Ohio
POPULATION: __71,552__ 1960-70 change: __+13.6__ %
__0.9__ % non-white. __9.2__ % over 65.
REAL ESTATE: Median value, $__23,000__ . __77__ less than
$10,000, __8,443__ $10,000 to $25,000, __4,652__ $25,000 and
over. Median gross rent, $__136__ . __1,802__ less than $100,
__5,444__ . $100 to $150, __3,152__ $150 and over.
EDUCATION: Median school years completed, __12.2__ .
__59.6__ % high school graduates.
INCOME: Median family income, $__11,830__ . __6,972__ less than
$10,000, __11,951__ $10,000 to $25,000, __951__ $25,000 and over.
EMPLOYMENT: __33,382__ in labor force, __43.7__ % in manufacturing, __2.5__ % unemployed.

7 PROVO, Utah

Provo is one of the few cities outside the Northeast or Midwest to make our list of safest cities, and we undoubtedly have the Mormons to thank for that. While Cambridge and Berkeley are among the most dangerous cities in the nation, conservative, peaceful Provo is home to an equally large but vastly different academic population—Mormon-run Brigham Young University and the 22,000 students that make it the largest private university in the United States.

There are 53,131 residents in addition to the students, and they have one of the lowest family-income averages of the safest cities—$7,167 a year—yet this is a city without slums. Unemployment is high, but if you're out of a job you can rest in the sun, which shines 72 percent of the possible time, or take advantage of the 12,000-foot-high snowcapped peaks outside the city, or the spectacular Utah Canyonlands and national parks to the south.

The Geneva Plant of U.S. Steel Corporation, largest steel mill west of the Mississippi, is the major employer in Provo. Other industries range from heavy industrial plants like Pittsburgh–Des Moines Steel and Pacific States Cast Iron Pipe Company to fabricating firms like

Barbizon Corporation (women's lingerie) and Signetics Corporation (microscopic electronics systems for space and industry).

Utah County is also the leading agricultural county in the state. It produces more strawberries, raspberries, apples, pears, and prunes than the rest of the state combined. It ranks first in the production of peaches and cherries. In addition it produces sugarbeets, vegetables, canning crops, hay and grain, livestock, poultry, and dairy products.

According to Mayor Verl G. Dixon, "Housing costs are average. A comfortable three-bedroom home can be purchased for around $30,000. Rentals for a two-bedroom apartment or home would be around $125 upward. Taxes are generally below the average for comparable communities."

Police Chief Jesse W. Evans, discussing the lack of crime with me, placed greatest emphasis on the city's many programs to combat juvenile delinquency. During the 1940s and early 1950s, he said, "we had a tremendous crime problem of malicious destruction of property and many burglaries. We learned that the majority of the crimes were being committed by juveniles and teenagers." The police, courts, civic groups, churches, service clubs, schools, and parks department put together an ambitious youth program that is still in effect, and their cooperation is paying dividends today.

"When problems arise that involve our youth in a delinquency problem," Evans says, "we notify the parents to either bring or send the child to police headquarters for an interview with a detective. When questioning a suspect that is in class at one of the public schools, we dispatch a plainclothes officer to the school in an unmarked police car and the child is called into a room where the officer is awaiting him for an interview.

"During the interview of any suspect," he adds, "a written statement of purported facts is taken and reduced to writing. In cases involving juveniles, a written statement is furnished the Juvenile Court on each and every juvenile handled. In those cases set by the court for official hearing, either one or both parents or guardian must accompany the child to court. Our policy of referring all delinquent children to the court leaves no chance for people to accuse the Provo Police of showing favoritism to any particular person or group."

Utah leads all states in the average years of school completed, and Provo is especially high, with a median figure of 13.3. The city's public school system consists of ten elementary schools, two junior high schools, and one high school. There is also a Seventh-Day Adventist

School. Huge Brigham Young University has already been mentioned. Another 2,400 students attend Utah Technical College in Provo.

Fifty-nine physicians and surgeons and 37 dentists practice in Provo. Among the medical facilities is Utah Valley Hospital.

The sun shines 325 days a year, and the residents enjoy 72 percent of possible sunshine. With an altitude of 4,553 feet above sea level, Provo has low humidity in all seasons—relative humidity at noon is a low 45 percent. In 1970, the hottest days were 99 degrees, the coldest −2 degrees. Provo is so dry, however, that even when winter temperatures fall below freezing, there is no frost. Low-temperature periods are brief, and deep snow seldom remains long. Average annual precipitation is around 13 inches.

Located 44 miles south of Salt Lake City, Provo is served by Interstate 15. Its local newspaper is the *Daily Herald*.

With a major university in town, cultural activities are plentiful. A university symphony orchestra, a concert band, many choruses, guest appearances by major-city orchestras, a Community-University Lyceum, the nearby Springville Art Gallery—these are just some of them. The libraries, both public and university, have a total of way over 500,000 volumes.

The Church of Jesus Christ of Latter Day Saints is dominant, of course, but various Protestant denominations and the Catholic faith are also represented by the community's churches.

The city's recreational program is extensive, and the municipal golf course (there are three additional courses in the area) hosts dozens of tournaments, five golf leagues, and three clinics annually. An active senior citizens program has 1,000 members participating.

Few cities in the country offer such a variety of natural and accessible recreational opportunities as does Provo. Nestled between the majestic Wasatch Mountains and Utah Lake, the city maintains mountain parks a few miles out of town. Adjacent to spectacular Mt. Timpanogos are 23 developed campgrounds and numerous scenic wonders—among them Timpanogos Cave National Monument, Deer Creek Dam and Lake, Bridal Veil Falls (with a 430-foot drop), and the Sundance ski area. Deer, pheasant, quail, ducks, and geese are close at hand, and in the mountain wilderness you'll find deer, elk, cougar, and bear. The Provo River is noted for its fine catches of German Brown and Rainbow trout. Catfishing is popular on Utah Lake in summer, bass can be taken in winter, and early spring brings the Walleye run on the lower Provo River.

FOR FURTHER INFORMATION Write to the Provo Chamber of Commerce, P.O. Box 738, Provo, Utah 84601, and ask for *Statistics* (information-sheets), the *Provo City Street Guide*, and *Discover Provo, Utah*, an illustrated color brochure.

CITY/STATE: Provo, Utah
POPULATION: __53,131__ 1960-70 change: __+47.4__ %
__1.8__ % non-white. __5.3__ % over 65.
REAL ESTATE: Median value, $__17,600__. __515__ less than $10,000, __3,195__ $10,000 to $25,000, __1,329__ $25,000 and over. Median gross rent, $__82__. __4,345__ less than $100, __1,188__. $100 to $150, __727__ $150 and over.
EDUCATION: Median school years completed, __13.3__.
__78.7__ % high school graduates.
INCOME: Median family income, $__7,167__. __6,821__ less than $10,000, __2,982__ $10,000 to $25,000, __321__ $25,000 and over.
EMPLOYMENT: __18,395__ in labor force, __12.8__ % in manufacturing, __6.7__ % unemployed.

8 GREENWICH, Connecticut

Greenwich is perhaps the biggest surprise on this list. After all, affluence attracts criminals and Greenwich is estate country. Then there are the spoiled and bored children of the executive class—and juvenile delinquency and drug usage are said to be rampant on the Connecticut Gold Coast. Maybe they're too stoned by now to cause any trouble.

Greenwich is the sort of town where a network of bridle trails affords about the only way to see many of the beautiful estates; where there are several hundred *private* fire hydrants; and where the police have a Scuba Team on duty. And as the town's chamber of commerce puts it, "There is no heavy industry in Greenwich and therefore no noise or odors." It does have a flourishing retail trade, however, as well as professional offices, light industry, and technical-research laboratories. In recent years many corporate headquarters have been moved to Greenwich, and the city now is home to such companies as Chesebrough-Pond, U.S. Tobacco, and the General Reinsurance Corporation.

In addition to its physical beauty, Greenwich's appeal to the executive class includes the lack of a state income tax and the relatively low local taxes. The community is on a pay-as-you-go basis, with the cost of schools and other public buildings as well as all welfare and relief costs being paid out of current income.

The U.S. Census statisticians, you will note, apparently gave up trying to figure the median value of Greenwich homes; it is listed merely as "$50,000 plus." (Even back in 1970, there were 10,635 houses worth $25,000 or more compared with 526 valued at less than $25,000. And 5,000 Greenwich families had an income of $25,000 or more annually.)

The police force has 147 persons on its rolls. There are also special officers, patrolling various residential sections, who work in cooperation with the police department.

In education, there are 12 elementary schools, three junior highs, and one high school. These are supplemented by 15 independent and parochial schools with a combined private registration of over 5,000 pupils.

Greenwich Hospital has 350 beds and 34 bassinets, and such advanced facilities as a cobalt-therapy unit, an intensive-care unit, a modern teaching auditorium, and an extensive medical library. The outpatient department has more than 30 clinics.

The Boston Post Road (Route 1), Merritt Parkway, and Connecticut Turnpike all cut through town. Greenwich is also on the New Haven line of the Penn-Central Railroad, and has a daily newspaper, *Greenwich Time*. Reception of New York City television and radio stations is excellent.

There are 35 churches and chapels in Greenwich representing nearly all denominations, and more than 150 civic, social, and neighborhood associations. Its library has over 217,000 volumes. A variety of cultural activities are sponsored by the Connecticut Playmakers of Old Greenwich, the Greenwich Art Society, and other groups. Bruce Museum contains a number of valuable exhibits, and the Greenwich Historical Society is located in the Bush-Holley House, classified by the National Trust as one of the nation's 300 most important historic buildings.

Greenwich recreation facilities include nine golf and country clubs; five boat and yacht clubs; several riding clubs; a number of beach clubs; tennis clubs; lawn bowling, rifle club, and skeet clubs; and one municipal golf club. The city also owns four beaches, all restricted to the use of residents and their guests. One of them is an island two miles out in Greenwich harbor. The town operates two boats on a half-hourly schedule to and from the island between June and September.

FOR FURTHER INFORMATION Write to the Chamber of Commerce of the Town of Greenwich, Inc., Greenwich, Conn. 06830, and ask for *Facts About Greenwich, Connecticut.*

CITY/STATE: __Greenwich, Connecticut__
POPULATION: _59,755_ 1960–70 change: _+11.1_ %
_2.5_ % non-white. _11.0_ % over 65.
REAL ESTATE: Median value, $_50,000+_. _9_ less than $10,000, _517_ $10,000 to $25,000, _10,635_ $25,000 and over. Median gross rent, $_147_. _886_ less than $100, _1,818_. $100 to $150, _2,528_ $150 and over.
EDUCATION: Median school years completed, _12.8_. _71.8_ % high school graduates.
INCOME: Median family income, $_18,024_. _3,463_ less than $10,000, _7,213_ $10,000 to $25,000, _4,993_ $25,000 and over.
EMPLOYMENT: _24,646_ in labor force, _22.0_ % in manufacturing, _2.4_ % unemployed.

9 FLORISSANT, Missouri

Florissant is one of those "cities" that wasn't there the last time you looked: it grew 72.7 percent between 1960 and 1970, and back in 1950 it was a small town of 3,737. Today a suburban neighbor of St. Louis and Missouri's fifth largest city, it is primarily residential, with a great many shopping areas. The new population explosion is deceptive, however, for Florissant has been around for a very long time.

In Florissant, for example, you will find the oldest Catholic edifice between the Mississippi River and the Rockies, built in 1819-20. Jesuit Father Pierre Jean DeSmet, the beloved Black Robe of the Indian nations, was ordained at Old St. Ferdinand's in 1827 and used Florissant as his base of operations. St. Stanislaus Seminary is a Jesuit Novitiate established in 1823. Sacred Heart Church (the German Church) was established in 1866, and the First Protestant Church in Florissant was built around 1895. There is even a link with the Spanish—the front portion of Casa Alvarez, which was built about 1790 for Eugene Alvarez, military storekeeper for the King of Spain, and which is open by appointment. At least seven Revolutionary War soldiers are believed to be buried in Cold Water Cemetery, and a number of old Florissant homes are also standing—bearing birthdates of 1830, 1836, and 1856. The Florissant Valley Historical Society has restored one aristocratic structure, Taille de Noyer, and opened it to the public. With its earliest section dating back to 1790, it is believed to be one of the oldest remaining homes in St. Louis County.

If the town has an old lineage, its present population is young—with a median age of 21.3 years, compared to 29.5 for the nation. Most breadwinners commute to work elsewhere—Florissant has no major industries, but is close to a dense industrial area just outside the city limits. Almost all the homes are valued between $10,000 and $25,000, and almost all the families have annual incomes in that range.

D.L. Brazie, the Planning and Research Officer for the Police Department, says: "Although we have an excellent record of crimes cleaned up, averaging between 30 percent and 50 percent in our cleanup rate, we concentrate on the preventative side of law enforcement. One method which we feel has been effective has been the use of the ten-hour-day, 40-hour-week schedule for the members of the uniformed patrol. In the use of this schedule, the prime hours from 8 P.M. to 2 A.M. are covered by a double shift of men, thus allowing one man assigned to a patrol sector to concentrate on patrol while another man assigned to the same sector handles calls for police service. Also we carry on a constant program of public education. That is, we attempt to educate the public in what they themselves can do to help prevent crime.

"We know for a fact that our preventative patrol methods work," Brazie adds, "as we have had professional criminals, apprehended for other offenses, admit to us that they have planned burglaries and robberies in our city and then abandoned the plans because 'too many cops come around too often.' Of course, the fact that we have a reputation for a high rate of crimes cleaned up is also a deterrent to those who would otherwise commit a crime here."

The Florissant area is served by two public school districts, with 35 elementary schools, six junior highs, three high schools, and two special schools for the physically and mentally handicapped between them. Also in the area are one Lutheran and eight Catholic elementary schools, a Catholic high school, and a preparatory seminary. Florissant Valley Community College enrolls over 9,000 students, and St. Louis Christian College is a four-year Bible college. Gateway College of Evangelism is affiliated with the United Pentacostal Church, which has established its world headquarters in Florissant. And a few miles away in St. Louis are many more educational institutions, among them the University of Missouri—St. Louis, St. Louis University (Jesuit), and Washington University, noted for its medical and law schools.

Medical facilities in the Florissant Valley include 255-bed Christian Hospital Northwest, with another hospital in the planning stage. A number of medical, osteopathic, and chiropractic clinics are in the area.

In addition to three local newspapers, the area is served by St. Louis newspapers, radio stations, and television stations. The St. Louis County Library District operates a Florissant Valley Branch.

Florissant has many organizations, including a number devoted to the preservation and operation of the community's historical sites, and its 39 churches represent Assembly of God, Church of Christ, Baptist, Methodist, Lutheran, Catholic, Nazarene, Christian, Community, Presbyterian, Episcopal, and Unitarian congregations.

Florissant's six major parks and seven neighborhood parks are unequaled in the county, with extensive facilities ranging from swimming pools and gymnasiums to barbecue and picnic areas. The city's pride is 55-acre Sunset Park, a forest preserve and wildlife refuge located on the Missouri River bluffs. Here you can see a large expanse of the river, and walk down to its banks.

Sports are emphasized in the Florissant Valley's recreational life— and in one recent year, the area produced the National Junior College soccer champions, the Missouri High School Athletic Association soccer champions, and the Flower Bowl football champions. Florissant is home to the St. Sabina Invitational Junior Soccer Championships, the Flower Bowl Football Festival, and the Amateur Softball Association of America National 16-inch Slow-Pitch Championships—and claims to have more organized boys and girls baseball, softball, soccer, ice hockey, football, and bowling teams than any other place, anywhere. Nonathletic annual events in the area include Missouri's Junior Miss Pageant, the Valley of Flowers Festival, a Fourth of July fireworks display, a Fall Festival, a Festival of Fun, and, during the Christmas season, the Home and Business Lighting Contests.

FOR FURTHER INFORMATION Write to the Florissant Chamber of Commerce, 1060 Rue Ste. Catherine, Florissant, Mo. 63031, and ask for its *Municipal Information* leaflet, *Directory of Florissant Churches, Schools and Organizations, Business and Professional Directory, Green Line Tour of Florissant;* and the folder on Taille de Noyer.

CITY/STATE: Florissant, Missouri
POPULATION: __65,908__ 1960-70 change: __+72.7__%
__0.5__% non-white. __3.1__% over 65.
REAL ESTATE: Median value, $__18,000__. __109__ less than $10,000, __12,627__ $10,000 to $25,000, __1,234__ $25,000 and over. Median gross rent, $__132__. __175__ less than $100, __1,650__. $100 to $150, __511__ $150 and over.
EDUCATION: Median school years completed, __12.4__. __65.7__% high school graduates.
INCOME: Median family income, $__12,452__. __4,364__ less than $10,000, __10,882__ $10,000 to $25,000, __497__ $25,000 and over.
EMPLOYMENT: __24,717__ in labor force, __32.9__% in manufacturing, __3.6__% unemployed.

10 WESTLAND, Michigan

Incorporated only recently, in 1966, Westland is a bedroom community on the southwestern edge of the sprawling Detroit metropolitan region. In 1960 it didn't exist. In 1970 its population was 86,749, and zooming upward.

Driving time to downtown Detroit is a half-hour or less, so many commute to jobs there or elsewhere in the metropolitan area. General Motors does have a Chevrolet Warehouse in Westland, however, and the Oxbow Machine Company, R & A Tool Company, and other small industrial companies offer some local employment opportunities.

The price-range for housing in 1970 and 1971 showed 9 percent selling for $14,000 to $17,000; 15 percent in the $17,000 to $20,000 range; a major proportion, 46 percent, priced at $20,000 to $26,000; 16 percent costing $26,000 to $32,000; and 14 percent priced at $32,000 or more. Most apartment rentals range from $165 to $250 per month. Some have swimming pools, club houses, air-conditioning, and other attractions.

Located in the heart of the city is the modern Westland Shopping Center, home of J.L. Hudson and other popular stores. Modern and comfortable facilities for shopping are available within the enclosed complex.

The Wayne County-Westland Community School District enrolls over 23,000 pupils. There are two senior high schools, five junior highs, and 26 elementary schools, with adult education, special education, and junior college programs available to residents.

Area medical facilities include Wayne County General Hospital, Parkview General Hospital, and Annapolis Hospital. Westland also has five small medical clinics, two convalescent homes, two nursing homes, and an emergency squad.

Interstate 94 runs just to the south of Westland, I-96 to the north, and the proposed I-275 will run along its western limits. Bus service is available, and the huge Metropolitan Airport is just four miles south of Westland. In addition to community newspapers, residents receive Detroit newspapers, radio stations, and television channels.

One of Westland's major assets runs through its center—the William P. Holliday Nature Park, 500 acres of wildlife reserve with 10 miles of trails. In the northern section of the city is the Edward P. Hines Parkway, a recreational area equipped with facilities for picnics and other outdoor activities. A few miles south is Belleville Lake, a popular playground for boating, fishing, and water skiing. Recreational programs are offered by the city's Recreation Department, youth athletic associations, the Little League, hockey associations, the YMCA, and others.

Westland's 28 churches represent many denominations, and the array of organizations include Rotary, Lions, Masons, Knights of Columbus, Oddfellows, Jaycees, veterans organizations, Business and Professional Women, Soroptimist, Senior Citizens, youth groups, and many others.

Saundra Weed, Executive Secretary of the Westland Chamber of Commerce, proudly asserts that "Westland has a great bunch of citizens. The chamber office constantly receives phone calls from churches and youth groups offering volunteer help anywhere they are needed. Our community also provides our citizens a variety of activities that promote good old-fashioned community spirit."

As examples, she notes that the city sponsors an annual Spring Festival (50,000 participated this past year), a symphony orchestra, and an annual Christmas tree lighting ceremony. Senior citizens programs are being set up. And the chamber sponsors a Christmas carol pageant and Christmas parade to promote city pride.

FOR FURTHER INFORMATION Write to the Westland Chamber of Commerce, 33250 Warren Road, Westland, Mich. 48185, for *Westland Basic Information, History of Westland, Westland Apartments,* and its *Industrial List.*

CITY/STATE: Westland, Michigan
POPULATION: __86,749__ 1960–70 change: __Not Inc.__%
__3.1__% non-white. __3.9__% over 65.
REAL ESTATE: Median value, $__21,500__. __444__ less than $10,000, __11,837__ $10,000 to $25,000, __3,434__ $25,000 and over. Median gross rent, $__162__. __603__ less than $100, __1,529__. $100 to $150, __3,536__ $150 and over.
EDUCATION: Median school years completed, __12.2__. __56.9__% high school graduates.
INCOME: Median family income, $__12,687__. __5,719__ less than $10,000, __14,213__ $10,000 to $25,000, __667__ $25,000 and over.
EMPLOYMENT: __31,758__ in labor force, __41.7__% in manufacturing, __3.8__% unemployed.

11 ARLINGTON, Massachusetts

Arlington proudly refers to itself as the "birthplace of Uncle Sam," and if you thought Uncle Sam was just a cartoonist's creation—well, you have a second thought coming. Uncle Sam's real name was Samuel Wilson, he was born in Arlington, and during the war of 1812 he was a slaughterhouse operator (in Troy, New York), selling meat to the Army. All his meat was stamped with the initials *U.S.* for "United States," but the soldiers soon decided that the letters really stood for "Uncle Sam" Wilson, and he soon became a popular symbol. Uncle Sam was clean-shaven in the original cartoons, and dressed in a top hat and tail coat. The red pants were added during Andrew Jackson's presidency, and the beard during the Civil War.

Around 1638 the area that later became Arlington was purchased—as part of Cambridge—from Squaw Sachem for $10 and a new coat every winter. A mill site led to the town's development, and as it was a stopover point on the road to Boston, many taverns were built. It was at the Black Horse Tavern that the "Committee of Safety" was meeting on April 18, 1775, and high losses were suffered as the British marched through. Jason Russell and 11 others defending his home were killed. Today you can visit the site of the Black Horse Tavern (it is marked at 333 Massachusetts Avenue), the Jason Russell House on Jason Street, and the Old Burying Grounds where the early patriots rest. And you won't want to miss the site where the first prisoners of the Revolution were taken—by a grandmother.

Today's Arlington is primarily a residential community, though there is some light industry. The population is overwhelmingly Democratic in registration, and almost half is of foreign stock—mostly Canadian, Irish, Italian, English, and Swedish.

In 1970, a total of 594 firms employed over 4,000 persons and had a payroll of around $27 million. Wholesale and retail trade was the most important segment of the economy, followed by the service industries and the construction industry. Many residents, of course, find employment in Boston or elsewhere in the metropolitan area.

Arlington is a settled community, with approximately three-quarters of its homes built before 1940. A majority of the dwellings are single-family homes, but a good number (32.7 percent) are two-family dwellings. Of the occupied units—and there are very few vacancies—66 percent are owner-occupied, 34 percent rented.

The Police Department consists of the chief, two captains, eight lieutenants, 12 sergeants, and 67 patrolmen. Departments include a detective bureau, a traffic enforcement and safety bureau, a record bureau, and a juvenile bureau.

Ferdinand A. Lucarelli, Chief of Police, stresses the role of education in his department. "We maintain an in-service training program which has been in effect since 1968," he says. "This program keeps our personnel abreast of all new laws, procedures, Supreme Court decisions, and other law enforcement-related subjects.

"About 51 percent of our force," he adds, "are presently enrolled in universities and community colleges for study toward an associate degree in law enforcement. This is done on their own time. We take advantage of all seminars and courses offered by federal and state law enforcement agencies by having as many of our personnel attend as possible."

In regard to anticrime programs, Chief Lucarelli reports that "the department has initiated a 'Project Identification' program, whereby it loans to residents of the town an instrument to inscribe their Social Security number on all their easily removable property, and then list the property and numbers with this department. This project is meant to discourage house breaks.

"I cannot pinpoint any one thing" that results in the low crime, he concludes, "but I would say that the dedication shown by our officers in their chosen field of law enforcement does definitely have a bearing on our showing."

About 9,600 students attend the city's public schools, with another 2,000 in the parochial system. Arlington Technical and Vocational High School is located here, and the many higher educational facilities of the metropolitan Boston area are within easy commuting distance.

Arlington Hospital is a fully accredited institution, and again there is a wealth of facilities available in the metropolitan area.

The average temperature in January is 27.7 degrees, in July 72.0 degrees. Average annual precipitation is 43.02 inches.

Arlington offers easy access to Boston, seven miles east, mostly by Routes 2 and 3. Route 128, circling the metropolis, is also easily accessible, as is Logan International Airport. Boston newspapers, radio stations, and television channels are received here.

Many parks and playgrounds have been built, and winter skating is popular on the four lakes within the city limits. The Robbins Library and its branches house 140,000 books, and community activities include the Golden Age Club, the Arlington Philharmonic Society, and "Friends of the Drama." Residents also have available all the cultural, athletic, and recreational attractions of the Boston area.

FOR FURTHER INFORMATION Write to the Arlington Chamber of Commerce, 1052 Massachusetts Avenue, Arlington, Mass. 02174, for its brochure, *Arlington, Mass.—In Pace with History,* and for the monograph on Arlington published by the Massachusetts Department of Commerce and Development.

CITY/STATE: ___Arlington, Massachusetts___
POPULATION: ___53,524___ 1960-70 change: ___+7.1___ %
___1.0___ % non-white. __14.0__ % over 65.
REAL ESTATE: Median value, $__25,800__. ___16___ less than $10,000, __3,428__ $10,000 to $25,000, __3,883__ $25,000 and over. Median gross rent, $__143__. __1,214__ less than $100, __2,835__. $100 to $150, __3,136__ $150 and over.
EDUCATION: Median school years completed, __12.5__.
__71.6__ % high school graduates.
INCOME: Median family income, $__12,247__. __4,727__ less than $10,000, __8,520__ $10,000 to $25,000, __899__ $25,000 and over.
EMPLOYMENT: __23,266__ in labor force, __19.1__ % in manufacturing, __2.7__ % unemployed.

12 WEST HARTFORD, Connecticut

One of New England's most beautiful cities also ranks as one of its safest. West Hartford is basically a residential suburb in the Hartford metropolitan area, with most of its breadwinners working as executives in the area's insurance companies and industries, or as professional people. The 1970 census revealed that over 70 percent of the city's working population is engaged in technical and professional, managerial, sales, or other white-collar occupations.

In addition to its role as a plush bedroom community, however, West Hartford does have some industry of its own. Some of the larger firms and their products include the Pratt & Whitney and Chandler-Evans companies (machine tools, gauges, aircraft accessories), Dunham-Bush, Inc. (commercial refrigeration), Holo-Krome Corporation (socket screws), Wiremold Company (electrical outlets), Jacobs Manufacturing Company (chucks), Colt Industries (firearms), and Whitlock Manufacturing Company (coiled heating units).

West Hartford is primarily a community of single-family homes located in uncrowded neighborhoods. Because of farsighted planning, there is a minimal amount of traffic congestion and a virtual absence of blighted or deteriorated areas. The value of the homes ranges from $28,000 to over $100,000 and new homes are generally priced $55,000 and up. Efficiency apartments rent from $115 to $165 monthly, and a four- or five-room apartment varies from $175 to as high as $550 monthly in a new luxury apartment house.

Uniformed patrol is the major activity of West Hartford's Police Department. Constant 24-hour police vigilance is provided by the ten foot and nine motor patrols covering the nine geographic areas of the town.

Based on overall student rankings on national achievement tests, West Hartford's public school system ranks among the top 1 percent of all school systems nationwide. It has the lowest dropout rate in the state, and over 80 percent of its graduates continue their education. In addition to the public system of 16 elementary schools, four junior high schools, and two senior high schools, there are three parochial elementary schools, one parochial high school, and 11 private schools. Also located in West Hartford are various branches of the University of Connecticut (including its Law School), the University of Hartford, and St. Joseph College. Trinity College and Hartford College for Women are in the immediate area.

Residents of the city are within a ten-minute drive of four major hospitals, including Hartford Hospital, one of the nation's largest, with 1,024 beds. Adjacent to the city in Farmington is the new $60 million University of Connecticut Health Center, housing the university's School of Medicine and School of Dental Medicine, a 200-bed teaching hospital, ten medical and ten dental outpatient clinics, and extensive medical and dental research facilities.

West Hartford also boasts some of the finest shopping facilities in the state, with a well-developed town center and three major shopping plazas serving various neighborhoods. Since the town center is just four miles west of the center of Hartford, there is easy access to the stores and offices there, including those in the modern Constitution Plaza.

Interstate 84 bisects the city, and Bradley Field, a major international airport, is a half-hour from the center of West Hartford. The *West Hartford News* is a weekly, and the area is served by Hartford's two dailies, five radio stations, and five television channels.

Recreation in the city is varied and highly developed, with facilities that include five parks, 13 neighborhood playgrounds, 22 small greens, nine softball and 11 baseball diamonds, one indoor and four outdoor swimming pools, 33 tennis courts, an indoor skating rink, four outdoor skating ponds, a supervised area for coasting activity and ski instruction, and two public and two private golf courses. The public library has over 200,000 volumes. With a program as broad as the interests of its residents, the Department of Parks and Recreation presents such activities as a ground flight school, a horsemanship course for local students, self-defense training for teenagers and housewives, a riflery program for teens, a cross-country and pre-ski fitness program for ladies, and a safe-sailing course. An intensive swimming program includes learn-to-swim classes, recreational and competitive programs, preschool adjustment classes, synchronized swimming and diving classes, scuba diving instruction, and lifesaving and instructor courses.

West Hartford is ideally and centrally located in New England— the ocean beaches of Long Island Sound are about 80 miles and an hour's drive away, and Boston and New York, both slightly over 100 miles distant, are easily accessible through the Interstate system of highways. Within a comfortable driving distance are the Berkshire Mountains, Green Mountains, and White Mountains.

FOR FURTHER INFORMATION Write to the Office of the Town Manager, Town Hall, 28 South Main Street, West Hartford, Conn. 06107, for *A Look at West Hartford.* Write to the West Hartford Chamber of Commerce, 29 North Main Street, West Hartford, Conn. 06107 for *Our Town,* a booklet published by the *West Hartford News.*

CITY/STATE: ___West Hartford, Connecticut___
POPULATION: __68,031__ 1960–70 change: __+9.1__ %
__0.7__ % non-white. __15.2__ % over 65.
REAL ESTATE: Median value, $__33,100__ __23__ less than $10,000, __3,202__ $10,000 to $25,000, __12,188__ $25,000 and over. Median gross rent, $__148__ . __682__ less than $100, __2,043__ . $100 to $150, __2,496__ $150 and over.
EDUCATION: Median school years completed, __12.8__ . __73.8__ % high school graduates.
INCOME: Median family income, $__15,451__ . __4,160__ less than $10,000, __10,277__ $10,000 to $25,000, __3,929__ $25,000 and over.
EMPLOYMENT: __29,504__ in labor force, __18.0__ % in manufacturing, __1.8__ % unemployed.

13 GREEN BAY, Wisconsin

In 1634, just 14 years after the Pilgrims landed at Plymouth Rock, French explorer Jean Nicolet stepped from his birch-bark canoe onto the shore of the Green Bay of Lake Michigan, and claimed the area in the name of his king. Others followed and soon Green Bay was a busy fur-trading center for the Northwest Company. With the Northwest Ordinance of 1787, the territory, including present-day Wisconsin, was annexed to the United States.

Green Bay today is an industrial and manufacturing center with a population of over 160,000 in its metropolitan area. A major Great Lakes seaport, ships from around the world reach it via the St. Lawrence Seaway. Yet it is probably best known around the country as the home of the Green Bay Packers. The Packers claim numerous professional football titles, and every year all 56,262 seats of Lambeau Stadium are sold out—all on a seasonal basis.

"Season tickets are a subject for divorce cases around here," quips Don Russell of the chamber of commerce. "Who cares about the kids—it's who gets the tickets!"

Football-mad Green Bay also serves as the port of entry for northern Wisconsin's hunting and fishing country, and for the wild Upper Peninsula of Michigan. Just north of the city are the fast-flowing waters of the Wolf River, winding its way through stately stands of Norway pine, hemlock, spruce, and birch. Farther up are the North Woods—a fish and game paradise of dense pine and birch forests threaded with a network of lakes, rivers, and streams. And still farther north, Lake Superior's rugged Apostle Islands and Pictured Rocks National Lakeshore. To the northeast, jutting out into Lake Michigan, is the Door Peninsula, with a variety of sandy beaches, a picturesque rocky coastline, and villages and white church steeples reminiscent of New England.

Green Bay's principal industry is papermaking. The city has four large paper mills, three pulp mills, and four paper-converting companies. Fort Howard Paper Company, with a work force of 1,800, is the largest employer in town. Other major paper-products plants are those of the American Can Company, Charmin Paper Products Company, and Green Bay Packaging.

Nonelectrical machinery and food processing are also major industries. The city has three food-canning and food-packing companies with nationwide distribution. Northwest Engineering Corporation and the Paper Converting Machine Company are among the machinery manufacturers. Other important industries are furniture factories, automobile parts plants, cold storage plants, dairy products plants, and fisheries.

There are over 45,000 dwelling units in the metropolitan area, and for $25,000 one can purchase a fairly nice home. Older two- or three-bedroom homes are also available, at prices beginning around $12,000. Two-bedroom apartments usually rent for $150 to $175, duplexes for $135 or $140.

Belgian, Dutch, French, German, and Polish are the most prevalent nationality backgrounds of Green Bay's citizens. (In fact, Green Bay is the only place I've found where *Belgians* are the butt of ethnic jokes!) Some persons attribute the low crime-rate to this ethnic background. Elmer A. Madson, the Chief of Police, takes another approach by noting that "we have a very localized population. And our geographical location does not lend us readily to association with other cities in the high-crime areas. By localized population, I mean that most of our people are second, third, and fourth generation. And although the city has grown substantially, a large part of this is normal and has not been caused by any sudden influx or industrial expansion."

Another factor behind the low crime-rate, he says, "would have to be economic. Green Bay is the center of an agricultural area but also has very diversified industrial activity. This diversification naturally provides fairly steady income and resulting living conditions."

Chief Madson adds that "our police planning and organization are also involved. We have public relations areas in the student groups, both at the University of Wisconsin in Green Bay and in our local high schools, with police and student representatives meeting as a body to discuss possible problems and methods of cooperating to prevent them." The public is also involved with the police through such programs as the auxiliary force, driving roadeos for young people, and hunter safety classes. "These create a citizen backing for the police which aids tremendously in enforcement."

In Green Bay's public school system, there are 29 elementary schools, four junior highs, and four high schools. Parochial schools consist of 14 grade schools and two high schools. Higher education facilities include the University of Wisconsin at Green Bay, St. Norbert College, and the Northeast Wisconsin Technical Institute.

Green Bay's major hospitals have a bed capacity of over 900. Two of them, a Lutheran and a Catholic hospital, are across the street from each other and share their more expensive equipment, thus freeing money for expansion of other facilities. In addition, the area has 19 nursing homes with more than 1,200 beds. Practicing in Green bay are 121 physicians and 71 dentists.

The climate consists of "four distinct seasons," as the chamber of commerce puts it, and no doubt the most distinct season of all is winter—with a January mean temperature of 7.2 degrees. Average annual precipitation is 27.87 inches, average annual snowfall, 39.9 inches. Green Bay's altitude is 582 feet above sea level.

Air passenger service consists of some 30 flights daily by North Central Airlines. Green Bay has two daily newspapers, the *Press-Gazette* and the *Daily News.* It has three AM radio stations, two FM stations, three local television stations (affiliates of each of the networks), and an educational television channel.

The 77 churches represent 22 denominations, and the population is about 60 percent Catholic, 25 percent Lutheran, and 5 percent Jewish, with the balance made up of various other denominations. The libraries house over 238,000 volumes. Cultural fare is served by the Neville Public Museum, the Next Door Theater, the Green Bay Community Theater, the Brown County Civic Music Association, the Green Bay Symphony Orchestra, and the University of Wisconsin campus. The city provides a full year-round recreational program, and more than 230 clubs and organizations offer plenty of opportunities for a wide variety of community and social activities.

FOR FURTHER INFORMATION Write to the Green Bay Area Chamber of Commerce, 400 South Washington Street, Green Bay, Wis. 54305, and ask for its two illustrated folders, *Green Bay Wisconsin—The Gateway to the Great Seaway* and *Green Bay Map & Street Guide;* also available are *Welcome to the Friendly Green Bay-Depere Area* (an information folder), *Green Bay Fact Summary,* and information-sheets on Green Bay's history, industries, tax rates, and the economy in general.

CITY/STATE: _____Green Bay, Wisconsin_____

POPULATION: __87,809__ 1960-70 change: __+39.6__ %
__1.1__% non-white. __9.5__% over 65.

REAL ESTATE: Median value, $__15,800__. __1,911__less than $10,000, __12,080__$10,000 to $25,000, __1,440__$25,000 and over. Median gross rent, $__85__. __5,419__less than $100, __2,396__. $100 to $150, __644__$150 and over.

EDUCATION: Median school years completed, __12.2__. __57.7__% high school graduates.

INCOME: Median family income, $__9,975__. __10,487__less than $10,000, __9,814__$10,000 to $25,000, __575__$25,000 and over.

EMPLOYMENT: __33,332__in labor force, __27.2__% in manufacturing, __4.3__% unemployed.

14 BRISTOL, Connecticut

Located midway between Boston and New York, and 18 miles west of Hartford, Bristol is home to three large international concerns—the New Departure-Hyatt Bearings Division of General Motors (ball and roller bearing manufacturers), the Associated Spring Corporation (world's largest producer of precision-mechanical springs), and the Superior Electric Company, manufacturers of special motors and tape-controlled machinery.

Arthur J. Crowley, Sr., Community Development Coordinator, reports:

"We are proud of our fine educational system, and our Bristol schools rate among the finest in New England. Sixteen public and six parochial schools and a new regional Catholic high school provide an excellent educational climate in our city.

"Our city government is the mayor-council type and is a well-administered management team. Our conservative policies last year produced a $638,000 surplus, and city spending has been reduced without any alteration in services. New methods of increasing our tax-base, reducing unemployment, and providing additional services for senior citizens, youth, and the handicapped are constantly being studied and improved.

"The 27 places of worship represent most denominations. Most of these churches are new and add much to the architectural beauty of the community.

"Bristol has an excellent hospital and recently increased the number of beds to 275 with new and expanded facilities, with special emphasis on emergency and outpatient treatment, laboratories, and the X-ray department.

"The hospital's educational program includes a school for X-ray technicians, as well as practical nurse and intern training programs. It houses an auditorium with a seating capacity of 125, which provides an excellent facility for medical seminars, staff meetings, and so forth.

"Bristol has two of the most beautiful parks in the state and has facilities for swimming, picnicking, skating, tennis, baseball, and all types of playground activities.

"To conclude, our police and fire departments are modern, are continually being updated, and we are proud of the fact that our energetic fire chief is the youngest in the country."

Chief of Police William J. Mead, Jr., notes the middle-class nature of the city—primarily single-family homes, 85 percent owner-occupied. There is almost no substandard housing in the city, he says, due to a redevelopment program started several years ago. "I feel that we have escaped many problems," he concludes, "because potentially delinquent youth travel to the three larger surrounding cities. I would also like to point out that we are not on a limited access highway."

Only 20 minutes from Hartford by the nearby Interstate 84, however, Bristol residents can partake of the cultural activities in that metropolitan area. Bristol itself has a daily newspaper, the *Bristol Press;* a radio station; three golf courses; and various cultural activities presented by the Bristol Civic Theater Workshop, the Bristol Art League, and the Women's College Club.

Bristol is home to the American Clock and Watch Museum, the only museum in the country devoted exclusively to the history of American clock-making. The location is appropriate, since nineteenth-century Bristol was a noted clock-making center, with the famous names of Ingraham and Sessions having their beginnings here.

Another local attraction has led to Bristol's designation as "Mum City, U.S.A." Much of the pioneer breeding and development of the chrysanthemum was done at the Bristol Nurseries, and each fall a two-week Chrysanthemum Festival features numerous activities in the fields of art, music, theater, the dance, and athletics. You will not want to pass up the gardens of Bristol Nurseries, known to be the largest display of garden mums in the world—over six acres with more than 75,000 plants of about 121 varieties and colors.

FOR FURTHER INFORMATION Write to the Bristol Chamber of Commerce, 81 Main Street, Bristol, Conn. 06010, and ask for *Bristol—In the Heart of Industrial Connecticut; Mum City, U.S.A.; American Clock & Watch Museum,* and *A Special Happening . . . Bristol Mum Festival.*

CITY/STATE: Bristol, Connecticut
POPULATION: 55,487 1960–70 change: +22.0 %
1.3 % non-white. 8.1 % over 65.
REAL ESTATE: Median value, $21,200. 137 less than $10,000, 6,360 $10,000 to $25,000, 2,440 $25,000 and over. Median gross rent, $89. 3,469 less than $100, 1,888. $100 to $150, 498 $150 and over.
EDUCATION: Median school years completed, 11.7.
47.9 % high school graduates.
INCOME: Median family income, $11,835. 5,010 less than $10,000, 8,813 $10,000 to $25,000, 585 $25,000 and over.
EMPLOYMENT: 23,475 in labor force, 49.5 % in manufacturing, 4.1 % unemployed.

15 ARLINGTON HEIGHTS, Illinois

Chicago's Loop is 36 minutes away by commuter train. O'Hare International Airport is a 20-minute drive. In less than an hour you can enjoy all the cultural and entertainment activities of the Chicago metropolitan area. Yet the 65,000-acre Cook County Forest Preserves are also nearby, and a herd of elk is ten minutes away.

Arlington Heights offers that sort of convenient access to both the metropolis and the country, which helps to account for its skyrocketing growth—an increase of 132.7 percent in the past decade. "Arlington Heights is not an industrial town," I was informed by Earl Johnson, Executive Manager of the chamber of commerce. "We have only one employer with over 1,000 people. There are several smaller companies employing from ten to two hundred persons. A good portion of our workers commute to Chicago daily. As compared to some of our adjacent towns, Arlington Heights could be classified as a residential village."

He adds that with a median family income of $17,034, Arlington Heights ranks fourth highest in the country for cities with a population of more than 50,000.

Honeywell, Inc., is the largest employer, providing work for 1,200 locally in the production of commercial control systems and products. Among the other, smaller manufacturers are the Capitol Fixtures and Construction Corporation (store equipment, furnishings, and fixtures), Weber Marking Systems (marking machines and devices), and Amersham-Searle Corporation (radiochemicals, radiopharmaceuticals, and nuclear supplies and accessories).

New homes in Arlington Heights start at about $37,500 and go up to $65,000. Custom-made homes may go to $100,000.

L.W. Calderwood, the Chief of Police, says: "The people of this community are involved in government without monetary compensation, and with home associations, schools and churches that want and demand law and order with justice for all. We try our damnedest to keep them well informed on what is happening in our community.

"I might say," he adds, "that we will see a marked reduction in crime in Cook County when the Assistant States Attorneys become career persons and are paid salaries that are commensurable with the presiding judges."

Arlington Heights has 19 elementary schools, nine junior high schools, and seven high schools. Parochial schools are also available. William Rainey Harper College, a community college, is in the nearby town of Palatine. Also readily accessible are the more than 50 institutions of higher learning in the Chicago area—including the University of Chicago, Northwestern University, the University of Illinois Chicago Circle Campus, Loyola University, Roosevelt University, De Paul University, and Illinois Institute of Technology.

Northwest Community Hospital has 223 beds and provides 24-hour emergency service. Holy Family, St. Alexius, and Lutheran General hospitals also serve the area. All are new and modern. Approximately 60 doctors and 36 dentists practice in Arlington Heights itself.

The Illinois Tollway (Northwest) borders Arlington Heights on the south, and O'Hare International Airport is ten miles away. In addition to the *Arlington Heights Herald,* there are the newspapers, radio stations, and television channels of Chicago and the surrounding area.

The city's 25 churches represent 13 denominations, and more than 70 civic, fraternal, neighborhood, and cultural clubs and organizations are active in Arlington Heights. Community recreation is centered around five city and 26 neighborhood parks, six large swimming pools (one of them an indoor pool), 36 tennis courts, 23 softball diamonds, and four baseball diamonds. Many golf courses and skating rinks are close at hand.

Major league baseball, football, basketball, and hockey are all available in Chicago, of course, but within Arlington Heights itself is a major sports attraction—Arlington Park Race Track, one of the country's leading thoroughbred tracks. Operating since 1927, it is the home of the $100,000 American Derby, Chicago's first stakes race, and the $100,000-added Arlington Classic. In the past, crowds of better than 50,000 have cheered the exploits of Armed, Assault, Citation, Round Table, Swaps, Buckpasser, and Dr. Fager, who established the present world record for a mile at Arlington.

FOR FURTHER INFORMATION Write to the Arlington Heights Chamber of Commerce, P.O. Box 6, Arlington Heights, Ill. 60006, for its illustrated color booklet, *Arlington Heights, Illinois—City of Good Neighbors.*

CITY/STATE: __Arlington Heights, Illinois__
POPULATION: __64,884__ 1960–70 change: __+132.7__ %
__0.5__% non-white. __4.7__% over 65.
REAL ESTATE: Median value, $__35,500__. __17__less than $10,000, __1,783__$10,000 to $25,000, __11,027__$25,000 and over. Median gross rent, $__194__. __121__less than $100, __461__. $100 to $150, __3,870__$150 and over.
EDUCATION: Median school years completed, __12.9__.
__82.8__% high school graduates.
INCOME: Median family income, $__17,034__. __1,953__less than $10,000, __11,396__$10,000 to $25,000, __2,324__$25,000 and over.
EMPLOYMENT: __25,486__in labor force, __27.2__% in manufacturing, __1.8__% unemployed.

16 APPLETON, Wisconsin

The Fox River Valley of Wisconsin is recognized as the papermaking capital of the world, but it is also an urban area with pleasant homes, a nationally recognized liberal arts college, and a seasoned cultural life. Located on the edge of Lake Winnebago, Appleton also enjoys easy access to the vast northern Wisconsin recreational empire.

Papermaking is by no means the only industry, though it is the most important one and is supplemented by related industries supplying it with machinery. Metal fabrication, farm and road machinery, food processing, knitting, and concrete and lumber companies contribute to the financial base of the area. Several insurance companies have their home offices here.

Among the major employers in the area are Appleton Papers, George Banta Company (printers of educational books and periodicals), Bergstrom Paper Company, Kimberly-Clark Corporation (book paper and pulp, household, and feminine hygiene products, nonwoven materials), Miller Electric Manufacturing Company (electric arc welders and accessories), Neenah Foundry Company (ductile iron castings, patterns—heat treating), Thilmany Pulp & Paper Company, Zwicker Knitting Mills (knit gloves and mittens, headwear, and accessory items), Wisconsin Michigan Power Company, and Aid Association for Lutherans (life insurance). Home Mutual Insurance Group and Integrity Mutual Insurance Company also have home offices in Appleton.

According to the Multiple Listing Service of Fox Valley, the median price for single-family residential homes, as of October 1972, was $25,169. The average sale price was $24,214. Over 250 new housing units are built annually, and more than 70 percent of Appleton's residents own their own homes.

Public schools include two senior high schools, two junior high schools, 16 elementary schools, a school for retarded children, and a vocational, technical, and adult education school. Their total enrollment is 14,334. Parochial schools consist of seven Catholic and four Lutheran elementary schools, and both Lutheran and Catholic high schools. Total parochial enrollment is 4,396.

Lawrence University is a highly regarded educational center, with approximately 1,500 students. Academically affiliated with it is the Institute of Paper Chemistry, a graduate school in the natural and biological sciences. Adjacent Menasha is the home of the University of Wisconsin Center—Fox Valley.

Eighty-eight physicians and 50 dentists practice in Appleton. The city has two general hospitals—St. Elizabeth, with 320 beds and a staff of 93 doctors, and Appleton Memorial, with 255 beds and 104 doctors—plus Outagamie County Health Center, offering a full range of psychiatric services and specialized rehabilitation for alcoholism. In the area are Kaukauna Community Hospital (72 beds), Theda Clark Hospital in Neenah (510 beds), and 14 nursing homes.

Appleton is 714 feet above sea level. The mean daily minimum temperature in January is 9.8 degrees, the mean daily maximum in July 82.6 degrees. Average annual precipitation is 28.45 inches, including an average annual snowfall of 43.4 inches.

Centrally located in Wisconsin, Appleton is 31 miles southwest of Green Bay and 100 miles north of Milwaukee. The county airport offers 22 flights daily on Air Wisconsin, with the principal routes being to Chicago, Minneapolis–St. Paul, Detroit, and Milwaukee. Additional commercial service via North Central Airlines, serving 12 cities in five states, is available nearby in Oshkosh and Green Bay.

The *Post-Crescent* is published daily (evenings) and Sunday, and three additional dailies are published in the area. Seven AM and five FM radio stations broadcast locally. There is reception of CBS, NBC, and ABC television channels from Green Bay, and of an independent television channel in Fond du Lac.

Appleton has 54 churches, including Assembly of God, Baptist, Catholic, Christian Science, Church of the Nazarene, Episcopal, Four-Square Gospel, Greek Orthodox, Jehovah's Witnesses, Lutheran, Mormon, Pentecostal, Salvation Army, Seventh-Day Adventist, Unitarian-Universalist, United Church of Christ, United Methodist, and Wesleyan congregations. There are three Jewish congregations—Orthodox, Conservative, and Reform.

The city has wide-ranging cultural activities, many of them originating with Lawrence University's Worcester Art Center, Music Drama Center (including three public auditoriums), and University Theater Group. Other activities and exhibits are sponsored by the Appleton Gallery of Art, the Attic Theater, the Fox Valley Symphony Orchestra, the Dard Hunter Museum (Institute of Paper Chemistry), and the Bergstrom Art Center in Neenah. Library facilities include the Appleton Public Library (127,000 volumes), Lawrence University (170,000 volumes, 110,000 government documents, 30,000 maps), and Kimberly Memorial Library (35,000 volumes) at the Institute of Paper Chemistry.

A wide range of recreational activities is also available in the area, including five outdoor and five indoor swimming pools, eight public and five private golf courses, a curling club, a yacht club, a racquet club, and 25 outdoor tennis courts. Boating and fishing are only minutes away on Lake Winnebago, Lake Poygan, Butte des Morts, and the Wolf and Fox rivers. The Green Bay Packers make their home a few miles northeast, and to the north is the famous lakes-and-rivers vacation country of northern Wisconsin.

FOR FURTHER INFORMATION Write to the Appleton Area Chamber of Commerce, P.O. Box 955, Appleton, Wis. 54910, and ask for four brochures: *Appleton, Come and Share It With Us, Appleton Wisconsin Historical Background, Appleton Wisconsin U.S.A.*, and *About the Appleton Area;* also *Fox Cities Guide to Principal Industries* ($2), *Profile for Industry* ($3), a current issue of *The Fox Valley Guide*, and lists of real estate brokers, employment agencies, schools, and hospitals. If you move to Appleton, be sure to obtain a copy of the very attractive and informative booklet, *This Is Appleton*, published by the League of Women Voters—and printed, naturally, on paper manufactured in Appleton.

CITY/STATE: Appleton, Wisconsin
POPULATION: 57,143   1960–70 change: +18.0 %
  0.5 % non-white. 9.6 % over 65.
REAL ESTATE: Median value, $ 18,200 , 728 less than $10,000, 8,226 $10,000 to $25,000, 2,223 $25,000 and over. Median gross rent, $ 94 . 2,593 less than $100, 1,559 . $100 to $150, 452 $150 and over.
EDUCATION: Median school years completed, 12.3 .
  62.6 % high school graduates.
INCOME: Median family income, $ 10,864 . 5,920 less than $10,000, 7,029 $10,000 to $25,000, 764 $25,000 and over.
EMPLOYMENT: 22,278 in labor force, 31.6 % in manufacturing, 2.7 % unemployed.

17 ALBANY, Georgia

One of the few Southern communities to qualify as one of the nation's safest cities, Albany is 172 miles south of Atlanta and is the fifth-largest city in Georgia. A Brandeis University study selected it as one of the country's 20 top growth areas of the future, and figures from *Sales Management*'s "1972/1973 Survey of Buying Power" rank it sixth in percentage growth among the fastest-growing metropolitan markets in the nation.

Firestone Tire & Rubber is the largest employer in Albany. Other major industries include Charmin Paper Products ("Please don't squeeze the Charmin," and other household paper products), Lilliston Corporation (farm implements), Flint River Cotton Mill (cotton sheeting), Aero Commander (airplanes), and MacGregor-Brunswick (golf clubs). Two medium-size military installations also make Albany their home—a U.S. Naval Air Station and a Marine Corps Supply Center.

Albany's neighborhoods include many that are beautifully landscaped and wooded, offering a variety of architectural styles. A number of apartment complexes have rentals from $120 to $195.

In reference to the low crime-rate, Mayor Motie Wiggins informed me that the police force grew from 66 men in fiscal year 1962 to 131 men in fiscal year 1972. During that period its budget was increased from $430,000 to $1,343,000. And in 1973 the force was augmented to 144 men with a budget of $1,692,000.

Albany's public school system includes four high schools, eight junior highs, and 24 grammar schools. A parochial school, a private school, nine private kindergartens, and a day school for retarded children are also operated here. In addition to two area-vocational schools and a privately owned business school, Albany Junior College and Albany State College are located here.

Phoebe Putney Memorial Hospital, a 450-bed facility, has well-equipped X-ray rooms, a pharmacy, a pediatrics section, a cobalt room, and a fully staffed emergency section. The hospital maintains heart, cancer, and mental health clinics, as well as a special clinic for less fortunate children, which is supported by the local Kiwanis Club. A new 250-bed private hospital, the clinics of the area's two military installations, a 125-bed nursing home, and a 150-bed nursing home round out the medical facilities. Sixty physicians and surgeons, including specialists in every area of modern medicine, and 25 dentists practice in Albany.

The climate is Southern—long, warm summers and short, mild winters, with snow rarely seen. The July mean temperature is 95.5 degrees, the January mean temperature 39.3 degrees. Normal annual rainfall is 49 inches.

Three airlines—Eastern, Air South, and Southern—serve the city. The daily *Albany Herald* and three weekly newspapers are published here. Broadcasting locally are six radio stations and one television channel, affiliated with the NBC and ABC networks, but five channels are received by antenna and ten with cable.

Golf is a year-round sport in Albany's mild climate, and challenging the player are six local courses, including the ones at Doublegate and Radium country clubs. Local fishing is for bass, crappies, and a great variety of pan fish. The Albany area is a mecca for bird and upland game hunting, with the city hosting the Southern Field Trials for hunting dogs. Gulf of Mexico and Atlantic Coast beach and fishing resorts are within easy weekend reach. But just four miles south of town in Radium Springs, the largest in the state, providing swimming, golfing, and fishing facilities; and Chehaw State Park is located one mile north of the city, with facilities for all kinds of recreation, including swimming, boating, fishing, picnicking, and camping.

For the culturally minded, there are the programs of the Community Concert Association, Albany Theater, Carnegie Library, Albany Symphony, Community Choruses, and Southwest Georgia Art Association. The city has an abundance of dogwood, magnolias, and live oak trees, with azaleas and camellias blooming in profusion in the open, so it should be no surprise that more than 38 garden clubs help to make Albany a delightful place to live.

FOR FURTHER INFORMATION Write to the Albany Chamber of Commerce, P.O. Box 308, Albany, Ga. 31702, for its *Map of Albany and Dougherty County, Georgia* (which includes much helpful information), *Albany, Georgia—The City of Opportunity in a Progressive State* (a 52-page illustrated booklet), *A Brief History of Albany, Georgia; Helpful Moving Hints*, a Bureau of the Census summary on the city, *Local Taxes, Manufacturing Plants in Albany*, an *Economic Development Profile*, and lists of clubs and organizations, real estate firms, apartment complexes, shopping facilities, and banks and financial institutions.

CITY/STATE: ___Albany, Georgia___

POPULATION: __72,623__ 1960-70 change: __+29.9__ %
__38.3__ % non-white. __6.3__ % over 65.

REAL ESTATE: Median value, $__15,700__. __1,454__ less than $10,000, __5,809__ $10,000 to $25,000, __1,397__ $25,000 and over. Median gross rent, $__55__. __8,828__ less than $100, __1,227__. $100 to $150, __304__ $150 and over.

EDUCATION: Median school years completed, __11.5__. __46.4__ % high school graduates.

INCOME: Median family income, $__7,551__. __11,337__ less than $10,000, __5,538__ $10,000 to $25,000, __452__ $25,000 and over.

EMPLOYMENT: __25,380__ in labor force, __19.0__ % in manufacturing, __4.6__ % unemployed.

18 OAK LAWN, Illinois

The community of Black Oaks in old "Horse Thief Hollow" eventually became known as Oak Lawn, and as the village grew, most of the black oaks were replaced with utility poles. Its growth has continued, rapidly and unabated, throughout the twentieth century.

There is very little industry in Oak Lawn itself, but a major industrial complex and center is located about a ten-minute drive away from town. Several hundred acres of undeveloped industrial property are available, for both light and heavy industry.

Oak Lawn is a residential community; 95 percent of its citizens own their own homes, and 90 percent of the existing housing units are in structures built since 1940. Between 1961 and 1970 some 3,500 new homes and 3,400 new apartment-units were built. Housing costs are typical of a Midwestern suburb—homes range from $20,000 to $150,000, apartment rentals from $180 to $350.

Gerhard A. Hein, Chief of Police, believes that "aggressive preventive patrols by all uniformed personnel are the primary reason" for the low crime-rate. His department's patrol schedules place selective emphasis on areas or districts as required. "The daily plotting of known offenses permits pressure to be brought to bear where necessary. The cooperation of our Detective and Juvenile departments with our patrols helps the preventive effort, to say nothing of their own success on apprehension.

"Secondary reasons," he continues, "could be the increased emphasis on training of recruits through longer courses and making refresher sessions available for the seasoned veteran. The investment in training pays dividends, whether nine-month-long command courses or the daily roll-call short subject methods are implemented. Having a Village manager, mayor and board of trustees who are receptive to the use of funds for education aids immeasurably.

"Maintenance of adequate records," he continues, "is a help to all concerned by keeping personnel informed. Dissemination of educational material through the news media is a must, and public appearances by qualified speakers at church, school or other civic groups bears out the old adage of 'Forewarned is forearmed.' Good community relations builds confidence and respect, but must be earned.

"Additional reasons come to mind, but I do believe our situation could be improved through more vigorous action by the judiciary," Hein concludes. "The recidivism rate of many offenders could be reduced substantially, were more severe penalties assessed. The search for Utopia continues, but meanwhile we'll continue to strive for improvement, and perhaps that might be a summation of our good record. There is no 'batting average' that cannot be improved."

Oak Lawn's public schools—16 grammar schools and three high schools—are supplemented by four parochial grammar schools. Special instruction is provided for the hard of hearing, blind, and educable mentally handicapped. The Oak Lawn School District ranks in the upper 10 percent in National Merit examinations.

Christ Community Hospital has 349 beds, plus 35 beds in the pediatric wards and three in isolation wards. There are 162 staff doctors affiliated with the hospital, and 95 student nurses in training. Practicing in Oak Lawn are 46 doctors, 39 dentists, and nine optometrists.

Oak Lawn is accessibly located in the southwest suburban area of Chicagoland. The area is served by Illinois 50 (Cicero Avenue), U.S. 12-20 (95th Street), Dan Ryan Expressway, and Interstate 294. Two railroads, each within 15-minutes travel time, connect with public transportation to downtown Chicago. In addition to a number of weekly newspapers in the area, there is full newspaper, radio, and television coverage from Chicago.

Recreational facilities in the community's 21 parkland areas include an Olympic-size swimming pool and 10 playgrounds featuring tennis instruction, summer softball, band concerts, a winter program, and various other activities. Eleven public and private golf courses are within a 20-minute drive. Oak Lawn is also easily accessible to extensive forest preserves for picnicking, a nature museum, fishing, horseback riding, skiing, and other recreational pursuits.

FOR FURTHER INFORMATION Write to the Oak Lawn Chamber of Commerce, 5251 West 95th Street, Oak Lawn, Ill. 60453, and ask for its brochure and fact-sheet on the community.

CITY/STATE: Oak Lawn, Illinois
POPULATION: 60,305 1960-70 change: +119.5 %
0.3 % non-white. 7.5 % over 65.
REAL ESTATE: Median value, $26,500. 199 less than $10,000, 5,439 $10,000 to $25,000, 6,875 $25,000 and over. Median gross rent, $171. 185 less than $100, 626. $100 to $150, 2,130 $150 and over.
EDUCATION: Median school years completed, 12.3. 60.9 % high school graduates.
INCOME: Median family income, $13,824. 3,428 less than $10,000, 10,175 $10,000 to $25,000, 1,261 $25,000 and over.
EMPLOYMENT: 23,463 in labor force, 25.3 % in manufacturing, 2.6 % unemployed.

19 KETTERING, Ohio

Kettering is mainly a residential suburb with most of its citizens employed in the Greater Dayton area. During World War II, a great influx of people moved into this area, and with the end of the war, demands for housing and services grew and birth-rates soared. Kettering was incorporated in 1952, and was named in honor of its most outstanding citizen, the famous philanthropist and inventor of the automotive self-starter, Charles F. Kettering.

Kettering's largest local employer is the Delco Division of General Motors, with a work force of over 2,000. Other industrial concerns include such industries as tool and die manufacturing, data processing, electronics, and communications. Among the major firms, and the number of persons employed by them, are National Cash Register Company (251–500), Top Value Enterprises (425), Cassano Enterprises (326), the Borden Company (211), Dayton Reliable Tool and Manufacturing Company (180), H & H Machine Tool Company (165), and Hilltop Concrete Corporation (115). The federal government also operates a Defense Electronics Center here.

The average cost of a home is approximately $23,000. Almost all of the potential residential land has been built upon, and the largest vacant tract is 687 acres owned by the State Department of Mental Hygiene. Studies are presently underway for a comprehensive plan for this entire acreage. Apartment projects are becoming more and more popular, too, with approximately 19 such projects containing 20 or more units located in Kettering. Rents average $150 a month.

Kettering has no downtown business district, but a number of new business and shopping concentrations with adequate parking are located at convenient points throughout the city. Twelve shopping centers occupy a total of 131.5 acres, or 38 percent of the commercially used land.

John R. Shryock, Chief of Police, says that "the reason for our low crime-rate must, out of necessity, be attributed to the citizenry of Kettering. You no doubt are aware that we are a relatively new city and our residents take pride in their homes and property. We are also noted for having very strict entrance requirements for our police officers, and a large percentage are actively pursuing additional formal education."

The Police Department was one of the first in the area to make use of computer operations to assist in record keeping and information retrieval. Another first, a police helicopter, was put into operation early in 1971 to aid in the abatement of crime and to provide greater protection. Also, an organizational change took place in 1970. This was the *ARGUS* concept, which has resulted in round-the-clock coverage of the city by uniformed officers, resulting in a 5.2 percent *decrease* in major crimes in 1971. Adult criminal arrests were up 3.7 percent over 1970, and juvenile criminal arrests were up some 17 percent over 1970.

Kettering has 14 elementary schools, four junior high schools, and two senior high schools. The estimated enrollment for Fairmont East High School is 1,815; for Fairmont West, approximately 1,800.

Medical and health facilities are provided by Kettering Memorial Hospital, which contains 401 beds plus diagnostic and treatment facilities. Cox Coronary Heart Institute and Kettering Medical College are also part of this medical complex.

Kettering has easy access to Interstate 75. Both air and rail passenger service are available in Dayton.

The city has a twice-weekly newspaper, the *Kettering-Oakwood Times*. Kettering is also served by two Dayton papers—the *Journal Herald* and the *Dayton Daily News*. There is reception, of course, of all the television and radio stations broadcasting from Dayton.

Kettering has both Catholic and Protestant churches, with most of the major Protestant denominations represented by congregations here. There are two branches of the Montgomery County Public Library in the city.

Recreational facilities and activities include several swimming pools, swimming and diving instruction, a recreation center for teens and senior citizens, structured classes in various arts and crafts, an indoor ice skating rink, Pee Wee baseball and football, and a 36-hole community golf course.

FOR FURTHER INFORMATION Write to the Kettering Chamber of Commerce, Inc., 40 Southmoor Circle, Kettering, Ohio 45429, and ask for *Industrial Firms in Kettering, Ohio* and its mimeographed information-sheets on the city.

CITY/STATE: ___Kettering, Ohio___

POPULATION: ___69,599___ 1960-70 change: ___+27.8___ %
___0.6___ % non-white. ___6.6___ % over 65.

REAL ESTATE: Median value, $___22,900___. ___213___ less than $10,000, ___9,142___ $10,000 to $25,000, ___6,281___ $25,000 and over. Median gross rent, $___129___. ___1,444___ less than $100, ___2,501___. $100 to $150, ___2,023___ $150 and over.

EDUCATION: Median school years completed, ___12.6___.
___73.1___ % high school graduates.

INCOME: Median family income, $___13,708___. ___4,584___ less than $10,000, ___12,553___ $10,000 to $25,000, ___1,827___ $25,000 and over.

EMPLOYMENT: ___29,443___ in labor force, ___35.2___ % in manufacturing, ___2.3___ % unemployed.

20 CLIFTON, New Jersey

Only 14 miles from Times Square, Clifton sits in the midst of the sprawling metropolitan potpourri known as northern New Jersey. It is a middle-class city without slums—bordered, however, by several neighbors that do have blighted areas.

While some residents commute to jobs in Newark, other northern New Jersey cities, or New York City, many choose to work close to home. Clifton has a remarkable diversity of industry for a community of its size, totaling approximately 30,000 jobs with an annual payroll of $300 million. In addition, some 1,000 retail stores in the city bring in $200 million annually in sales.

Among the larger firms of nationwide reputation are Hoffman-La Roche, ITT Federal Laboratories, Fairchild Camera & Instrument, the du Pont Corporation, Wilson Sporting Goods, General Foods, Fruehauf Corporation, Oneida Paper Products Company, the Polymer Chemicals Division of W.R. Grace, the Miles Chemical Division of Miles Laboratories, Walter Kidde Company, Allstate Can Corporation, Automatic Data Processing, Inwood Knitting Mills, and many others.

More than half of the houses here are multiple-family dwellings. Approximately 10,000 rental units are also available, but among them are just two high-rise apartment houses. There is no central shopping area, but rather a diversity of shopping areas—both in Clifton itself and in the cities that surround it on all sides.

Chief Joseph A. Nee heads a police force of 131 officers and 30 reserves. He finds a number of reasons for the city's relatively low crime, in an area where many neighbors have much higher crimerates—the middle-class ethnic makeup of the population, "rigid enforcement of narcotics laws," the fact that his force "is one of the highest paid police departments in the state," and the additional fact that "many of our police officers are lifelong residents of the city—and pride, ambition and drive to keep the city safe is foremost in their minds."

Clifton's population, Chief Nee told me, "is composed of many residents of different ethnic backgrounds. In the majority of cases these people have been residents for many years, with sons and daughters remaining after school and marriage. This is important, for stability in our residents provides a firm basis for respect for law and order. These are people who are proud homeowners and citizens, and a ride through the city quickly shows this pride. Where this civic spirit may be lacking, a gentle prod by city officials to 'keep up your property' usually corrects the situation."

Beginning in 1959, he says, the force instituted the one-man patrol. "To date this has been effective, doubling patrol coverage and creating police omnipresence. Our one-man patrol system permits smaller posts, faster response, and better patrol." He adds that by having policemen travel alone in their cars, they "realize that if there is a job to be done, they have no one to rely on but themselves."

"The night hours," he adds, "are handled by what we consider an elite group. This unit is a tactical squad comprised of five men who have produced a record of accomplishment both in arrests and in prevention. We deploy them immediately to areas of reported crime, and give them far reign to develop tactics and select areas for coverage. Its operations are covert, using unmarked cars, civilian clothes, and long hair and beards if necessary. Their responsibility for efficient performance is controlled only by the Chief of Police, and we eliminate services not connected with crime."

Chief Nee directed my attention to several other factors. "We have complete radio communications with every officer," he explained, "whether he is in the patrol car or out of it. All men are equipped with walkie-talkies." And "we encourage members of the department to pursue their education on the college level. In 1959 the administrators decided that training on a college level would be beneficial. Presently over 30 officers are pursuing Associate and Baccalaureate degrees. Seven officers hold B.A. degrees with majors in criminal justice and police science."

Clifton was also one of the first cities in the nation to deploy its 155 firemen as public safety officers. This means that when they are not on actual call, they cruise around the city handling many police duties as well as fire prevention chores.

Clifton's public school system is the seventh largest in the state, consisting of 13 grammar schools, two junior highs, and a high school. There is also a special school for victims of cerebral palsy. Many physicians and dentists practice throughout the Jersey metropolitan area, and while there are no hospitals within the city, nearby hospitals serving Clifton residents include Mountainside in Montclair; Passaic General, St. Mary's, and Beth Israel in Passaic; Barnert Memorial, Paterson General, and St. Joseph's in Paterson; Clara Maas in Belleville; Hackensack General in Hackensack; and Chilton Memorial Hospital in Pompton Plains.

For automobile transportation there is easy accessibility to Route 80, the Garden State Parkway, the New Jersey Turnpike, and Routes 3, 46, 20, and 21. Commuter passenger service is available on the Delaware, Lackawanna & Western Railroad. Bus service is plentiful, and the city is conveniently near Newark Airport.

Clifton residents have available not only their own daily newspaper and three weeklies, but also all the communications media of the metropolitan area—both New York City and New Jersey newspapers, radio stations, and television channels.

Clifton's 32 churches include many Protestant denominations and a number of Catholic parishes, as well as Russian Orthodox and Ukrainian Orthodox congregations and a Jewish synagogue. The municipal Recreation Department sponsors sports clinics, leagues, and tournaments, plus many special events, organizations, and clubs. Facilities include 16 indoor community centers, 31 playgrounds, and a special center for retarded children. Also in Clifton is Botany Village, a nostalgic cameo community capturing the flavor of the gay nineties; it has become a major tourist attraction.

FOR FURTHER INFORMATION Write to the City Manager, City of Clifton, Clifton, N.J. 07015, and request the several fact-sheets available on the city.

CITY/STATE: _____Clifton, New Jersey_____
POPULATION: ___82,437___1960-70 change: __+0.4__%
__0.6__% non-white. __11.8__% over 65.
REAL ESTATE: Median value, $_27,100_. ___38___less than $10,000, _5,472_$10,000 to $25,000, _7,725_$25,000 and over. Median gross rent, $__107__. _4,170_less than $100, _4,374_. $100 to $150, _1,352_$150 and over.
EDUCATION: Median school years completed, __11.6__.
__46.9__% high school graduates.
INCOME: Median family income, $_11,947_. _8,225_less than $10,000, _13,467_$10,000 to $25,000, _1,715_$25,000 and over.
EMPLOYMENT: _37,988_in labor force, _40.3_% in manufacturing, _3.4_% unemployed.

21 EAST HARTFORD, Connecticut

Opposite Hartford on the Connecticut River, East Hartford is a city with modern downtown skyscrapers and fine residential neighborhoods. But it is best known as an industrial center, with more than 110 manufacturing establishments producing many products.

United Aircraft Corporation is the most prominent of these in the city's economy. Founded in 1925, it still maintains its corporate and executive headquarters—as well as its main plant—in East Hartford. United Aircraft Corporation has become greatly diversified in both military and commercial fields. One of the world's foremost aircraft-engine manufacturers and the maker of Sikorsky helicopters, this firm is also active in turbine engines, development of commercial uses for the fuel cell, turbine-powered trains and automobiles, and application of marine versions of the gas-turbine engine, and maintains a wide-ranging space program.

Other leading taxpayers in the city include the Fuller Brush Company, Republic Steel Corporation's Union Drawn Steel Division, IBM Corporation, First National Stores, Hartford Electric Light Company, and A & P Food Stores.

The police force has 96 uniformed and civilian personnel. A new IBM communications terminal was installed at the complaint desk recently, allowing the officer on duty to make immediate and direct connection with all records on file in the State Motor Vehicles Department. In about 90 seconds, information can be obtained on a vehicle's registration or the status of a person's operator's license. If a vehicle is stolen, that information is also available quickly. In the future, the department expects to be connected with the state's National Crime Information Center and FBI office, and will be able to obtain almost immediate information as to whether a person is involved in, or wanted for, any crime.

East Hartford has 20 elementary schools and two high schools. Additionally, two parochial elementary and one parochial junior high school are located in the city. All the Hartford-area colleges and universities are within easy commuting distance.

Activities for citizens of all ages are sponsored by the Department of Parks and Recreation. Facilities include 24 parks and playgrounds, four outdoor and two indoor-outdoor swimming pools, three outdoor wading pools, ice skating and skiing areas, a boat-launching area, a public clubhouse, and a music shell. And whatever the cultural or athletic activity you desire, if you cannot find it in East Hartford you undoubtedly will find it across the river in Hartford, the second-largest metropolis of New England.

FOR FURTHER INFORMATION Write to the Town of East Hartford, 740 Main Street, East Hartford, Conn. 06108, for a copy of the city's most recent annual report.

CITY/STATE: _____East Hartford, Connecticut_____
POPULATION: __57,583__1960–70 change: __+30.9__%
__1.3__% non-white. __7.4__% over 65.
REAL ESTATE: Median value, $__22,900__. __62__less than $10,000, __5,817__$10,000 to $25,000, __3,340__$25,000 and over. Median gross rent, $__133__. __1,966__less than $100, __2,968__. $100 to $150, __2,653__$150 and over.
EDUCATION: Median school years completed, __12.2__. __55.9__% high school graduates.
INCOME: Median family income, $__11,771__. __5,139__less than $10,000, __9,576__$10,000 to $25,000, __485__$25,000 and over.
EMPLOYMENT: __27,223__in labor force, __33.8__% in manufacturing, __2.1__% unemployed.

22 BAYONNE, New Jersey

Bayonne sits within sight of the Statue of Liberty, and is directly opposite New York City's Borough of Brooklyn across the bay. Geographically it is a peninsula—bounded on the west by Newark Bay, on the east by Upper New York Bay, on the south by the Kill Van Kull (which separates it from Staten Island), and on the north by Jersey City. This geographic isolation, plus the social and cultural traditions of its ethnic populace, has resulted in a small-town atmosphere and a degree of cohesion uncommon in a metropolitan sea.

"The residents of Bayonne," says Mayor Francis G. Fitzpatrick, "are truly representative of the proverbial melting pot so often referred to in our history books. Over the years these people migrated to Bayonne, and each group in turn offered its talents and wisdom, culminating in a community of hard-working, sincere and understanding individuals." About half the population is of foreign stock, meaning it is either foreign-born or of foreign or mixed parentage. The largest segment is Polish, the Italians second, and other nationalities prominent in the community are the Irish, Russian, Austrian, English, Czech, German, Lithuanian, and Hungarian.

"For a number of years," explains Mayor Fitzpatrick, "Bayonne was considered the oil refining capital of the world because such giants of the oil industry as Standard Oil of New Jersey, Asiatic Petroleum, Gulf Oil, Tidewater Associated Oil Company, and Texaco maintained large industrial plants in the city. Many of these firms are still with us. Fortunately the city, as a result of its geographical location, is endowed with a tremendous deep-water harbor providing access to the large ocean-going tankers so vital to the oil industry.

"Just prior to the start of World War II," he continues, "the city built a huge marine facility which was taken over by the United States Navy and used as the Naval Supply Depot. This was, and still is, the largest maritime supply depot in the world, and it contains the world's largest drydock facility.

"After World War II there was an exodus of several of the large oil refineries to other areas. This, in turn, resulted in a conversion of large industrial complexes to some smaller manufacturing enterprises. Actually, the industrial fiber of the city of Bayonne now consists of diversified industries encompassing chemical, electronic, needlecraft, and various specialized activities. Since 1962 the city has pursued a landfill policy, reclaiming an area that for 66 years was a burning municipal dump and successfully converting it to an industrial park."

Unemployment is low, and the primary job market for Bayonne is one of skilled labor.

The city consists primarily of one- and two-family dwellings that are owner-occupied. Most are in good repair, indicating a high degree of civic pride. Land values in Bayonne, however, are the highest in New Jersey. For example, the minimum building lot of 25 feet by 100 feet averages between $13,000 and $15,000.

Of Bayonne's school population, approximately 9,300 students attend the public schools and 5,600 the parochial schools. There are 11 elementary schools and a high school in the public system, and seven elementary schools plus two high schools (one for boys and the other for girls) in the Catholic system.

The Bayonne Free Public Library, recently rebuilt, began as a small Workmen's Library. Beginning with the Dutch Reformed Church of 1828, Bayonne now has 20 Protestant, four Orthodox, 11

Catholic, and eight Jewish congregations. Large community centers are maintained by the two YMCA's, the Jewish Community Center, and the Knights of Columbus.

FOR FURTHER INFORMATION Write to the Bayonne Chamber of Commerce and Tax Research Council, 17 West 25th Street, Bayonne, N.J. 07002, and ask for the Hammond map of the city of Bayonne, *Market Data Information on Bayonne, New Jersey,* and the Regional Plan summary entitled *Bayonne, New Jersey—Gateway to the New York-New Jersey Market.*

CITY/STATE: Bayonne, New Jersey
POPULATION: 72,743   1960-70 change: -2.0 %
 4.6 % non-white. 10.9 % over 65.
REAL ESTATE: Median value, $ 23,000 . 84 less than $10,000, 1,887 $10,000 to $25,000, 1,299 $25,000 and over. Median gross rent, $ 88 . 9,198 less than $100, 4,274 . $100 to $150, 1,013 $150 and over.
EDUCATION: Median school years completed, 11.4 . 46.0 % high school graduates.
INCOME: Median family income, $ 10,542 . 9,126 less than $10,000, 10,013 $10,000 to $25,000, 678 $25,000 and over.
EMPLOYMENT: 31,119 in labor force, 36.2 % in manufacturing, 3.3 % unemployed.

23 MANCHESTER, New Hampshire

Manchester, the largest city in New Hampshire and the three northern New England states, has emerged as the northern terminus of the East Coast supercity strip. Yet the surrounding countryside is mostly rural and wooded, with numerous lakes and ponds. Within an hour's drive are Boston, the Atlantic coast, the White Mountains ski country, a hundred mountain lakes, and New Hampshire's beautiful "Currier & Ives" countryside.

More than 210 manufacturing firms and over 1,800 wholesale and retail services provide the employment opportunities. "Soft goods" still predominate in manufacturing, but there has been rapid growth recently in durable goods manufacturing—with the greatest growth in electronics.

Among the nationally known firms with plants in the area are Pandora Industries (Pandora Knitwear), Chicopee Manufacturing Corporation (Johnson & Johnson), Edison Electronics Division (McGraw-Edison Company), Foster Grant Company, General Electric, International Paper, J.F. McElwain Company (Thom McAn Shoes), Moore Business Forms, Raytheon, Scovill Aerosol Products, Sweetheart Plastics (Maryland Cup Corporation), and Sylvania Electric Products (General Telephone).

Housing costs are relatively low in Manchester—a recent report ranked it as the fifth-cheapest city in that regard, among the 21 cities listed in New England. Ample housing is available in the city and its suburbs, and recent construction has included multiunit apartment complexes.

Thanks to the continuing vigilance of William Loeb, publisher of the *Manchester Union Leader*, New Hampshire is the only state in the union with neither a state income tax nor a sales tax. New Hampshire citizens pay the 13th-lowest per capita state and local taxes in the nation ($333) and the lowest in New England.

John A. Stips, Chief of Police, credits the local population for the low crime-rate. "Manchester has always enjoyed an excellent reputation," he says, "and we attribute it to the citizens who reside here; many who have 'roots' here for generations and are good, honest, hard-working, and family-devoted people. Over the years I have found them to be law abiding, willing to get involved in assisting their fellow men, and lacking the feeling of apathy which we see in many parts of our nation. Our police department could not function properly without the support of all our citizens and we do have their support when we need it."

Manchester's public school system consists of 21 elementary schools, three junior highs, and three high schools, with an enrollment of 16,786 students. There is also a complete parochial system of 17 elementary schools, two junior highs, and two high schools, with 6,371 students enrolled. The Derryfield School is a private coeducational institution.

Three liberal arts colleges—St. Anselm's, Notre Dame, and Mount St. Mary's—make this their home. Also in Manchester are the Merrimack Valley Branch of the University of New Hampshire, the New Hampshire Vocational Institute, two business colleges (New Hampshire College, an accredited four-year institution, and Hesser Business College), and specialized schools including a data-processing and computer-programming school (Concord Commercial College).

The 128 practicing physicians and surgeons in Manchester give it a favorable ratio of one doctor per 763 persons. The four hospitals in the area—a Veterans Administration Hospital plus Elliot, Sacred Heart, and Notre Dame hospitals—have a total of 683 beds, with modern cardiac and cancer wards.

Average temperatures range from 21.1 degrees in January to 69.6 degrees in July. Annual snowfall averages 60.6 inches, and the average annual precipitation is around 39 inches.

Manchester is bisected by a number of major highways, including the Frederick E. Everett Turnpike and Interstate 93. In addition to bus service, there is air passenger service with Delta Airlines (formerly Northeast Airlines) flights to New York, Boston, Detroit, and Chicago, as well as Trans East Airlines flights to Portland, Maine, and Albany, New York. Limousine service is available to Boston's Logan International Airport.

The *Manchester Union Leader* is the state's only daily and Sunday newspaper—the Sunday edition is called the *New Hampshire Sunday News*. Four radio stations and a television station broadcast from the city.

With more than 200,000 volumes, Manchester's city library is the largest in northern New England. Seventy-three churches and synagogues reflect a wide range of religious denominations. Cultural affairs are sponsored by the Manchester Historical Society, the Institute of Arts and Sciences, the Currier Gallery of Art, and other groups.

Recreational activities to meet all tastes will be found here—social and athletic clubs, the Manchester Ski Club and Massabesic Yacht Club, and diversified facilities ranging from 735 acres of parks and playgrounds to swimming pools, tennis courts, golf courses, gymnasiums, basketball courts, a hockey rink, horseshoe pits, and much more. Excellent boating and fishing is available at Lake Massabesic and other lakes and streams in the area, and everything from the Atlantic coast to the White Mountains is within an easy drive.

FOR FURTHER INFORMATION Write to the Manchester Chamber of Commerce, 57 Market Street, Manchester, N.H. 03101, and ask for *Finger Tip Facts on Manchester, New Hampshire, This Is Manchester—The Four Seasons Crossroad of New England* (a 28-page illustrated booklet), a street map of the city, and fact-sheets on taxes, real estate agents, employment agencies, and rentals. Also, if you are a businessman thinking of relocating here, the Manchester Industrial Council, 57 Market Street, Manchester, N.H. 03101, has a most attractive packet of .materials for you.

CITY/STATE: _____Manchester, New Hampshire_____
POPULATION: __87,754_____1960–70 change: ___-0.6__%
__0.4__% non-white. __12.7__% over 65.
REAL ESTATE: Median value, $__17,300_. ___837___less than $10,000, __8,568__$10,000 to $25,000, __1,566__$25,000 and over. Median gross rent, $__69___. __10,795_less than $100, __2,417_. $100 to $150, __432___$150 and over.
EDUCATION: Median school years completed, __11.5__.
__47.5__% high school graduates.
INCOME: Median family income, $__9,489__. __12,041_less than $10,000, __9,510__$10,000 to $25,000, _646___$25,000 and over.
EMPLOYMENT: __37,011_in labor force, __33.6___% in manufacturing, __3.4___% unemployed.

24 MIDLAND, Texas

Midland is oil country—no two ways about it. The place was a sleepy town nobody had ever heard of until 1923, when oil was discovered near Big Lake. Midland quickly became the administrative center, with tall office buildings rising upwards on the flat Texas prairie. The population doubled each decade from the 1920s through the 1960s.

The economic base for Midland is still petroleum, as the Permian Basin area, in which it is situated, contributes almost one-fifth of the total crude oil, gas liquids, and natural gas produced in the United States. More than 750 oil companies and related firms have offices in Midland, mostly for exploration but also for production, processing, and marketing. Twenty-second in population in Texas, Midland ranks fifth in the amount of office space and has more (nearly 3 million square feet) than any city between Fort Worth and Los Angeles.

Some of the nationally known oil companies with offices here (and the numbers they employ in Midland) are Atlantic Richfield (225),

Chevron (80), Cities Service (73), Continental (100), Getty (52), Gulf (200), Humble (325), Marathon (20), Mobil (350), Pennzoil (24), Phillips (83), Shell (506), Skelly (86), Sohio (44), Sun (55), Superior (96), Texaco (336), and Union Oil Company of California (190).

Other prominent employers in town are Dotty Dan, Inc. (children's clothing), Drilco (industrial mining and drilling tools), Levi Strauss & Company (jeans), Midland Homes (mobile homes), and the Printing Division of West Texas Office Supply (business forms and commercial printing).

H.A. Tuck, Public Relations Director of the Midland Chamber of Commerce, says that "currently, Midland has only 2.7 percent unemployed, with a critical shortage of workers in the building trades (carpenters, plumbers, electrical workers, masons, etc.). We are also short of doctors, primarily general practitioners. There are many jobs available for unskilled female workers in a first-class garment plant. There is also quite a demand for clerical workers, mostly secretaries, and a shortage of oilfield drilling crew workers."

Housing, Tuck adds, "is quite reasonable in Midland. Three-bedroom houses sell for $12,000 to $35,000. New three-bedroom homes are selling for about $15 per square foot of living space. More than 350 apartment units are under construction now. Apartments rent for $125 to $450 per month. Average for a two-bedroom apartment is about $150 per month."

The public school system consists of 20 elementary, three junior high, two freshman, and two high schools. With one of the highest pay schedules in the state, 15 percent of the classroom teachers annually receive merit pay supplements and 10 percent annually are given grants for graduate study. Seventy percent of the school system's graduates attend college. There are also nine private and parochial schools in Midland, two of them teaching through the eighth grade.

Midland College is a community junior college. The University of Texas of the Permian Basin was created by the Texas Legislature in 1969, and began classes in 1973. The Permian Basin Graduate Center is an extension service provided by area colleges and universities.

Midland Memorial Hospital is community owned and contains 180 beds. Parkview Hospital is privately owned and has 60 beds. Midland has five medical clinics, one osteopathic clinic, and two modern nursing homes with a total of 160 beds. There are 23 dentists and 58 physicians and surgeons.

Located in the High Plains area of Texas, Midland is 2,779 feet above sea level. Annually there are an average of 168 clear days and 99 partly cloudy days. The January mean minimum temperature is 31 degrees, and the July mean maximum is 95 degrees. Average annual precipitation is 14.7 inches. The growing season averages 218 days.

Midland is on Interstate 20, and the Midland-Odessa Regional Air Terminal has more than 30 jet flights per day on Continental and Texas International airlines.

Communications media include an afternoon daily newspaper, four AM radio stations, one FM radio station, and three television stations, each affiliated with one of the national networks. Cable television is also available, and brings in 10 channels.

Midland's 100 or more churches represent 25 faiths and denominations. A vigorous cultural calendar includes productions of the Midland-Odessa Symphony Orchestra, Chorale, and Ballet, the Midland Community Theatre Center (with its Children's Theater program), various art galleries, the Midland Civic Concerts Association, the Midland Art Association, and the Summer Mummers, who present "Mellerdrammer" productions. The Midland County Library has some 110,000 volumes, with outstanding business, scientific, and petroleum collections. Museums include the Museum of the Southwest, with its Planetarium and Lancaster Garden Center; the Permian Basin Petroleum Museum, Library, and Hall of Fame; the Abell-Hanger Foundation's Pliska Museum (housing an early airplane); and the Midland County Historical Museum, home of the skull of a 20,000-year-old Midland Man. (Actually she was a woman, and is commonly called "Midland Minnie.")

City recreation facilities include 28 parks, six swimming pools, an 18-hole municipal golf course, 27 softball and baseball fields, and 14 tennis courts. The YMCA, a Youth Center, the City of Midland Swim Team, an annual Soap Box Derby, boys' clubs, the Midland Junior Baseball Association, and various softball leagues provide competition for children and adults. "Super Summer" is a summer recreation spectacular, and the Midland Cubs play in the Texas Baseball League. Other spectator sports range from rodeos to quarterhorse racing at Midland Downs and motorcycle and stock-car racing. Private facilities include two country clubs, a racquet club, and a polo club, and fishing, boating, and water sports are available on four lakes within two hours' drive of Midland.

FOR FURTHER INFORMATION Write to the Midland Chamber of Commerce, P.O. Box 1890, Midland, Tex. 79701, and ask for its brochure *Midland, Texas, City Map and Tourist Guide*, and its *Directory of Manufacturers, Processors, Oil Companies and Related Firms in Midland County, Texas.*

CITY/STATE: ＿＿＿＿Midland, Texas＿＿＿＿
POPULATION: ＿59,463＿＿1960-70 change: ＿-5.0＿%
＿11.3＿% non-white. ＿5.2＿% over 65.
REAL ESTATE: Median value, $＿13,900＿. ＿4,243＿less than $10,000, ＿6,675＿$10,000 to $25,000, ＿1,873＿$25,000 and over. Median gross rent, $＿86＿. ＿2,623＿less than $100, ＿994＿. $100 to $150, ＿939＿$150 and over.
EDUCATION: Median school years completed, ＿12.6＿. ＿68.1＿% high school graduates.
INCOME: Median family income, $＿10,616＿. ＿7,200＿less than $10,000, ＿7,231＿$10,000 to $25,000, ＿1,073＿$25,000 and over.
EMPLOYMENT: ＿24,216＿in labor force, ＿5.9＿% in manufacturing, ＿3.7＿% unemployed.

25 WEST ALLIS, Wisconsin

Although some still speak of West Allis as a suburb of Milwaukee, developments since the 1950s have placed it solidly in the city classification. Now the sixth-largest city in Wisconsin, it is highly industrialized and has a primarily blue-collar population. It ranks 16th among 18 Milwaukee County suburbs in average income, and a quarter of its residents are foreign-born or the children of foreign-born parents.

Mayor Arnold H. Klentz says that "industry and commerce are enjoying an improved economy, which does result in more job opportunities." The major employer is the huge Allis-Chalmers Manufacturing Company, established here at the turn of the century. The Kearney & Trecker Corporation, manufacturers of machine tools, is another major employer. Others include the Wisconsin Milk and Ice

Cream Division of the Borden Company, Seven-Up Bottling Company, Hansen Laboratory (a research laboratory center), Godfrey Company, Crestwood Bakery, Gateway Transportation, the Alumatic Corporation of America, the Drug Division of McKesson & Robbins, RBP Chemical and Supply, American Motor Sales Corporation (warehouse and offices), and the factory branch of Fruehauf Trailer Company.

Of the residential acreage in West Allis, 96 percent is already developed. Sixty percent of all housing units are single-family units, with 23 percent duplex units and 17 percent apartments, rooming houses, or other multiunit complexes. About 65 percent of the units are owner-occupied, and 33 percent are rented.

West Allis is part of a school system that also includes West Milwaukee and parts of Greenfield and New Berlin. In the system are 18 elementary schools, four junior highs, three high schools, a vocational school, and an orthopedic school. The 11 parochial schools consist of seven Catholic and four Lutheran schools. Marquette University and the University of Wisconsin—Milwaukee are located in Milwaukee. Other colleges in the area include the Milwaukee School of Engineering, Mount Mary College, Alverno College, and Cardinal Stritch College. The University of Wisconsin is just 70 miles away in Madison.

West Allis Memorial Hospital is a 300-bed facility built by the city in 1961.

The average January temperature is 20 degrees, and the average temperature in the summer months is near 70 degrees. Rainfall averages about 30 inches per year, and while snowfall varies considerably from year to year, it averages about 46 inches annually. West Allis is 670 feet above sea level.

West Allis is served by Interstates 94 and 894. It is easily accessible to General Mitchell Field, where commercial air service is provided by four of the nation's largest trunk air lines and two feeder airlines.

"Our kids would rather become champion ice skaters or baseball players than tough guys," says F.W. Zirkel, Director of the Recreation Department. As proof, winning national recognition for championship baseball and ice skating has become a West Allis habit. Facilities include seven parks, 21 playgrounds, and 18 field houses, gymnasiums, and recreational centers. The range of adult and children's activities is wide, covering arts and crafts, dramatics, family camping, fun and figure clubs, golden-age clubs, golf, guitar lessons, home economics, dancing, nature study, sewing classes, woodwork, baseball, softball, basketball, volleyball, skating, and sledding. Metropolitan area facilities within easy access include the Milwaukee County Zoo and Mitchell Park Conservatory, swimming pools, golf courses, and parkways. Lake Michigan and the many lakes located close to the urban area provide ample water recreation opportunities.

FOR FURTHER INFORMATION Write to the West Allis Chamber of Commerce, 3125 South 108th Street, West Allis, Wis. 53227, and ask for *History of West Allis* and *West Allis, Wisconsin—A Good Place to Live—to Work—to Do Business.* Businessmen interested in possible relocation may want to request a copy of the most recent annual report of the city, and a copy of the January 20, 1973, *Bulletin* of the Citizens' Governmental Research Bureau, available from the office of Mayor Arnold H. Klentz, City of West Allis, West Allis, Wis. 53227.

CITY/STATE: West Allis, Wisconsin
POPULATION: __71,723__ 1960-70 change: __+5.2__ %
__0.4__% non-white. __10.7__% over 65.
REAL ESTATE: Median value, $__19,000__. __212__ less than $10,000, __10,399__$10,000 to $25,000, __2,163__$25,000 and over. Median gross rent, $__109__. __3,116__ less than $100, __3,731__. $100 to $150, __941__$150 and over.
EDUCATION: Median school years completed, __12.1__. __54.7__% high school graduates.
INCOME: Median family income, $__11,050__. __7,580__ less than $10,000, __10,862__$10,000 to $25,000, __540__$25,000 and over.
EMPLOYMENT: __30,587__ in labor force, __38.5__% in manufacturing, __3.8__% unemployed.

26 WILKES-BARRE, Pennsylvania

Wilkes-Barre was having enough problems, adjusting its economy to a vanishing coal industry, when tropical storm Agnes hit it in June 1972. One of the worst natural disasters in the nation's history, Agnes aimed her wrath particularly at Wilkes-Barre.

With the Susquehanna River sweeping over its banks, 100,000 people had to be evacuated from their homes, including 16,000 who were over 60 years old. Every downtown business was buried under mud and water. Also inundated were 150 manufacturing firms, with damage to railroads intensifying the industrial impact. (And all the major railroads affected were in bankruptcy.) The flood hit commercial firms representing 80 percent of the business in the area, and directly across the river, in the upper-middle-class suburb of Kingston, all but 20 of the 7,167 buildings were swamped. Total property damage was estimated at $1.2 billion.

The people of Wilkes-Barre have worked valiantly to recover from the effects of Agnes, and in some important areas they have met with more success than would have been predicted after the storm. A *New York Times* report in December 1972 told how more than two-thirds of the stores had been redecorated and opened, and how most residents who wanted work could get it. President Nixon personally delivered a $4 million federal assistance check to a local college that had been hard-hit. At a Christmas party, Santa Claus distributed 5,000 toys to children who were victims of the previous spring's flood. Many of the toys were provided by residents of the Mississippi gulf coast, which had been devastated by hurricane Camille in 1969.

Initially the area's economy was agrarian. The discovery of anthracite coal in 1808, however, opened it to the mining industry and a great network of railroads. The coal industry in this area reached its zenith in 1918, when 37.7 million tons of coal were mined. Peak employment was 67,207 workers in 1926, but the decline had already begun—and it accelerated. By 1970 tonnage reached an all-time low of 2,719,940, and mining employment was down to 2,038—barely 2 percent of the total work force.

But just as the late thirties marked the waning years of mining, they also marked the beginning of the area's economic renaissance. An industrial development program launched at that time, and continued to the present, helped transform the area's once narrow-based economy into one that is much more widely diversified.

As the mines closed, apparel manufacturers moved into the area and became the major source of factory jobs—constituting a third of the manufacturing employment today. The other major industries in the Wilkes-Barre/Scranton area are food processing, fabricated metals, electrical machinery, leather, paper, tobacco, printing and publishing, textiles, and nonelectrical machinery. It should be noted, however, that in the dominant apparel industry, the majority of workers are women and wage-rates are low.

Persons of foreign birth or parentage comprise 29.1 percent of Wilkes-Barre's population, with the largest groups being Polish and Italian. Housing is still badly affected by flood damage, with thousands of victims living in mobile homes and long waiting lists for the services of plumbers, electricians, and so forth, but in normal times the city offers a good choice of urban living or suburban living in mountain, country, and lake areas.

Both public and parochial school systems are available. Wilkes College and Kings College (coeducational) and Misericordia College (women) offer graduate degrees. Penn State University Center and Luzerne County Community College provide two-year continuing education programs with an emphasis on technical curriculum. Also in the area are two new vocational-technical schools, a business college, and Wyoming Seminary, a coeducational preparatory school.

The area is served by four hospitals—Nesbitt, Wyoming Valley, Wilkes-Barre General, and Mercy. A regional Veterans Administration hospital is also located here. Kirby Memorial Health Center, fully supported by private endowment, houses many of the community's health and welfare agencies. Valley Crest is a $4 million, 300-bed home for the indigent and infirm, serving all of the county.

Wilkes-Barre is accessible in minutes to Interstates 80, 81, 84, and the Pennsylvania Turnpike's Northeast Extension. Bus schedulees include express service to New York, 100 air miles away, and to Philadelphia, 90 air miles to the south. The Wilkes-Barre/Scranton airport is served by major and feeder airlines, including Eastern and Allegheny.

Cultural activities include a Fine Arts Fiesta and the programs of the Philharmonic Orchestra, Oratorio Society, chamber music groups, Art League, Little Theater, Historical Society, Ballet Guild, Orpheus Choral Society, and Mozart Club.

Sports range from golf and tennis to a wide variety of water sports and winter activities. Pocono Downs, one of the nation's newest tracks, provides harness and flat racing. Hunting and fishing abound. Situated on the rim of the Pocono Mountains resort area, you enjoy its many outdoor-oriented attractions.

FOR FURTHER INFORMATION Write to the Greater Wilkes-Barre Chamber of Commerce, Chamber of Commerce Building, Wilkes-Barre, Pa. 18701, and ask for *Greater Wilkes-Barre Pennsylvania— A Good Place to Visit . . . a Great Place to Live!* (an illustrated color folder), a stapled series of information-sheets, and the *Community Profile* sheet. Businessmen interested in possible relocation should also contact the Economic Development Council of North-eastern Pennsylvania, Inc., P.O. Box 777, Avoca, Pa. 18641.

CITY/STATE: ___Wilkes-Barre, Pennsylvania___

POPULATION: __58,856__ 1960–70 change: __-7.4__%

__1.8__% non-white. __14.9__% over 65.

REAL ESTATE: Median value, $__9,300__. __4,801__ less than $10,000, __3,376__$10,000 to $25,000, __311__$25,000 and over. Median gross rent, $__62__. __7,512__ less than $100, __770__. $100 to $150, __145__$150 and over.

EDUCATION: Median school years completed, __11.5__. __46.3__% high school graduates.

INCOME: Median family income, $__8,047__. __9,888__ less than $10,000, __4,752__$10,000 to $25,000, __277__$25,000 and over.

EMPLOYMENT: __23,930__ in labor force, __35.0__% in manufacturing, __4.2__% unemployed.

27 ALTOONA, Pennsylvania

Jim Marks was a railroad man, and when he first saw the famed Horseshoe Curve of the Pennsylvania Railroad he was enthralled. He asked that when he died, his body be cremated and the ashes scattered around the Curve. That day came in 1941, and railroad officials accompanied his widow in a business car when she carried out this sad rite in fulfillment of his request.

Railroad men aren't the only persons fascinated by Horseshoe Curve—the public is too, with more than a quarter of a million visitors seeing it each year. The Alleghenies were the greatest obstacle to the railroad in its western push, and in 1847 a railroad engineer devised the vast semicircular route as a means of keeping the grade of the track to no more than 1.75 percent, rather than the 4.37 percent grade of a route directly across the valley of the Juniata River. That difference in grade has immense practical effects—allowing the usual three-unit diesel engine, for example, to take 125 cars up the slope rather than 43. It is a construction wonder, too, built entirely by men with picks, shovels, horses, and drags, before the day of the bulldozer and the steamshovel.

Altoona, Pennsylvania, has always been a railroad town, but 20 years ago it faced a bleak future as employment at its vast railroad shops dwindled with the passing of steam. Altoona Enterprises was organized to turn the economy around, and it did that through diversification.

Altoona's most interesting product today is undoubtedly Slinky, the toy that walks downstairs, but it is also home to the Butterick Division of American Can Company (dress patterns), Crane Company (plumbing, heating, and air-conditioning equipment), PPG Industries, Proctor-Silex, Puritan Sportswear, Saf-T-Bak (men's work and hunting clothes), RSL Shuttlecocks, SKF bearings, Sylvania Electric Products, U.S. Envelopes, and Veeder-Root (computers). Other manufacturers produce brass and copper extrusions, mattresses, steel fabrications, coal-mining equipment, truck bodies, clay products, shoes, washers, clothing, tank-car coatings, foundry pieces, boilers, machine products, paper goods, tubing, electrical fixtures, and specialized machinery.

The city's public schools include a very large high school, three junior high schools, a number of elementary schools, and a new $7 million area vocational-technical school. Altoona also has parochial schools and Pen-Mont Academy, a private Montessori-system school for grades one to four. The Altoona Campus of Pennsylvania State University enrolls about 1,000 full-time day students and 800 adults in the continuing education division.

Medical facilities include two city hospitals, Altoona and Mercy, with a total of about 650 beds. In the immediate area are a U.S. Veterans Hospital and the Pennsylvania State Mental Hospital. Within a few miles are Nason Hospital in Roaring Springs and Tyrone Hospital in Tyrone. The chamber of commerce lists 18 dentists and 21 doctors available for taking new patients.

The city is 30 miles from the Pennsylvania Turnpike and 43 miles from Interstate 80. As befits a railroad town, it still has rail passenger service—a remarkable (for our day) six trains eastbound and seven westbound daily. The airport is serviced by Allegheny Airlines, Pennsylvania Commuter Airlines, and KMK Airlines.

Altoona has one television channel (a CBS affiliate), four AM and three FM radio stations, and two dailies in the county—the *Altoona Mirror* and the *Daily Herald*.

In cultural affairs, Altoona boasts of a great restoration—the old Mishler Theater, which hosted Sara Bernhardt, the Barrymores, Otis

Skinner, Lillian Russell, and many others. Spearheading the restoration was the Blair County Arts Foundation, whose participating organizations include the Alto Artists Guild, the Altoona Blair County Photographic Society, the Altoona Choral Society, the Community Theater, the Altoona Mannerchor, the Altoona Symphony League and Symphony Society, the American Guild of Organists, the Baldwin Organ Club, the Blair County Civic Music Association, the Lyric Choraleers, and a number of other groups. An arts festival is held annually in the downtown area.

Recreation in the city centers around the parks and playgrounds, swimming pools, tennis courts, and four indoor recreation centers. Six country clubs and golf courses are found here, as well as archery, rifle, revolver, trap, and skeet layouts. A Hunt Club keeps alive the tradition of riding to hounds. Lakemont is a restored amusement park in the grand tradition of the turn of the century. And the surrounding mountains supply ski centers, caverns, springs, lookouts and scenic drives, hunting lodges, and magnificent fall foliage tours.

FOR FURTHER INFORMATION Write to the Altoona Area Chamber of Commerce, 1107 12th Street, Altoona, Pa. 16601, and ask for the 52-page illustrated color booklet, *Altoona, Pennsylvania* ($1), as well as mimeographed, stapled information-sheets for tourists, *It's in Blair County, Pa.* (a tourist guide), the *Visitors Guide, World Famous Horseshoe Curve* (a folder), *Clean Water, Clean Air, Clean Fun* (a brochure on Blair County), and *History of Blair County.*

CITY/STATE: ___Altoona, Pennsylvania___

POPULATION: __62,900__ 1960-70 change: __-9.4__% __1.4__% non-white. __15.0__% over 65.

REAL ESTATE: Median value, $__7,700__. __8,793__ less than $10,000, __4,307__ $10,000 to $25,000, __558__ $25,000 and over. Median gross rent, $__57__. __5,618__ less than $100, __306__. $100 to $150, __95__ $150 and over.

EDUCATION: Median school years completed, __11.7__. __47.9__% high school graduates.

INCOME: Median family income, $__7,979__. __10,944__ less than $10,000, __5,265__ $10,000 to $25,000, __258__ $25,000 and over.

EMPLOYMENT: __22,958__ in labor force, __26.1__% in manufacturing, __3.4__% unemployed.

28 SIOUX FALLS, South Dakota

South Dakota is often referred to as the nation's most agricultural state. Its business and industrial economic development is tied directly to an expanding agricultural base and especially to the livestock industry.

The economy of Sioux Falls reflects the state's agricultural orientation, but it is branching out in new directions as well. Its largest employer, with a work force of 4,200, is John Morrell & Company—fourth-largest meat-packer in America. And based on receipts, the Sioux Falls stockyards are the ninth-largest in the nation. But the city has also become the retailing, wholesaling, and communications center of an entire region. Electronics, steel fabrication, plastics, millwork, the manufacture of farm machinery and road equipment—these are now all part of the Sioux Falls scene. And in 1973 Sioux Falls entered the space age with the opening of the Interior Department's Earth Resources Observation System (EROS) Data Center, staffed by some 150 specialists who will evaluate and process scientific data collected by orbiting satellites.

The production of cattle, hogs, and lambs remains important in the region. Leading items in export trade are feed grains, soybeans, tallow, lard, and flaxseed. The agricultural lands immediately surrounding Sioux Falls grow abundant crops of corn, rye, soybeans, wheat, oats, barley, flax, and alfalfa hay.

The Police Department has 113 full-time officers, and is equipped with 35 radio cars and four motorcycles. Mayor M.E. Schirmer considers it "among the best in the Upper Midwest. We carry on a continuous training program and do an outstanding job in recruitment," he says. "Also, it is significant that we have between 20 and 30 of our police officers attending local colleges, taking subjects dealing with their profession and also other subjects leading to a degree. Many of our police officers are college graduates."

In the Sioux Falls public school system are 20 elementary schools, four junior highs, and two high schools. The parochial system has seven elementary schools and a high school. An Episcopal elementary day school is also in operation, as are special schools for deaf and crippled children. Augustana College (Lutheran) has some 2,000 students, and Sioux Falls College (Baptist) about 1,000. Business and trade educational facilities include the Southeast Area Vocational-Technical School and Nettleton Commercial College. And within an hour's drive of the city are four more colleges and universities.

Two large general hospitals, a Veterans Administration hospital, and a crippled children's hospital have a total capacity of nearly 1,000 beds. Other facilities in Sioux Falls include eight medical clinics, eight nursing homes, facilities for the training and care of the mentally handicapped, and 23 pharmacies. More than 150 physicians and 43 dentists practice in the city.

In transportation, Sioux Falls is located at the junction of Interstates 90 and 29. The city airport is served by Western, North Central, and Ozark airlines, with 40 flights daily, including direct flights to Washington, New York, and St. Louis. Minneapolis is 210 miles northeast, and Chicago is 510 miles southeast.

Sioux Falls has a daily newspaper, the *Argus-Leader*, and a weekly, the *Suburban News*. Eight radio stations broadcast from the city. There are two local television stations, affiliates of CBS and NBC, with reception also of an ABC-affiliated channel from Mitchell, South Dakota.

The 89 churches in Sioux Falls include congregations of nearly 40 denominations, with Lutheran churches predominating. The public library system has over 100,000 volumes, with another 200,000 volumes in the college libraries. Cultural activities include a concert and lecture series and the productions of the Sioux Falls Augustana Symphony Orchestra, the Municipal Band, the Community Playhouse, the Community Concert Association, the Civic Fine Arts Center, and the two colleges. Pettigrew Museum features exhibits on history and the natural arts.

Recreation includes amateur competition in a wide array of sports, the facilities of 26 parks, and Northern League baseball play. A ski center, four swimming pools, skating rinks, and five golf courses are other attractions. Children enjoy the Great Plains Zoo and Dennis the Menace Park, where they can play in real-life objects—including a jet airplane, a fire engine, an army tank, and other fascinating "toys." Sioux Falls is approximately an hour away from a region known as "the heart of the pheasant country," with duck and goose hunting an additional challenge, and the Great Lakes of South Dakota—created by dams on the Missouri River—offer superb fishing.

FOR FURTHER INFORMATION Write to the Chamber of Commerce, P.O. Box 1425, Sioux Falls, S. Dak. 57101, and ask for *This Is Sioux Falls* (both a printed folder and a mimeographed sheet), *You Will Enjoy Seeing . . .* , *O Beautiful for Spacious Skies* (a bro-

chure on the space data center), *Historical Review of Sioux Falls,
Tour Guide of Sioux Falls,* the brochure on the Pettigrew Museum,
Siouxland Ecumenical Association (a listing of churches), *List of
Manufacturers and Processors,* a city map, a current issue of the
Sioux Falls Guide, and information-sheets on schools, employment
agencies, real estate agencies, general information, and legal infor-
mation. If you are a businessman thinking of relocation, *Horizons—
Sioux Falls in the 70's* is a 69-page booklet available from the Sioux
Falls Development Foundation, 101 West 9th Street, Sioux Falls, S. Dak.
57102.

CITY/STATE: Sioux Falls, South Dakota
POPULATION: ___72,488___ 1960–70 change: ___+10.7___%
___1.0___% non-white. ___10.3___% over 65.
REAL ESTATE: Median value, $___16,000___. ___1,987___less than
$10,000, ___9,294___$10,000 to $25,000, ___1,891___$25,000 and
over. Median gross rent, $___85___. ___5,099___less than $100,
___2,121___. $100 to $150, ___550___$150 and over.
EDUCATION: Median school years completed, ___12.4___.
___65.4___% high school graduates.
INCOME: Median family income, $___9,617___. ___9,361___less than
$10,000, ___7,708___$10,000 to $25,000, ___510___$25,000 and over.
EMPLOYMENT: ___29,920___in labor force, ___16.2___% in manufacturing, ___4.3___% unemployed.

29 ROCHESTER, Minnesota

World famous for the Mayo Clinic, Rochester is truly an excep-
tional city. In dining, cultural life, and transportation—and in many
other areas as well—its concentration of professional population has
resulted in facilities and opportunities far superior to what one
would expect in a city of 54,000.

The Clinic itself employs 1,200 physicians and some 3,000 other
workers. Another 3,000 medical and paramedical personnel are employed by the hospitals affiliated with the Clinic. And the Clinic con-

tributes in still another way to the community's economy: it is the principal reason Rochester has an estimated 500,000 visitors annually, resulting in the great variety of lodging, dining, and transportation facilities.

The IBM Corporation is another major contributor to the economy, for its Midwest manufacturing and research plant in Rochester employs some 5,000 persons. Libby, McNeill & Libby (canned vegetables), the Johnson Company (A. B. Dick and printing), and other smaller firms are also located here.

The average cost of homes in Rochester is about $20 per square foot of living area. In two-story houses, the cost for the first floor remains $20, while the cost per square foot on the second floor is $12. Apartments range from efficiencies to three-bedroom units, with many renting in the $150 to $175 range. High-rises, garden apartments, and multiple-unit buildings are available, many of them featuring wall-to-wall carpeting, draperies, air-conditioning, swimming pools (both indoor and outdoor), barbecue areas, indoor recreation rooms, saunas, and tennis courts.

Public education facilities consist of 27 elementary, three junior high, and two senior high schools. There are also five Catholic and Lutheran elementary schools and a Catholic high school. Adult and higher education opportunities are provided by Rochester State Junior College, an extension center of the University of Minnesota, the Rochester Area Vocational-Technical Institute, various medical training programs, and schools of art, dancing, music, and beauty culture.

Rochester's medical facilities, of course, are unsurpassed. The Mayo Clinic, with its 1,200 physicians, is the world's largest association of physicians in a coordinated group practice of medicine. Affiliated with the Clinic are Saint Mary's Hospital and Rochester Methodist Hospital, with a combined capacity of more than 1,500 beds and the most advanced facilities. Olmsted Community Hospital and Rochester State Hospital (for the emotionally and mentally ill) bring the total number of beds to more than 3,000. Among the training facilities are the Mayo Graduate School of Medicine (largest in the world), the Mayo Medical School for Undergraduates, and three nurses' training programs.

In climate, Rochester has four distinct seasons. The average winter temperature is 16.1 degrees, the average summer temperature 69.7 degrees. On the average, 35 days a year have subzero temperatures, and five have temperatures of 90 degrees or more. Average annual snowfall is 41.9 inches, with an annual precipitation of 28.46 inches. The altitude is 1,021 feet above sea level.

Rochester, 80 miles south of the Twin Cities of Minneapolis and St. Paul, is nine miles from Interstate 90. There is excellent bus and limousine service, including limousine service to the Twin Cities. And Rochester's Municipal Airport is the second-largest airport in the state, with more than 30 flights daily on Northwest Orient, North Central, and Ozark airlines.

The *Rochester Post Bulletin* is a daily newspaper, and Minneapolis and St. Paul newspapers are also available. The city has four radio stations and an NBC-affiliated television channel, with reception of Twin Cities radio and television stations.

Rochester's more than 45 churches represent some 25 denominations. Organizations of all kinds abound. The Rochester Symphony Orchestra, the Symphony Choral, five vocal choruses, the Civic Theater, the Municipal Band, the Oratorio Society, and the Diversified Art Center contribute much to the cultural life of the city. Cultural activities range from summer open-air concerts and carillon concerts three times a week to a Beaux Arts Ball, the seasonal presentation of *The Messiah*, and an annual Festival of the Arts. Of particular interest is Mayowood, the beautiful estate of Doctors Charles W. and Charles H. Mayo, now a state historical site. Rochester also has a library with more than 117,000 volumes, and three museums—treating medical science, local history, and antique vehicles.

For recreation and entertainment there are movie theaters, nightclubs, and more than 80 restaurants. Golfers will find three 18-hole public courses and a private golf and country club. Twenty city parks, 12 areas with athletic facilities, a youth hockey arena, paved tennis courts, an indoor tennis club, ski slopes and snowmobile trails, and outdoor and indoor swimming pools—these are just some of the many recreational facilities, both private and public. Silver Lake, in the center of the city, is a winter refuge for some 17,000 giant Canadian geese, and the surrounding countryside delights the visitor, with gently rolling lands swelling into the high hills of the Hiawatha Valley of the mighty Mississippi.

FOR FURTHER INFORMATION Write to the Rochester Area Chamber of Commerce, 212 First Avenue Southwest, Rochester, Minn. 55901, and ask for *Rochester Welcomes You* and *Rochester Facts and Figures* (two illustrated color brochures), *Profile of a City* (a 12-page factual leaflet), the *Visitor Map* and a current issue of the *Rochester Guide Magazine*, its *Hotel Motel Guide* and *Directory of Guest Homes & Apartments*, and folders on Mayowood and the Hemp Old Vehicle Museum.

CITY/STATE: _____Rochester, Minnesota_____

POPULATION: __53,766__1960–70 change: __+32.2__%
__1.2__% non-white. __9.8__% over 65.

REAL ESTATE: Median value, $__20,900__. __258__less than
$10,000, __6,595__$10,000 to $25,000, __2,733__$25,000 and
over. Median gross rent, $__125__. __1,984__less than $100,
__2,267__. $100 to $150, __1,874__$150 and over.

EDUCATION: Median school years completed, __12.7__.
__74.0__% high school graduates.

INCOME: Median family income, $__11,563__. __4,674__less than
$10,000, __7,019__$10,000 to $25,000, __716__$25,000 and over.

EMPLOYMENT: __23,417__in labor force, __16.0__% in manufacturing, __3.0__% unemployed.

30 LA CROSSE, Wisconsin

Founded as a trading post in 1841, La Crosse has grown into the largest city in Wisconsin on the Mississippi River. The setting is magnificent, for here the Black and La Crosse rivers merge with the mighty Mississippi, framed by bluffs and hills that break into brilliant hues of reds, browns, and yellows in the fall. Grandad Bluff is a park area on one of those ridges, hundreds of feet above the river, and from it your view extends to the city below, Minnesota and Iowa on the other side of the Mississippi, and wooded coulees (or valleys) headed inland.

Prominent among the diverse industries located here are the Trane Company (air-conditioning and heating equipment), G. Heileman Brewing Company (beer), La Crosse Rubber Mills (rubber footwear), Dairyland Power Coop, La Crosse Garment Company (clothing), and La Crosse Telephone Company. Other important employers are La Crosse Cooler Company (refrigeration equipment), Machine Products (machine parts), Northern States Power, U.O.P. Norplex Corporation (plastics), and—in nearby Onalaska—Metallics, Inc. (metal stamping) and Outers Laboratories (gun products).

Of the 16,000 housing units, 68 percent are owner-occupied. Unlike most cities, the residential areas close to downtown have not de-

teriorated but reflect generations of pride on the part of their own-
ers. You can trace the city's growth as you proceed from the older
residential areas in the center of town to the newer ones toward the
bluffs. In recent years families have begun to build up the steep
ridges and in the wooded coulees, enjoying the panoramic views. And
instead of high-rise apartments, many choose to live in town houses
with patios and balconies that take advantage of the beautiful sur-
roundings.

Fifteen elementary schools, three junior highs, and two high
schools enroll about 10,000 students in the public educational system.
Catholic schools enroll another 4,000 in seven elementary schools,
a high school, and Holy Cross Seminary, a live-in preparatory school.
The Lutheran school system consists of three grade schools and
a high school in Onalaska. There is also a Seventh-Day Adventist
school, as well as a school for the physically handicapped and another for the hard of hearing and deaf.

La Crosse is home to a branch of Wisconsin State University,
enrolling some 7,000 students in its undergraduate and graduate programs; to Viterbo College, a four-year coeducational college specializing in teacher training; and to the Western Wisconsin Technical Institute, offering vocational and technical programs in 40 fields.

Three hospitals and a number of excellent clinics provide first-rate
medical facilities for the area, which is served by 130 physicians, 56
dentists, and nine chiropractors. St. Francis Hospital has 340 beds, a
Newborn Center, a 67-bed nursing home, and a halfway house for
former mental patients. It operates four schools, and is staffed by 60
physicians and 27 dentists. La Crosse Lutheran Hospital, staffed by
72 physicians, is an ultramodern facility with 350 beds, 14 bassinets,
10 operating rooms, and three training schools. La Crosse Hospital
has 42 beds with emergency, operating, and acute-care facilities,
staffed by 27 doctors. Affiliated with it is the 112-bed Eleanora Gund
Nursing Home. Gundersen Clinic, with 70 physicians and surgeons,
is considered one of the best clinics in the nation. Also in La Crosse
are the Skemp Grandview Clinic, La Crosse Clinic, Barge Chiropractic Clinic, and La Crosse Neuropsychiatric Clinic.

Normal temperatures range from 16 degrees in the winter to 70
degrees during the summer. Average annual precipitation is about
30 inches, with plenty of snow during the winter. The average elevation is about 650 feet above sea level.

Transportation facilities include Interstate 90 and air passenger
service by North Central Airlines and Mississippi Valley Airways.
The Milwaukee Road, Burlington Northern, and Chicago & North

Western railroads provide freight service and an amazing (for this day) 15 passenger trains daily.

The *La Crosse Tribune* is a daily newspaper. There are also four weeklies, four radio stations, and two television stations. Cable TV subscribers receive another nine channels.

More than 60 churches represent some 30 denominations and faiths. In addition to the modern city library, the one on the Wisconsin State University campus houses more than 208,000 volumes. Cultural life centers around the La Crosse Community Theater, the Coulee Region Symphony Orchestra, the Fine Arts Association, the La Crosse County Historical Society, and the La Crosse Society of Arts and Crafts. For three weeks each year the Coulee Region Festival of Arts features pop and symphonic music concerts, art exhibits, choral performances, and a symphony summer school.

Municipal and private recreation programs take full advantage of the many facilites, including pools and beaches, tennis courts and ball fields, ice rinks, 19 parks, numerous public golf courses and a private country club, a zoo, an aquarium, and a wildlife refuge on Goose Island. At the first sign of spring, La Crosse's residents invade the river by motorboat, houseboat, sailboat, or on an old-fashioned paddle-wheeler. Fishing, sailing, and water skiing all have their devoted fans, while others head for the hills to hike, hunt, or enjoy the 22 coulee-country motor trails. Winter doesn't slow the pace: there's ice fishing, skating, skiing on Mt. La Crosse, and snowmobiling. Clubs abound, including enough square dance clubs to make this the "Square Dance Capital of the World." And among the highlights each year are the Stars of Tomorrow Baseball Tournament, the Apple Festival (across the river in La Crescent, Minnesota), the Horse Show, the Interstate Fair, and the Oktoberfest—five days of impromptu concerts by German bands, a queen's pageant, a parade, name entertainers, and lots of consumption of the popular local beers.

FOR FURTHER INFORMATION Write to the Greater La Crosse Chamber of Commerce, Box 842, La Crosse, Wis. 54601, and ask for its 84-page illustrated color booklet on the city ($1.50), and for the *Recreation Guide to La Crosse* (an illustrated color brochure), the *Industrial Directory* ($1), *Facts on La Crosse, Wisconsin,* and tourist folders on *The Hixon House, Guide to Dining, Motel Hotel Guide, La Crosse County Camp Sites,* and *The Big Indian Boat Lines.*

CITY/STATE:　　　La Crosse, Wisconsin
POPULATION: _51,153_____1960–70 change: __+7.5__%
__0.5__% non-white. __12.7__% over 65.
REAL ESTATE: Median value, $_16,500_. _1,206_less than
$10,000, _6,685_$10,000 to $25,000, _1,253_$25,000 and
over. Median gross rent, $__79__. _4,108_less than $100,
_1,170_. $100 to $150, _386_$150 and over.
EDUCATION: Median school years completed, __12.3__.
_60.8_% high school graduates.
INCOME: Median family income, $_9,099_. _6,806_less than
$10,000, _4,746_$10,000 to $25,000, _438_$25,000 and over.
EMPLOYMENT: _19,623_in labor force, _25.3____% in manufacturing, __6.3__% unemployed.

31 CEDAR RAPIDS, Iowa

The U.S. Department of Commerce refers to the Cedar Rapids economy as one of the most depression-proof in the country. *Life* magazine described Cedar Rapids as one of the nation's four most livable communities. They must be doing something right, here in the midst of the Iowa corn fields.

More than 200 manufacturing and processing firms make economic conditions good indeed. There is always a demand for professional, skilled, and semiskilled workers (and, conversely, very little demand for the unskilled). The population is increasing at about 5,000 persons per year, retail sales increase about $25 million each year, and the manufacturing payroll increases by $25 million to $50 million annually.

No one industry dominates the economy, but the larger ones include Collins Radio (makers of the astronauts' radio equipment), the Wilson-Sinclair Company (meat-packers), with a plant that slaughters 1,200 cattle and 10,000 hogs a day, and Quaker Oats, with the world's largest cereal mill. Eighteen miles south of town is Amana Refrigeration (refrigerators, freezers, microwave ovens, air-conditioners, furnaces).

Housing is varied in price range and style, and more than 10,000 rental units are available. Nearly 70 percent of the homes are owner-occupied, and another 600 to 800 homes are built each year to meet the demands of the expanding population. Prices are average for a Midwestern metropolis of 100,000.

Cedar Rapids' public schools are rated among the top 5 percent in the nation, and the Catholic school system is complete from first grade through high school. The public system includes three senior high schools, six junior highs, and 30 grade schools; there are two parochial high schools and eight parochial grade schools. The city also benefits from the presence of three colleges—the highly respected Coe College, Mount Mercy College, and Kirkwood Community College, where the enrollment has mushroomed to nearly 2,000 full-time students and 18,000 adult and continuing education students. Kirkwood's major divisions are vocational-technical, adult education, and arts and sciences. Nearby, too, are Cornell College (17 miles away) and the University of Iowa (26 miles).

Two modern hospitals and 191 physicians and surgeons serve the medical needs of Cedar Rapids. St. Luke's Hospital, with 650 beds, and Mercy Hospital, with 390 beds, have tried to avoid duplication of costly equipment and services, and thus provide the city with a wider range of facilities. And 26 miles south is the University of Iowa Medical Hospital and a Veterans Administration Hospital.

United Air Lines and Ozark Air Lines provide passenger service at the municipal airport, and railroad passenger service is provided by the Chicago, Milwaukee, St. Paul & Pacific Railroad. There are ample bus connections, and Interstate 80 is located 18 miles south of the city. The *Cedar Rapids Gazette* is published daily and on Sunday, and four radio stations and four television stations broadcast from Cedar Rapids. The TV stations have affiliations with all three networks and with National Educational Television.

The 109 churches in Cedar Rapids represent 54 denominations. Cultural activities—many of them related to the three colleges—include the programs of the Cedar Rapids Art Association, the Children's Theater, the Cedar Rapids Symphony Orchestra, the Municipal Band, a Community Concert series, the Art Center, a Community Theater, the Coe Promenade Orchestra, and the Coe College Fine Arts Festival. In addition to the city's public library system and the college libraries, the Iowa Masonic Library and Museum welcomes visitors.

Cedar Rapids' recreational facilities are spread over 59 parks covering 2,232 acres, 35 playgrounds, 30 tot-lots, 12 ice rinks, four swimming pools, and four recreation centers (including one for senior citizens). Other facilities include Memorial Baseball Stadium, Kingston Stadium, tennis courts, and archery ranges. Team sports competition is keen, and special classes are offered in such activities as speed skating, tobogganing, tennis, square dancing, softball, drama, arts and crafts, and gardening. Water sports are highly popular— swimming in the pools; boating, water skiing, and fishing on the Cedar River in the center of the city; and boating, camping, and picnicking at spots farther along the river.

August brings the annual festival known as Venetian Nights on the Cedar, with a parade of boats and floats, and water sports performances, on the Cedar River. The All-Iowa Fair is also held in August, at Hawkeye Downs, the scene too for big-car and stock-car racing, the Kennel Club dog show, the Shrine horse show, and the Boy Scout Exposition. A short drive away are the attractions of the Mississippi River and Iowa's state parks. Particularly recommended is a visit to the Amana Colonies, 20 minutes from Cedar Rapids. The restaurants and shops here will introduce you to the fascinating culture of these colonies founded by pioneers of German, Swiss, and Alsatian ancestry.

FOR FURTHER INFORMATION Write to the Cedar Rapids Chamber of Commerce, 127 Third Street, N.E., Cedar Rapids, Iowa 52401, and ask for their 132-page illustrated color booklet, *Cedar Rapids, Iowa . . . City of Five Seasons;* also of interest: *Manufacturers of Cedar Rapids and Marion* and the fact-sheet on taxes.

CITY/STATE: Cedar Rapids, Iowa
POPULATION: __110,642__ 1960–70 change: __+20.2__ %
__2.0__ % non-white. __9.5__ % over 65.
REAL ESTATE: Median value, $__18,100__. __1,581__ less than $10,000, __17,507__ $10,000 to $25,000, __4,123__ $25,000 and over. Median gross rent, $__105__. __4,836__ less than $100, __4,339__. $100 to $150, __1,421__ $150 and over.
EDUCATION: Median school years completed, __12.4__.
__68.1__ % high school graduates.
INCOME: Median family income, $__10,900__. __11,786__ less than $10,000, __14,874__ $10,000 to $25,000, __1,104__ $25,000 and over.
EMPLOYMENT: __46,229__ in labor force, __34.5__ % in manufacturing, __4.1__ % unemployed.

32 MEDFORD, Massachusetts

While I was writing this book, news leaked to the *Medford Mercury* that their city was being listed as one of the nation's safest. A local resident sent me a tearsheet with an article about this, and a note recording her "amusement"—"because it has been a long-standing joke around here that the reason we are safe is because the Mafia live here."

Intrigued, I read the newspaper, and next to the article about this book was an article with the headline, "Teresa . . . A Hunted Man!" The Teresa in question was a fellow author, Vincent "Big Vinnie" Teresa. A self-professed Mafia leader who turned state's evidence, Teresa has recorded his life in the underworld in a most interesting—and amusing—book, *My Life in the Mafia*. Of particular interest to Medford, however, was the fact that this infamous resident still owed $201.30 for his 1966 automobile excise tax. Teresa apparently has been more concerned over the $500,000 price-tag he claims the underworld has put on his head.

Whatever the truth—or lack of it—in my correspondent's bit of gossip, it was not one of the factors mentioned by Chief John C. Kirwan as he outlined the reasons for Medford's low crime-rate. He noted how Medford is a "bedroom" community three miles northwest of Boston, with an income level about the same as Boston's, that it is the home of Tufts University, and that it is a "dry" city—though he doesn't necessarily see a correlation between that factor and the lower crime.

The nearness to Boston *is* a definite factor, says Kirwan, "inasmuch as the majority of criminals apprehended by this department are residents of other cities, with the highest proportionate number living in Boston."

The impact of Medford's minority population "on our overall crime incidence is negligible," he adds. "I am sure that the principal credit for this happy situation must be given to our minority citizens themselves, who traditionally have demonstrated a law-abiding nature. However, it may also be proper to give some credit to the staff of our police training academy who, often in the face of much local criticism, have enriched the training curriculum with the inclusion of materials on community relations."

The subject turned to Tufts, and its impact on the police. "In my judgment," says Kirwan, "a most compelling factor is the excellent working relationship existing between this department and the administrators, faculty, and student body of the university. An example illustrative of this positive relationship is that on the occasion of a recent 'nonviolent' demonstration, focused on ending the Vietnam War, a number of Tufts students picketed our local military recruiting offices for a period of five days. During this period my response was not to activate our Tactical Unit, but rather to assign a single officer in civilian clothes to this group. This officer's instructions were to initiate and maintain a dialogue with the students, to develop as many reasonable mutual guidelines as possible, and to remain with the students during the hours they were demonstrating to insure that their right to lawful free expression was not interfered with.

"This strategy had a positive 'payoff' both to the community and to the students," Kirwan claims. "Although the demonstration took place in the heart of our business district during busy afternoon hours, disruption to traffic and normal shopping activity was minimal, the expense to the taxpayers normally incurred when the Tactical Unit is activated was avoided, and the vandalism and violence which sometimes follows this type of activity did not occur. On the other hand, the students were satisfied that they had received an opportunity to dramatize their issues without even the threat of police over-reaction or what they usually perceive as harassment by the police. (During this period, no arrests were made.)"

"A highly visible police presence" is also important to crime prevention, according to Kirwan—and 72.2 percent of his personnel are assigned to patrol. He concludes that "a possible effect of the reputation this department has earned for aggressive and successful investigation of serious crimes is that most 'professional' criminals avoid Medford as a target for their crimes."

CITY/STATE: Medford, Massachusetts
POPULATION: __64,397__ 1960–70 change: __-0.9__%
__3.0__% non-white. __13.0__% over 65.
REAL ESTATE: Median value, $__22,500__. __154__ less than
$10,000, __4,486__ $10,000 to $25,000, __2,480__ $25,000 and
over. Median gross rent, $__103__. __3,508__ less than $100,
__3,578__. $100 to $150, __581__ $150 and over.
EDUCATION: Median school years completed, __12.2__.
__59.8__% high school graduates.
INCOME: Median family income, $__11,145__. __6,719__ less than
$10,000, __8,852__ $10,000 to $25,000, __746__ $25,000 and over.
EMPLOYMENT: __26,875__ in labor force, __22.1__% in manufacturing, __3.1__% unemployed.

33 ODESSA, Texas

Odessa is the home of the only Shakespeare Festival in the Southwest—and also hosts an annual rattlesnake hunt. One of its colleges has a School of Drilling Technology, which draws students from every major oil-producing nation in the world, and its rodeo is the first of the year for world-champion cowboys.

The city got its name from the Russian immigrant workers on the Texas & Pacific Railway, who were reminded of the region around their native Odessa, Russia, by the wide, flat prairies. But Odessa, *Texas,* is very much a showcase of capitalism. It is the home of the nation's largest inland petrochemical complex, with 16 plants producing synthetic rubber, polyethylene and polypropylene for plastic goods, nylon, styrene, butadiene, and agricultural fertilizers. The four major companies in this $300 million complex are El Paso Products (a subsidiary of El Paso Natural Gas), Rexene Polymers (a division of Dart Industries, Inc.), General Tire & Rubber, and Shell Oil.

In addition, the region has 17 other petroleum complexes, eight oil refineries, and 92 gas and gas products plants. Odessa alone has 592 service and supply centers that cater to the petroleum and petrochemical industry. The Permian Basin, of which Odessa is the center, has over 20 percent of the nation's discovered oil reserves and 13 percent of its gas reserves.

Odessa also has the largest steel service center between Houston and Phoenix, and the greatest number of highly skilled machinists and machine operators in that area. The largest machine shop in Odessa gets 30 percent of its contracts from Houston and the Chicago-to-Pittsburgh area.

Out on the plains, ranching continues to be important, and the Sandhills Hereford and Quarterhorse Show is dedicated to the cattlemen and their livestock—keys to the early development of the Southwest.

Average features of a $30,000 home in Odessa are 2,100 to 2,500 square feet on an 80-foot lot, four bedrooms, brick veneer, fireplace, all built-in appliances, two-car garage, and two and one-half baths. House payments (including taxes and insurance) would be about $270 per month. House rentals (unfurnished) range from $65–70 per month for two bedrooms to $200 per month for four bedrooms. Unfurnished apartments rent from $140 per month (one bedroom) to $170 per month (two bedrooms).

Chief of Police Jack Tomlin told me that "Odessa is a proud, competitive city," and "it is this spirit which carries over into our city's attitude on crime. Generally, this attitude may be described as intolerant. As a result of this intolerance, we receive a great deal of cooperation from all levels of our community in our efforts to prevent and suppress crime."

The stability of Odessa's economy and population, he believes, "is the second area that contributes to Odessa's low crime-rate. Odessa is a growing community, yet its population is not transient in nature. Those families that move here come with the idea of staying and making a home for themselves. Therefore, they have an interest in keeping the community as safe and low in crime as possible."

Chief Tomlin adds that "minority group reaction to the crime problem is exceptionally good, and cooperation from the minority areas is high. Odessa finds that its minority group problems are few as compared to other cities its size. No major minority problems have ever existed within the city." Also, "approximately 40 percent of our officers attend or have graduated from colleges, specializing in the field of law enforcement. They seek education as a response to the community's desire to acquire and hold the best trained officers possible."

Odessa has 23 elementary schools, seven junior highs, and three high schools in its public school system. In addition, there are four parochial schools, with Odessa Christian School and St. Mary's offering classes through the sixth grade. The city has 15 vocational schools. Odessa Junior College enrolls 2,700 students, and the University of Texas of the Permian Basin opened its doors in 1973, offering undergraduate and graduate programs.

Medical Center Hospital, with 373 beds, is the largest general hospital between Fort Worth and Phoenix. Private-room rates are $20 to $27. Odessa also has three clinics, two convalescent homes, and a rehabilitation center. Sixty-eight physicians and 24 dentists practice in town.

The climate is semiarid, with little allergy-producing pollen and over 300 days a year to enjoy outdoor activities. The average minimum temperature in January is 30.9 degrees, and the July average maximum is 94.5 degrees. (Humidity is low, however.) Average annual rainfall is 14.24 inches, including 3.4 inches of snowfall.

Odessa is located on Interstate 20, and the Midland-Odessa Air Terminal has 39 flights daily on Continental, Texas International, and Air Texas airlines.

The *Odessa American* is a daily and Sunday newspaper. Odessa has four AM radio stations, three FM radio stations, and three television channels (with affiliations with each of the networks). Three additional channels are available by cable TV.

There are more than 150 churches in the city representing 35 faiths and denominations. The library has 112,000 volumes, a Presidential Museum, and a Southwest Room with the largest genealogical collection in the Southwest. Cultural life includes a symphony, chorale, civic concert association, college fine arts series, ballet association, and art association. There are two live theaters—the Permian Playhouse and the Children's Theater—and the Shakespeare Festival, housed in the world's most authentic replica of the Bard's Globe Theater. Odessa College has an Indian museum, and another museum is located at the earth's third-largest meteor crater, eight miles west of Odessa.

Recreation is as varied as the culture. In addition to the usual range of city activities and facilities, children have an unusual playground—Prairie Pete Park. For thrill-seekers there is drag racing, with hot rods and funny cars, at the Odessa Raceway and Odessa Speed Bowl. There is excitement, too, in sail-planing, and Odessa is home to two holders of world soaring records—Al Parker and Wally Scott. And at Sandhills State Park, sand-surfing and dune buggies are what's happening.

Fishermen will find eleven lakes and reservoirs for weekend jaunts. Hunters find morning dove, blue quail, jackrabbits, squirrels, and prairie dogs locally; white tail and buck tail deer, antelope, and duck in West Texas; and black tail deer and black bear in New Mexico. New Mexico also offers good hunting for dove, quail, and duck.

Annual events range from the rodeo and Shrine Circus to a square dance festival, fine arts festival, jazz festival, rattlesnake roundup, and soap box derby.

FOR FURTHER INFORMATION Write to the Odessa Chamber of Commerce, P.O. Box 3626, Odessa, Tex. 79760, and ask for its detailed *Community Profile*, its foldout brochure *Odessa, Texas; Travel Tips—Odessa, Texas; Homes for Living*, and the city *Street Guide Map*.

CITY/STATE: Odessa, Texas
POPULATION: 78,380 1960–70 change: -2.4 %
6.5 % non-white. 4.9 % over 65.
REAL ESTATE: Median value, $11,000. 6,878 less than $10,000, 8,272 $10,000 to $25,000, 1,005 $25,000 and over. Median gross rent, $75. 4,742 less than $100, 1,046. $100 to $150, 598 $150 and over.
EDUCATION: Median school years completed, 12.1. 53.9 % high school graduates.
INCOME: Median family income, $9,385. 11,227 less than $10,000, 8,585 $10,000 to $25,000, 639 $25,000 and over.
EMPLOYMENT: 30,948 in labor force, 11.7 % in manufacturing, 4.5 % unemployed.

34 PARMA, Ohio

According to Mayor John Petruska, one of its chief boosters, Parma is a "typically American, truly cosmopolitan community. It is the ninth largest community in the state and larger in population than many entire counties in Ohio. We have hard-working, enthusiastic and conscientious homeowners, and we have families that derive a fine education from our school system and go on to greater achievements in other parts of the nation.

"Our community," he adds, "although pushed by rapid housing demands after the second World War, has still managed—through foresight on the part of many—to retain a fine residential atmosphere, a deep sense of culture, a pride in ethnic origins, a love for recreation and outdoor activities, and a respect for law and order."

Located just south of Cleveland, Parma's major industry is the Chevrolet-Cleveland Division of General Motors, which employs 9,000 in the production of transmissions, metal stampings, and prop shafts. Other major employers are Modern Tool & Die (tool and die metal stamping, consumer products); Union Carbide Corporation (research); and Ohio Bell Telephone Company.

The general price range for homes in Parma is $20,000 to $65,000. Eighty-eight percent of the homes are owner-occupied. Rental price ranges for apartments are mostly $125 to $185 for one bedroom, $150 to $240 for two bedrooms, and $195 to $310 for three bedrooms.

Parma's public schools include 21 elementary schools, five junior highs, and three senior high schools, with a total enrollment of over 26,000 and an instructional staff of 1,228. The schools have what is perhaps the best vocational program in the state, and in addition there is an adult education program with a total of over 15,000 enrolled. Another 10,000 students attend parochial schools, including 11 Catholic and Lutheran elementary schools and three Catholic high schools. The Western Campus of Cuyahoga Community College, a two-year public educational facility, is also located in Parma. It opened in 1966 with 2,800 students, and now has more than 5,000 full-time and part-time students. All of its faculty hold master's degrees or higher.

Parma Community General Hospital has 205 beds and a medical staff of 181. New construction will soon increase the numbers to 278 beds and 55 bassinets, including a new coronary and intensive-care section. Kaiser Community Health Foundation, a prepaid group-practice health-care plan, has two Parma-based facilities. Kaiser Foundation Hospital has 55 beds, and an outpatient health center has facilities for many medical departments. Holy Family Cancer Home is also located in Parma.

Cleveland-area weather statistics show a mean January temperature of 28.4 degrees, and a mean July temperature of 71.9 degrees. Average annual precipitation is 35.35 inches.

With Parma's location in the Cleveland metropolitan area, transportation facilities are complete. Cleveland's Hopkins International Airport, for example, is just to the north. The *Parma Sun Post* is a weekly newspaper, and Parma residents have available all the newspapers, radio stations, and television channels of the metropolitan area.

The 34 Protestant churches in the area include Assembly of God, Baptist, Christian, Christian Science, Church of Christ, Episcopal, Jehovah's Witnesses, Lutheran, Reformed, Presbyterian, Nazarene, and United Methodist congregations. There are 17 Catholic and Eastern Orthodox churches, including ones with Byzantine, Ukrainian, Syrian, Russian, and Serbian rites.

Parma's residents have at their disposal all the cultural fare of Cleveland, but their city itself has a Community Orchestra, a Little Theater, and the Southwest Music Association, bringing to Parma the Cleveland Orchestra with guest conductors and artists. The Parma Fine Arts Council and other such organizations add to the cultural scene. The two Parma branches of the county library system have over 188,000 volumes.

Recreational facilities include 320 acres of parks, three outdoor swimming pools, an 18-hole municipal golf course, an ice skating rink, picnic areas, a toboggan slide, and lakes stocked for fishing. Recently acquired from the government was a former Nike site of more than 92 acres, which will be developed into future recreational facilities.

FOR FURTHER INFORMATION Write to the Parma Chamber of Commerce, 5510 Pearl Road—Room 201, Parma, Ohio 44129, and ask for these mimeographed information-sheets: *Parma Statistics, History of Parma, Realtors in Parma, Apartments Located in the Parma Area, Industries in the Parma Area, Protestant Churches in the Parma Area, Catholic and Eastern Orthodox Churches in the Parma Area, Motels in the Parma Area, Emergency Information,* and *Utilities in Parma.*

CITY/STATE: Parma, Ohio

POPULATION: ___100,216___ 1960-70 change: __+21.0__ %
__0.3__ % non-white. __7.5__ % over 65.

REAL ESTATE: Median value, $__24,000__. ___106___ less than $10,000, __13,421__ $10,000 to $25,000, __10,015__ $25,000 and over. Median gross rent, $__133__. ___952___ less than $100, __2,363__. $100 to $150, __1,553__ $150 and over.

EDUCATION: Median school years completed, __12.2__.
__57.6__ % high school graduates.

INCOME: Median family income, $__12,438__. __7,973__ less than $10,000, __17,390__ $10,000 to $25,000, __1,195__ $25,000 and over.

EMPLOYMENT: __42,116__ in labor force, __34.8__ % in manufacturing, __2.2__ % unemployed.

35 CICERO, Illinois

Cicero's inclusion as one of America's safest cities will raise the eyebrows of many who have been reared on television's late-evening gangster movies. Actually, Cicero may have been even safer when the Big Guy was in charge—unless you crossed him, of course, in which case your best protection was plenty of distance. Whatever its past, Cicero's crime record today would make most communities envious.

Many authorities have noted the work of the Cicero Police Department, which must concern itself not only with the city's 67,058 residents but with an estimated 50,000 workers who commute into the city as well. For example, Clyde B. Vedder, Professor of Criminology and Corrections at Northern Illinois University, commented after a visit to the department and a tour of Cicero:

"Down through the many years of making similar tours of communities throughout the United States, I do not recall ever seeing a town less crime-ridden. Calls were few and far between, and concerned non-serious criminal activities, which is remarkable for a place the size of Cicero. Your official records reveal that the incidence of crime is considerably less than many communities much smaller than Cicero. There can be but one best explanation: competent police service by your department due to proficient and able supervision by your personnel on the command level. . . .

"The results speak for themselves, and other communities would do well to emulate law enforcement in Cicero."

Similarly, Cicero's Fire Department was one of the first in the United States to identify the homes of handicapped or invalid persons with special light-reflective emblems, to insure their safe evacuation in case of fire or other disaster. Cicero is considered one of the best-lighted communities in the nation—and was the first in the United States to have all its back alleys lighted.

There is more about Cicero that is surprising to the outsider. For example, it is the second-largest industrial center in the state of Illinois—it produces more, and pays out more and higher wages, than any Illinois city other than Chicago. There are more than 150 industrial establishments, with the largest being the Hawthorne Works of the Western Electric Company, where, incidentally, the first talking picture was produced. Hotpoint operates the world's largest range plant in Cicero, and Kropp Forge Company of Cicero has the largest forging operations in the United States. The first electric-arc furnace in the United States was produced by another Cicero plant, that of the National Malleable Steel Castings Company.

The most recent statistics I have seen are somewhat dated, but they show that about 85 percent of Cicero's residents own their own homes, and that 70 percent of these are mortgage-free. The general price range is $20,000 to $50,000, with Austin Boulevard enjoying a reputation as the local "Gold Coast" area. Many of the housing units here are two-family structures.

Cicero's public school system includes 13 elementary schools and one high school. In addition, there are nine Catholic and two Protestant schools in the city. Morton College, a community institution, is in Cicero.

Cicero is served by the 426-bed MacNeal Memorial Hospital in adjacent Berwyn, and 48 doctors and 46 dentists practice in town. Entrances to the Eisenhower Expressway are located just to the north, and Burlington Northern trains provide 12-minute express service to the Chicago Loop. O'Hare International Airport is 19 miles away.

Cicero has five parks in addition to the playgrounds maintained at each school. Facilities are available for tennis, baseball, softball, and skating. Two race tracks, Hawthorne Park and Sportsman's Park, are located at the southern edge of the city.

Community activities are plentiful and colorful, reflecting the heritage of the 27 nationalities identified among the local population. Avowedly patriotic, Cicero remains proud of the record of its residents in time of war, and of the fact that during World War II one of its draft boards went 14 months on enlistments without having to call on any draftees.

FOR FURTHER INFORMATION Write to the Cermak Road Business Association, 2130 South 61st Court, Cicero, Ill. 60650.

CITY/STATE: _____Cicero, Illinois_____

POPULATION: __67,058__ 1960–70 change: __-3.0__ %
__0.3__% non-white. __12.2__% over 65.

REAL ESTATE: Median value, $__21,000__. __126__less than $10,000, __5,777__$10,000 to $25,000, __1,505__$25,000 and over. Median gross rent, $__107__. __4,840__less than $100, __5,774__. $100 to $150, __1,019__$150 and over.

EDUCATION: Median school years completed, __10.7__. __39.2__% high school graduates.

INCOME: Median family income, $__11,265__. __7,439__less than $10,000, __11,154__$10,000 to $25,000, __513__$25,000 and over.

EMPLOYMENT: __30,978__in labor force, __44.4__% in manufacturing, __2.8__% unemployed.

36 WICHITA FALLS, Texas

Wichita Falls is located on the site where Indians, early settlers, and cattle herds on the Chisholm Trail crossed the Wichita River. Ranching dominated the area until the early 1900s, when oil booms in Electra, Burkburnett, and Kamay ushered in a prosperous oil era. The decline of the oil industry in this area was the most important factor in the city's loss of population between 1960 and 1970—two refineries closed down, and several major oil companies moved their district offices. But records show that the population reached its low point in 1965 and 1966, and has since started upward. Wichita Falls is still a major independent oil center, but its economy has branched out into many trade and manufacturing areas.

As evidence of the continuing importance of oil, Wichita County has over 400 oil production and oil service firms, the second-highest number of any county in the nation, and they employ 8,000 residents. More independent oil companies have headquarters here than in any other city. The world's largest manufacturers of oil field drilling rigs and catheads, along with 40 other oil industry equipment manufacturers, have plants here.

Among the major employers in Wichita Falls are Levi Strauss & Company (Western wear, jeans), Town & Country Mobile Homes, the Allis-Chalmers Corporation (industrial electrical controls), United Electric Company (air-conditioning and refrigeration), Cyrus W. Scott Manufacturing Company (men's casual dress slacks), Johnson & Johnson (hospital products), Washex Machinery Company (laundry and dry cleaning equipment), Ciba Pipe Systems, Westchester Homes (mobile homes), Sprague Electric Company (electronic components), Walker-Neer Manufacturing Company (oil well and water well drilling equipment), and the Wichita Falls Foundry & Machine Company.

Another major economic factor is Sheppard Air Force Base, a multimission base and second-largest of the Air Force's technical centers. Its military population of 17,600 contributes an annual payroll of $110 million to the economy.

Wichita County has 135,000 acres in cultivation, with the principal crops being wheat, cotton, alfalfa, and grain sorghums. Hereford cattle were introduced to Texas here at the turn of the century, and ranching remains an important part of the area's economy. The Angus breed has grown in importance in recent years.

Comprising the public school system are 24 elementary schools, six junior highs, three high schools, and a Vocational-Technical Training Center. Episcopal, Lutheran, and Catholic elementary schools, plus a Catholic junior high and high school, are available. The city has 26 private day nurseries and kindergartens, two schools for the handicapped, and a school for the trainable mentally retarded. Midwestern University offers an associate degree in nursing, seven B.A. programs, and seven M.A. programs.

More than 130 physicians and surgeons and 50 dentists practice in Wichita Falls. Two general hospitals, Wichita and Bethania, have a total of 575 beds, and five private clinics add another 300 beds. Sheppard Air Force Base also has a 400-bed hospital. A $1 million Medicenter was opened in 1972 to provide recuperative hospital care.

Wichita Falls is 946 feet above sea level. The mean minimum temperature in January is 30.3 degrees. The July mean maximum is 97.6 degrees. Average annual rainfall is 27.7 inches.

The Municipal Airport is served by Texas International, Continental, and Rio airlines. They offer 14 departing flights daily, with nine of these by jet.

Wichita Falls has two daily newspapers, the *Record News* (mornings) and the *Times* (afternoons). Three AM and two FM radio stations broadcast from the city. There are two local television stations, plus reception of a third station in Lawton, Oklahoma.

In addition to three Catholic churches and two Jewish synagogues, Wichita Falls has 132 Protestant churches representing 28 denominations. Cultural programs are made available by the Wichita Falls Symphony Orchestra, the Broadway Theater League, Civic Music, the Wichita Falls Museum and Art Center, the Wichita Falls Ballet Theater, and the fine arts department of Midwestern University.

Fifty-nine park areas include facilities for picnicking, baseball, and golf, with a total of four public and private golf courses in the area. Wichita Falls is one of the top tennis cities in Texas, with excellent facilities available. It is also the home of the NCAA Pioneer Bowl, played each December in Memorial Stadium. Championship rodeos are popular throughout the area. Professional football, baseball, and basketball are as nearby as Dallas, and winter sports in Colorado and New Mexico are becoming increasingly popular.

The Wichita Falls area has excellent quail hunting, with plenty of duck, whitetail deer, wild turkey, and goose hunting to the south. Rabbits, coyotes, and bobcats are found throughout the area. Fishermen will find black bass the most popular local catch, with four- to eight-pounders. Nearby lakes and some of their catches include Lake Kemp (Kentucky spotted bass), Lake Wichita (bass, cattails, crappie, channel catfish), Possum Kingdom Lake (black bass and white bass), and Lake Kickapoo (channel catfish, crappie). Skin and scuba diving are popular on Possum Kingdom Lake, and canoeing enthusiasts enjoy trips down the Brazos River below the dam.

FOR FURTHER INFORMATION Write to the Wichita Falls Board of Commerce and Industry, P.O. Box 1860, Wichita Falls, Tex. 76307, and ask for the *Welcome Book, Welcome to Wichita Falls, Gateway to Texas, Wichita Falls—The City With Happy Faces, It's Your Move . . . to Wichita Falls, Texas*, the *Industrial Index* (list of manufacturers), *General Business Statistics, Apartment Information, Capsule History of Sheppard AFB, Texas; Schools* (information-sheet), and *Good Fishing All Around Wichita Falls*.

CITY/STATE: Wichita Falls, Texas
POPULATION: 97,564 ___1960–70 change: ___-4.1___%
___10.3___% non-white. ___9.5___% over 65.
REAL ESTATE: Median value, $___10,300___. ___8,653___less than
$10,000, ___7,785___$10,000 to $25,000, ___1,580___$25,000 and
over. Median gross rent, $___69___. ___7,306___less than $100,
___1,510___. $100 to $150, ___782___$150 and over.
EDUCATION: Median school years completed, ___12.2___.
___56.0___% high school graduates.
INCOME: Median family income, $___7,972___. ___15,648___less than
$10,000, ___7,563___$10,000 to $25,000, ___970___$25,000 and over.
EMPLOYMENT: ___31,110___in labor force, ___10.3___% in manufacturing, ___3.8___% unemployed.

37 LYNCHBURG, Virginia

"The most interesting spot in the state" was the way Thomas Jefferson described Lynchburg on one of his frequent trips from Monticello to his other home at Poplar Forest, less than 10 miles from
the city. Today's Lynchburg, too, has many sights and attractions
of interest to both tourists and new residents. Located in the valley
of the James River, next to the Blue Ridge Mountains, scenic beauty
awaits you in all directions.

The city was founded by John Lynch, and John's older brother
Charles contributed to American history in a unique way by being
responsible for the term *lynch law*. Originally it did not connote mob
violence, but rather Colonel Charles Lynch's method of handling Tor-
ies during the American Revolution. Suspects were rounded up,
tried, and sentenced; they were then tied to a walnut tree in Lynch's
yard and given 39 lashes. After that they were compelled to prove
their patriotism by shouting, "Liberty Forever!"

Pipe, shoes, and tobacco are the traditional industries of Lynchburg. Shoes and pipe are still important local products, but so are
more than 150 other industries. The industrial community now includes General Electric, Babcock & Wilcox Company, H.K. Porter

Company, Weyerhaeuser Company, Gould National Batteries, Limitorque Corporation, E.F. Houghton & Company, Illinois Tool Works, Georgia-Pacific Corporation, and Burlington Industries. Meredith/ Burda has completed a $6 million rotogravure-printing plant, and Abbott Laboratories a $10 million plant for the production of infant formula. The Babcock & Wilcox facility built the atomic power-plant for the world's first nuclear-powered merchant ship, the *Savannah*, and the ship's first crew was trained here.

Important industrial classifications in Lynchburg today include foundries, fabricated metal, machinery and tool manufacturing, shoes, textile and garment manufacturing, pulp and paper, lumber and wood products, furniture, printing and publishing, chemicals and pharmaceuticals, mining, food processing, plastic and rubber products, concrete, stone and clay products, electrical and communications equipment, transportation equipment, display advertising signs, and milling. Lynchburg is also the international headquarters of First Colony Life Insurance Company, and regional headquarters for the Nationwide Insurance Group.

Beautiful housing sites and a wide variety of architectural styles in housing are available. There are a good number of apartment developments, too, with two-bedroom apartments usually renting from $90 to $175, and some luxury apartments renting at prices up to $300. Rentals for most three-bedroom apartments range from $200 to $375.

W.E. Gilliam, Chief of Police, credits both the community and the police protective services for the low crime-rate. "The key to operating an effective police department," he says, "is its men and their recruitment, training and equipment. All of our police candidates are required to pass physical and written examinations before appointment to the police department."

Gilliam continues:

"After a man becomes a police officer, he is thoroughly trained and retrained in all phases of police science. Selected officers are also sent to various state and national police schools for specialized training. The men are also encouraged to continue their academic studies as well. For instance, recently we have implemented a Police Educational Incentive Pay Program, which rewards individuals who have attained certain levels of academic achievement in police science curriculum with increased pay ranging from 3 percent to 12 percent, depending on their level of achievement.

"Equipment also plays a vital part in policing and we have endeavored to provide our officers with the best in the equipment which they need. . . .

"Re-study of our methods and operations has also played a significant part in our effort to provide quality protective services as a crime deterrent. Over the next several months, the International Association of Chiefs of Police will be conducting a Management and Operations Study of the Lynchburg Police Department. Implementation of their recommendations should make us an even more effective deterrent to crime."

Lynchburg has a public school system ranked as one of the state's best; it comprises 15 elementary schools extending to the eighth grade, with an enrollment of 5,779, and one high school with 4,859 students. Private and parochial secondary facilities include Holy Cross Academy (a Catholic elementary and high school), Lynchburg Christian Academy (kindergarten through 12th grade), Seven Hills School (a girl's prep school), Villa Maria (a Catholic girls school), the Virginia Episcopal School (a boys prep high school), James River Day School (grades one through six), and Timberlake Christian School (kindergarten through sixth grade).

Lynchburg is also a college center. Lynchburg College enrolls about 2,000 students, and Randolph-Macon Woman's College and Sweet Briar College have national reputations. Central Virginia Community College is a two-year institution with 1,700 students, and other educational institutions are Virginia College, Lynchburg Baptist College, and Phillips Business College.

More than 150 doctors and 53 dentists practice in Lynchburg. The two hospitals serving the city are Virginia Baptist Hospital and Lynchburg General-Marshall Lodge Hospitals, with 578 beds and extensive facilities between them.

Lynchburg's climate is pleasant—not too hot in the summer and not too cold in the winter. Average daily minimum temperature in January is 29.0 degrees; normal daily maximum temperature in July is 86.6 degrees. Normal annual precipitation is 40.3 inches, including a mean annual snowfall of 19.6 inches. Relative humidity is 78 at 7 A.M., 52 at 1 P.M., and 63 at 7 P.M.

The city has 96 Protestant churches representing many denominations, a Catholic church, a Greek Orthodox church, and a Jewish synagogue. The colleges contribute much to the cultural life, and art, music, and theatrical events are held in the Fine Arts Center. Lynchburg has a symphony orchestra, the nation's oldest continuous community little theater, a film society, literary and poetry groups, an art club, a community band, the Lynchburg Dance Theater Guild, a Community Concert Series, the Broadway Theater League, and a branch of the Association for the Preservation of Virginia Antiquities.

Recreational opportunities are no less extensive, with five golf courses (three of them open to the public), two putting courses, 32 municipal tennis courts, a number of swimming pools, and plenty of ideal spots for hunting, fishing, and hiking in the surrounding Piedmont region and Blue Ridge Mountains. The nation's capital is only about four hours away by car, Williamsburg approximately three. It will take you about 90 minutes to get to Thomas Jefferson's home, Monticello, or to Natural Bridge. Even nearer are Appomattox and an authentically reconstructed nineteenth-century village, restored James River canal locks, the Appalachian Trail, and the Peaks of Otter, highest point on the Blue Ridge Parkway in Virginia.

FOR FURTHER INFORMATION Write to the Greater Lynchburg Chamber of Commerce, Box 2027, Lynchburg, Va. 24501, and ask for *Lynchburg*, a deluxe 108-page illustrated color booklet; two brochures, *Lynchburg Tour Map* and *Guide to Attractions & Services;* a city map; *Local Climatological Data;* folders on *Taxes, Places of Worship, Food Service and Lodging, Real Estate, Apartment Directory,* and *No Parking Problems . . . Park & Shop Downtown;* and information-sheets on community data, educational institutions, population and effective buying income, the business index, employment agencies, and facilities for boating, fishing, and swimming.

CITY/STATE: _____ Lynchburg, Virginia _____
POPULATION: __54,083__ 1960–70 change: __-1.3__ %
__23.4__% non-white. __12.3__% over 65.
REAL ESTATE: Median value, $__13,400__. __3,341__ less than $10,000, __4,035__ $10,000 to $25,000, __1,849__ $25,000 and over. Median gross rent, $__64__. __5,485__ less than $100, __980__. $100 to $150, __221__ $150 and over.
EDUCATION: Median school years completed, __11.3__. __44.7__% high school graduates.
INCOME: Median family income, $__8,855__. __7,782__ less than $10,000, __5,240__ $10,000 to $25,000, __680__ $25,000 and over.
EMPLOYMENT: __22,644__ in labor force, __33.2__% in manufacturing, __2.5__% unemployed.

38 OSHKOSH, Wisconsin

Named for an Indian chief and once known as the "Sawdust City" because of its large number of sawmills, Oshkosh today is the site of diversified industries, the home of a major university campus, and a sailing and fishing center taking full advantage of its location on the upper Fox River and Lake Winnebago.

Of the more than 150 industries, only one—North American Rockwell—employs more than 1,000 persons. No one industrial classification comprises more than 20 percent of the total employment. Among the products manufactured in Oshkosh are furniture, concrete products, metal stampings, sash and doors, paints, transmissions, axles, ladders, castings, work and leisure clothing, boxes, and a great variety of trade-name products. Industries with nationwide and worldwide reputations manufacture heavy-duty trucks, refuse-collection units, electronic-component units, candles, and excelsior products.

The Oshkosh plant of North American Rockwell manufactures planetary axles, front-driving axles, and special gear-driving assemblies. Morgan Company produces doors and other woodwork items. Among the other major employers are the Leach Company (refuse-collection bodies), Lenox Candles (commercial and decorative candles), Medalist Industries (special woodworking and machinery), Mercury Marine (propellers, engine parts, accessories), Miles Kimball Company (Christmas cards and paper products), Oshkosh B'Gosh (work and casual wear), Oshkosh Truck Corporation (trucks and tractors), Pluswood Industries (plywood paneling and industrial boards), SNC Manufacturing Company (electrical transformers, coils, reactors), and Universal Foundry Company (ferrous and nonferrous castings, pattern equipment). The major governmental and nonmanufacturing employers are the University of Wisconsin at Oshkosh, Mercy Medical Center, Winnebago State Hospital, the City of Oshkosh, and Wisconsin Telephone Company.

Oshkosh has a good mixture of homes in the 20- to 50-year-old bracket as well as others built more recently. Some of the new subdivisions front on cul-de-sacs and back on man-made boat channels immediately accessible to Lake Winnebago. In recent years, many apartments and multifamily housing complexes have been constructed.

A diversity of shopping areas bid for the consumer's attention. In the central city is a recently built complex of 42 retail establishments with second-level parking, known as Park Plaza and financed entirely by private enterprise.

Both public and parochial school systems operate in the city, and among the three technical schools in the Fox Valley, one is in Oshkosh. Also located here is the University of Wisconsin at Oshkosh, which has expanded to 12,000 students.

Mercy Medical Center is a 452-bed facility staffed by more than 80 physicians, surgeons, and dentists. Schools of nursing, medical technology, anesthesiology, and X-ray technology train students there. Two facilities for the mentally ill are Winnebago State Hospital (800 beds) and Winnebago County Hospital (340 beds). Oshkosh also has several medical complexes—Doctors' Park and the Oshkosh Clinic—and eight nursing homes. Two are new church-sponsored centers providing around-the-clock nursing care together with extensive activity programs.

The average winter temperature is 22.8 degrees, the average summer temperature 79.2 degrees. Average annual rainfall is 28.67 inches, including an annual snowfall averaging 40.37 inches.

U.S. 41 is a four-lane highway providing a direct route south to Chicago and north to Green Bay. Wittman Field has 29 flights daily on North Central Airlines, with direct service to Milwaukee, Chicago, Green Bay, Marquette, and Minneapolis. A convenient 20-minute connection is provided at Milwaukee to North Central flights to New York and other cities.

Local communications media include the *Oshkosh Daily Northwestern,* two AM and three FM radio stations, and a campus Titan station. Three Green Bay television stations, representing all networks, are received in Oshkosh, as well as UHF channels from Green Bay and Fond du Lac. Cable television is being introduced.

Oshkosh's 57 churches include Assembly of God, Baha'i, Baptist, Catholic, Church of Christ, Christian Science, Congregational, Episcopal, Jehovah's Witnesses, Lutheran, Methodist, Mormon, Nazarene, Presbyterian, Quaker, Salvation Army, Unitarian, and Pentecostal congregations. Oshkosh also has a Jewish temple.

Cultural facilities include Paine Art Center and Arboretum, the university's Frederick March Theater, the Oshkosh Public Museum, the Civic Auditorium, and the Grand Theater. The Grand Opera House, built in 1883 and now a registered historical landmark, has seen performances by Caruso, Sara Bernhardt, Will Rogers, the Barrymores, and many others. The Oshkosh Symphony Orchestra, the Community and Junior theaters, the Town and Gown artists series, a Kiwanis-sponsored Travel and Adventure Series, the Community Chorus, and the Winnebago Art Fair provide a stimulating cultural calendar for residents.

Recreational facilities include public beaches on Lake Winnebago and the Fox River, indoor and outdoor swimming pools, golf and country clubs, tennis courts, marinas, and riding stables. Among the annual activities are sailboat races and regattas, the Miss Wisconsin Pageant, and the Experimental Aircraft Association Convention at the airport, which, each year, brings thousands of people to the nation's largest aeronautical convention. Winter sports activities range from ice skating at the city's 17 public rinks to snowmobiling, tobogganing, sledding, slaloming at nearby ski slopes and resorts, and fishing through the ice on Lake Winnebago for walleye, perch, and sturgeon.

FOR FURTHER INFORMATION Write to the Oshkosh Area Chamber of Commerce, 27A Washington Avenue, Oshkosh, Wis. 54901, and ask for its 64-page color booklet on the city, *Oshkosh—The Story of Oshkosh, Wisconsin, Hub of Winnebagoland Waterways*, as well as *What to See and Do, A Profile of Oshkosh Wisconsin* (a statistical report of interest to businessmen), and *Oshkosh Area Guide to Principal Manufacturers* ($3).

CITY/STATE: _____Oshkosh, Wisconsin_____
POPULATION: __53,221__ 1960–70 change: __+18.0__ %
__0.6__% non-white. __11.4__% over 65.
REAL ESTATE: Median value, $__14,900__. __1,785__ less than $10,000, __6,462__ $10,000 to $25,000, __1,087__ $25,000 and over. Median gross rent, $__94__. __2,965__ less than $100, __1,515__. $100 to $150, __878__ $150 and over.
EDUCATION: Median school years completed, __12.1__. __54.9__% high school graduates.
INCOME: Median family income, $__9,715__. __6,392__ less than $10,000, __5,377__ $10,000 to $25,000, __371__ $25,000 and over.
EMPLOYMENT: __21,236__ in labor force, __30.2__% in manufacturing, __4.5__% unemployed.

39 BERWYN, Illinois

Some of its citizens refer to Berwyn as the "Fort Lauderdale of the Midwest," but the reference is only to the large number of retired persons, for there the similarity ends. In climate, the adjective most often used by the devious chambers of commerce in the Chicago area is "vigorous"—and the weather can be vigorous indeed. Berwyn also sports none of the flashy affluence of Fort Lauderdale, presenting instead a facade of ethnic working-class stability. Then, too, and in Berwyn's favor, there is the matter of crime—for while Berwyn ranks No. 39, Fort Lauderdale ranks No. 353 among cities of 50,000 and over, down near the bottom of the heap.

Donald E. Pechous, Alderman of Ward 1, told me that "Berwyn is a stable community, which contributes greatly to its low crime rate. It is 99 percent built up. Most homes are single-family with detachable garages or else two flats. Apartment buildings are few."

Berwyn, he contends, "can be considered a safe city when compared to communities of like size because of its large ethnic Czech and Italian population. It is also a tribute to our fine fire and police departments. Residents are very concerned with rising crime rates elsewhere, and are urging that additional police be added to our force because Chicago's Austin neighborhood is having problems with 'changing conditions' which threaten to affect Berwyn in the future." He noted that adjacent Cicero serves as a buffer between Berwyn and the West Side slums of Chicago.

"Good law enforcement," Pechous adds, "is aided by citizen participation in calling the police department whenever the citizen notices a suspicious car, person or activity within his neighborhood. Berwyn residents have aided in this manner by reporting strange happenings directly to the police."

Berwyn is called "the city of homes," and has little industry of any consequence. But Western Electric's Hawthorne Works is next door in Cicero, and employs many Berwyn residents. Cicero also has many other heavy industries with excellent retirement programs. "Berwyn residents," according to Pechous, "are savers and thrift is encouraged. The standard joke is that Berwyn's time payment plan is 'cash.'"

There are 11 elementary schools and one high school in Berwyn, as well as three Catholic elementary schools and a special school for retarded children. Morton College is a two-year community institution in Cicero, with Berwyn part of the college district, thus assuring low resident tuition.

Average annual precipitation is about 32 inches, including an average annual snowfall of 34.6 inches. The altitude is approximately 700 feet above sea level, and the climate is described as "mainly mild, occasionally rigorous."

McNeal Memorial Hospital is located in the center of Berwyn. *Berwyn Life* is a newspaper published three times a week, and the city's location in the midst of the Chicago metropolitan region assures full newspaper, radio, and television coverage. South Berwyn has passenger stations on the Burlington Railroad, providing swift service to and from the Chicago Loop, 10 miles east. The trip time in modern double-decked coaches averages under 20 minutes.

Berwyn's churches include Adventist, Baptist, Christian Reformed, Christian Scientist, Episcopal, Independent Fundamental, Lutheran, Methodist, Presbyterian, Reformed, Roman Catholic, and United Church of Christ congregations—24 in all. There is a host of civic, cultural, and service groups, with more than 120 listed in the town directory. Many of them reflect the ethnic and working-class orientation of Berwyn, with names such as the Alois Jirasek Czek School Patronat Sokol, the American Hellenic Society of Berwyn, the La Sertoma Club, the Italian-American Civic Organization, the OBEC Barachniku Vysehrad, and the Pilsen Butchers Benevolent Association.

FOR FURTHER INFORMATION Write to the South Berwyn Business and Civic Association, 6843 West Stanley Avenue, Berwyn, Ill. 60402, for its 12-page brochure and directory to the city.

CITY/STATE: ___Berwyn, Illinois___
POPULATION: ___52,502___ 1960-70 change: ___+3.2___ %
___0.4___ % non-white. ___17.0___ % over 65.
REAL ESTATE: Median value, $___23,200___. ___70___ less than
$10,000, ___5,605___ $10,000 to $25,000, ___3,199___ $25,000 and
over. Median gross rent, $___121___. ___1,858___ less than $100,
___4,252___. $100 to $150, ___1,440___ $150 and over.
EDUCATION: Median school years completed, ___11.5___.
___46.0___ % high school graduates.
INCOME: Median family income, $___11,836___. ___7,827___ less than
$10,000, ___8,967___ $10,000 to $25,000, ___671___ $25,000 and over.
EMPLOYMENT: ___23,819___ in labor force, ___35.7___ % in manufacturing, ___2.2___ % unemployed.

40 PITTSFIELD, Massachusetts

The Berkshires, in the far western corner of Massachusetts, have long been a favorite haunt of poets, artists, and tourists. Actress Frances Kemble, a summer resident of Lenox, wrote that "few spots on earth can boast of a more perfect union of all the elements of natural beauty. . . . It is an enchanting region." And as William Cullen Bryant expressed it, "I was struck by the beauty of the smooth green meadows . . . and I admired no less the contrast between this soft scene and the steep craggy hills that overlooked it, clothed with their many-colored forests."

Pittsfield, 135 miles west of Boston and 135 miles north of New York City, is the largest city and commercial center of the Berkshires. It is a manufacturing city, its residents overwhelmingly Democratic in politics. Nearly a third of them are of foreign stock, mostly Italian, Canadian, Irish, Polish, and English.

The dominant employer is General Electric, with a work force of 9,000 at its three Pittsfield plants. That figure is 2,300 less than several years ago, a reduction caused by changing national and international markets, but GE still provides for a third of the area's employment and a payroll of more than $100 million.

Eaton Paper Corporation, now a division of Textron, is the second-largest employer (with 800), and manufactures converted paper products and leather desk sets. The A.H. Rice Company (industrial sewing thread) employs 330. Pittsfield also is the home of Berkshire Life Insurance Company, Berkshire Mutual Insurance Company, and Buttenheim Publishing Corporation.

Wages are relatively high at GE and other plants, and of 10 metropolitan core-cities in the state, Pittsfield has the highest family median income and the lowest rate of poverty.

Agriculture has declined in importance, though production per acre is rising along with the market value of products sold. Livestock, poultry, and their products bring the greatest income, followed by nursery, hay, and forest products.

Pittsfield is primarily a community of single-family homes, and three-quarters of the houses were built before 1940. Housing construction has not kept pace with demand. Most apartments on the market rent for $175 to $190 for one bedroom, or $170 to $225 for two bedrooms. Many persons commute to Pittsfield from Lenox, Lanesborough, Dalton, and, to a lesser extent, Lee.

Police Chief John J. Killeen reports that 65 officers of the force—the overwhelming majority—are furthering their education at Berkshire Community College. "We are proud of the safety record which we have established," says Mayor Donald G. Butler, "but are not at all happy with the fact that by doing so we have eliminated our community from receiving federal funds in the area of crime prevention."

Fire Chief John E. McDonough reports that the National Fire Protection Association ranks Pittsfield's department sixth among cities of all population classes in the nation, and first among U.S. cities in the 50,000 to 100,000 population category.

Approximately 12,000 students attend the public school system, which consists of 20 elementary schools, three junior highs, and three high schools. About 2,000 students attend the parochial system of five elementary schools and a high school. Taconic High School has a heavy vocational-technical orientation, and the dropout rate in the public schools has been kept to 3 1/2 percent. Miss Hall's School is an independent college-preparatory school for girls. Five private schools are located in nearby Lenox.

Berkshire Community College is located in Pittsfield, Berkshire Christian College (a theology school) in Lenox. The University of Massachusetts and Schenectady's Union College offer afternoon and evening courses in Pittsfield on demand.

Ninety-four physicians and 40 dentists practice in Pittsfield. Berkshire Medical Center has 431 beds and a medical staff of 171. Hillcrest Hospital, a private facility, has 144 beds and 155 doctors affiliated with it. Seven major outpatient clinics are also located in Pittsfield.

The average January temperature is 21.8 degrees, and the cool mountain nights keep the average July temperature at 67.8 degrees. Spring and fall are marked by rapid weather changes. Average annual precipitation is 44 inches, including an average yearly snowfall of 77 inches, generally anticipated between late November and March. The altitude of the city is 1,035 feet above sea level.

In addition to bus transportation, Command Airways has four round trips daily to New York, and limousine service is also available to New York City. The *Berkshire Eagle* is a daily and Sunday newspaper published in Pittsfield. Six radio stations broadcast from the Berkshires (three of them from Pittsfield), and in addition to a Pittsfield television channel there is coverage available from New York City, Boston, Hartford, Albany, Schenectady, and Springfield.

The 45 churches in Pittsfield include Catholic, Baptist, Methodist, Christian Science, Church of Christ, Mormon, Lutheran, Congregational, Greek Orthodox, Jehovah's Witnesses, Salvation Army, Ukrainian Catholic, Episcopal, Russian Orthodox, Seventh-Day Adventist, and Unitarian congregations.

Points of interest in and around Pittsfield include the Berkshire Museum, Arrowhead (Herman Melville's home), the Herman Melville Memorial Room of the Berkshire Athenaeum (Library), the Crane Museum (papermaking) in Dalton, and the Hancock Shaker Village. Cultural activities are sponsored by the Town Players, the Community Concerts, and the Holroyd and Canterella dance schools. The Berkshires are cultural beehives, with numerous art galleries and three summer theaters in the region. Lenox is the summer home of the Boston Symphony Orchestra and its Tanglewood concerts. In addition there are the Jacob's Pillow Dance Festival in West Becket; folk, blues, and country concerts at the Lenox Arts Center; the Red Fox Music Barn in New Marlboro; and chamber music concerts at Pittsfield's South Mountain Music Association.

Berkshire sports recreation is equally stimulating, with numerous golf courses (four around Pittsfield), a dozen ski areas, and lakes, beaches, waterfalls, and hiking trails everywhere. Bird and small game hunting are excellent, with deer also plentiful. The more than 30 lakes and ponds offer good fishing—with bullhead, pickerel, yellow perch, and bluegill the most plentiful—and the Deerfield, Farmington, and Konkapot rivers have excellent trout fishing.

FOR FURTHER INFORMATION Write to the Association of Business and Commerce of Central Berkshire County, Inc., 107 South

Street, Pittsfield, Mass. 01201, for a Berkshire County map, a real estate agency list, *Berkshire County Manufacturers*, and the monograph on Pittsfield published by the Massachusetts Department of Commerce and Development. If you want more detailed information, ask for the 120-page report of the Berkshire County Development Commission, *Community and Economic Data*. Even more detailed and useful is *Target '76*, a 113-page report available from the Urban Coalition, P.O. Box 1141, Pittsfield, Mass. 01201.

CITY/STATE: Pittsfield, Massachusetts
POPULATION: _57,020_ 1960–70 change: _-1.5_ %
_2.3_% non-white. _12.1_% over 65.
REAL ESTATE: Median value, $_18,000_. _655_ less than $10,000, _6,636_$10,000 to $25,000, _1,536_$25,000 and over. Median gross rent, $_80_. _5,092_ less than $100, _1,433_. $100 to $150, _392_$150 and over.
EDUCATION: Median school years completed, _12.2_. _58.6_% high school graduates.
INCOME: Median family income, $_10,678_. _6,560_ less than $10,000, _7,526_$10,000 to $25,000, _630_$25,000 and over.
EMPLOYMENT: _22,400_ in labor force, _39.5_% in manufacturing, _4.4_% unemployed.

41 FORT SMITH, Arkansas

Located on the western border of Arkansas, and cradled in a bend of the Arkansas River, Fort Smith is flanked by two mountain ranges and more than a million acres of national forest. To the south are the Ouachitas, and to the north the rugged Boston Mountains— the world-famous Ozarks of Arkansas.

Fort Smith's most famous historical site is the restored courtroom and gallows of "Hanging Judge" Isaac C. Parker, whose federal court brought law and order to the outlaw-infested Indian Territory until his death. Other reminders of frontier days include traces of the Butterfield Stage Route, which operated from 1858 through 1861 and constituted the nation's first coast-to-coast link.

One of the leading manufacturing cities of Arkansas, Fort Smith boasts more than 230 manufacturing plants, which employ over 16,000 workers. It is widely recognized as a major furniture manufacturing center. Also one of the major livestock markets of the Southwest, the Fort Smith area rounds out its economy with the production of fruits, vegetables, poultry, and dairy products.

Carl W. Beyer, Chief of Police, suggests that one reason for the low crime-rate is that "our patrol vehicles are highly visible to the population of the city and to transients passing on through. This is accomplished by demanding maximum time on the streets for the patrol vehicles in order to discourage criminal acts."

Chief Beyer also notes that "Our court system is dedicated to speedy trials when warranted. Consequently, there is no significant backlog of cases on our Municipal or Circuit Court dockets. This factor is an important deterrent to crime."

Fort Smith has a city curfew law for minors—10:30 P.M. Sunday through Thursday, and 12:30 A.M. Friday and Saturday. This law is enforced.

In addition to the public and parochial secondary schools, Fort Smith is home to Westark Junior College, which offers both day and night classes and a wide range of adult education and vocational-technical courses. The main campus of the University of Arkansas is only 60 miles away at Fayetteville.

Medical facilities include two hospitals and two clinics. More than 120 medical doctors and over 40 dentists practice here. The local *Southwest Times Record* is published twice daily. Broadcasting from Fort Smith are five AM radio stations, three FM radio stations, and two television channels. Eight out-of-town channels are carried on CATV. Braniff and Frontier airlines offer jet service.

On the average, Fort Smith has 72 days a year with temperatures of 90 degrees or above, and 81 days when the thermometer reads 32 degrees or below. From April through October, the average daily maximum temperature is 85.2 degrees and the average nightly minimum temperature is 61.4 degrees. From November through March, the average daily maximum temperature is 52.1 degrees, and the average nightly minimum temperature is 31.5 degrees. The normal annual precipitation is 42.22 inches, with an average annual snowfall of 5.0 inches. In mean number of days, there are 129 clear, 95 partly cloudy, and 141 cloudy; 93 have some precipitation, and 13 witness heavy fog.

Cultural activities are conducted by a number of active organizations, among them the Fort Smith Little Theater, the Broadway Theater League, the Fort Smith Symphony Association, the Associated Artists of Fort Smith, the Community Concert, and the Fort Smith Affiliation of the Arts.

Two highlights of the year's calendar are the Arkansas-Oklahoma Rodeo (May) and the Arkansas-Oklahoma Livestock Exposition and District Free Fair (September). Other annual events include a state industrial fair, an antique show, a dog show, and a horse show.

With the Ozarks so easily accessible, outdoor recreation is varied and plentiful. The city itself has more than 1,700 acres of parks, with swimming, picnicking, baseball fields, tennis courts, and golf courses. Four large lakes are within an hour's drive, and are perfect for water skiing from May to October. Fishermen test their skill with the elusive largemouth bass or the fighting rainbow trout in the lakes and mountain streams, and the prairies and woodlands around Fort Smith provide excellent hunting for small game. Quail hunting is a favorite winter sport. Delightful auto tours abound, too, with breathtaking panoramic views from Mount Gayler, highest point in the Ozarks, and the winding path of Talimena Skyline Drive.

FOR FURTHER INFORMATION Write to the Fort Smith Chamber of Commerce, 613 Garrison Avenue, Fort Smith, Ark. 72901. Materials include *Bonanza Land* (a color brochure on the attractions of this region of Arkansas), *Historic Fort Smith, Where to Stay and Dine and What to See, City Map, Fort Smith Fact Sheet, Industrial Directory* (25¢), *Fort Smith Church Directory, Fort Smith Tax Rate,* and *Climatological Data.*

CITY/STATE: Fort Smith, Arkansas
POPULATION: 62,802 1960–70 change: +18.5 %
7.6 % non-white. 11.1 % over 65.
REAL ESTATE: Median value, $11,900. 4,897 less than $10,000, 6,834 $10,000 to $25,000, 1,498 $25,000 and over. Median gross rent, $60. 6,030 less than $100, 628. $100 to $150, 138 $150 and over.
EDUCATION: Median school years completed, 12.1. 53.6 % high school graduates.
INCOME: Median family income, $7,975. 11,207 less than $10,000, 5,284 $10,000 to $25,000, 544 $25,000 and over.
EMPLOYMENT: 25,290 in labor force, 28.1 % in manufacturing, 4.2 % unemployed.

42 ANDERSON, Indiana

Archaeological finds in the summer of 1968 dated Anderson's first residents as members of a mound-building culture existing 2,000 years ago. Another historic moment took place in more recent times, when the discovery of natural gas propelled this sleepy farm community into an industrial economy. Anderson played a key role in the development of the early automobile industry, manufacturing such American classics as the Anderson carriage, the DeTamble roadster, and the Lambert towncar. The automotive industry still dominates, but 90 separate industries employing 28,000 persons operate in the city. Growth will undoubtedly continue as transportation and water surveys are completed, and construction is finished on Interstate 69.

Located 35 miles northeast of Indianapolis, Anderson's largest employers are two divisions of General Motors—Delco-Remy (automotive electrical equipment, batteries, generators, horns, regulators, coils and switches) and Guide Lamp (automotive and marine lighting equipment, rear view mirrors, plastics, die castings). The world's largest file plant is that of the Nicholson File Company, and the Brockway Glass Company manufactures glass containers. Other major employers include Warner Press (commercial printing, religious literature, and the Sunshine Line greeting cards), Emge Packing Company (meat-packing), the Container Corporation of America (corrugated paper boxes), the city utilities, and Anaconda Wire & Cable Company's Automotive and Magnet Wire Division.

Anderson has a wide spread in housing costs, but whatever neighborhood you pick, the price of new homes will probably be $3,000 or $4,000 less than in other Midwestern areas. More than 7,000 rental units are available too. Anderson has the third-lowest taxes of Indiana cities with a population of 35,000 or more.

Public educational facilities include two high schools, four junior highs, and 23 elementary schools. There are four parochial elementary schools and a private school for girls. The new area-vocational school also offers adult education programs. And Anderson College, with approximately 2,000 students, offers liberal arts and theology programs on its modern campus. It is affiliated with the Church of God, which maintains its world headquarters in Anderson and holds its international convention here each summer.

Two hospitals, Saint John's Hickey Memorial and Community Hospital, have a total of 550 beds. The city has two radio stations and two daily newspapers—the *Anderson Herald* (mornings and Sundays) and the *Daily Bulletin* (afternoons)—with additional newspaper, radio, and television coverage from Indianapolis, as well as cable television. Hub Airlines provides service at the municipal airport.

Approximately 100 churches and a multitude of organizations are active in Anderson, and cultural affairs center around the Anderson Community Concerts Series, the Chancel Organ Concerts, a symphony orchestra season, the exhibits at the Anderson Fine Arts Center, and the amateur productions of the Geeting Summer theater. Among the collections of the Anderson Library is the National Music Hall of Fame, the world's largest collection of American popular-music compositions.

Anderson's system of 14 municipal parks includes outdoor and indoor swimming pools, tennis courts, and an ice rink. Of the five golf courses and clubs, two are private, one is a municipal course, and the others are privately owned but open to the public. Babe Ruth and Little League baseball is popular (the 1965 Babe Ruth World Series was held here), and Sun Valley Speedway is home of the "Little 500" sprint-car classic and the National Crown, the oldest annual stock-car event in the country.

In May, 10,000 redbud trees blossom during the Redbud Festival. Other big events are the Fourth of July fireworks display and the Family Festival. On the edge of town, Mounds State Park has facilities for picnicking, hiking, archery, nature study, and horseback riding. Quail and pheasant shooting is a popular sport in this area, and as you head south or west from Anderson you will discover the covered bridges, forests, and state parks that attract artists and tourists from all over the Midwest.

FOR FURTHER INFORMATION Write to the Anderson Chamber of Commerce, P.O. Box 469, Anderson, Ind. 46015, for its 52-page illustrated color booklet on Anderson, the official city map, an *Industrial Directory*, and mimeographed sheets entitled *Information Concerning Anderson, Indiana.*

CITY/STATE: ___Anderson, Indiana___

POPULATION: __70,787__ 1960–70 change: __+44.3__ %
__10.5__ % non-white. __9.4__ % over 65.

REAL ESTATE: Median value, $__13,000__. __4,066__ less than $10,000, __9,294__ $10,000 to $25,000, __1,151__ $25,000 and over. Median gross rent, $__76__. __5,550__ less than $100, __1,527__. $100 to $150, __250__ $150 and over.

EDUCATION: Median school years completed, __12.0__. __50.2__ % high school graduates.

INCOME: Median family income, $__9,816__. __9,593__ less than $10,000, __8,640__ $10,000 to $25,000, __469__ $25,000 and over.

EMPLOYMENT: __28,046__ in labor force, __47.5__ % in manufacturing, __5.5__ % unemployed.

43 OAK PARK, Illinois

Oak Park has produced a number of famous sons and daughters. Among the most prominent ones are Frank Lloyd Wright, the father of modern architecture, who designed approximately 30 homes in Oak Park and adjoining River Forest; novelist Ernest Hemingway, who won both the Pulitzer and Nobel prizes for literature, and who was born at 339 North Oak Park Avenue; and Edgar Rice Burroughs, creator of Tarzan.

While a student at Oak Park–River Forest High School, Hemingway began his literary career by editing *Trapeze*, the school newspaper, and contributing to the literary magazine. He graduated in 1917.

Unity Temple, now a national historical landmark, was constructed in 1906. Designed by Frank Lloyd Wright, it was the first public building he executed, and he spoke of it late in life as a major achievement in his career. Guided tours are conducted here, and also in Wright's house and studio in Oak Park.

A middle-class suburban community, Oak Park has a good mix of 9,635 single-family homes and 13,175 apartment units, as well as retail shops and light industry. The village is served by two rapid transit lines (referred to as the CTA "els") which transport Oak Park commuters to downtown Chicago in 15 to 20 minutes. Also, bus transportation links Oak Park with Chicago, O'Hare Airport, and other suburban communities, and the Chicago & Northwestern Railway provides transportation to downtown Chicago and as far west as Geneva, Illinois.

Oak Park's Police Department has 94 law enforcement officers and a communications network linking it with state police and the FBI, making information available to the officer on the beat in a matter of 10 to 45 seconds. Special emphasis has been placed on advanced education and training regarding narcotics and drug abuse.

The city's fire fighting force consists of 95 men and seven pieces of equipment, including four pumpers, an aerial-ladder truck, an emergency squad, and a snorkel. "Baby Sitter Seminars," for teen and adult baby-sitters, emphasize precautions that are vital to fire safety. Its equipment and training have enabled Oak Park to achieve a Class 3 fire rating, assuring low fire-insurance premiums—and Oak Park is one of only six communities in the state to achieve that ranking.

Public school facilities include 10 elementary schools and the Oak Park-River Forest High School, where 80 percent of the faculty hold master's degrees, and half of the faculty have earned 30 or more hours beyond the M.A. Dr. James Bryant Conant included this school in the select group of high schools that were, in his judgment, conducting superior programs of education. Each year it has one of the largest number of National Merit Scholarship finalists in the nation, and 80 percent of its graduates enter college.

Also in the Oak Park area are eight Catholic elementary schools, three Catholic high schools, two Lutheran schools, and five additional private schools. Nearby colleges include Concordia Teachers College (Lutheran), Rosary College, and Triton Junior College.

Two modern medical complexes are Oak Park Hospital, with more than 400 beds, and West Suburban Hospital, also with more than 400 beds. Their medical staffs number 175 and 160, respectively, and they contain some of the metropolitan area's most sophisticated and modern medical facilities.

In addition to three local weeklies, another newspaper published three times a week, and an Oak Park radio station, there is complete media coverage with Chicago newspapers, radio stations, and television channels.

Oak Park has more than 40 churches, representing the Adventist, Assembly of God, Baptist, Bible, Christian Disciples of Christ, Christian Reformed, Christian Science, Congregational, Eastern Orthodox, Episcopal, Friends (Religious Society of Quakers), Lutheran, Methodist, Pentacostal, Presbyterian, Roman Catholic, Unitarian Universalist, United Church of Christ, and Unity denominations. There is also a Jewish synagogue. More than 150 societies, clubs, and organizations are active here, and the Oak Park Public Library houses approximately 160,000 volumes, 3,000 record albums, and 1,500 films. Rare book collections feature the works of Oak Park alumni Frank Lloyd Wright and Ernest Hemingway.

Oak Park's recreation system includes 12 park areas, three parkways, and seven recreation centers. In operation are several swimming pools, a skating area, a senior citizens center and historical museum, and a pistol range. The Oak Park Conservatory (greenhouses) and the Trailside Museum of Natural History are open to the public. Cultural programs include a Village Art Fair, a Concerts Under the Stars series, and an Art in the Park exhibition, plus the activities of the Historical Society, the Community Lecture Series, and the Civic Symphony.

FOR FURTHER INFORMATION Write to the Oak Park-River Forest Chamber of Commerce, 948 Lake Street, Oak Park, Ill. 60301, and enclose $1 for a copy of the 84-page *Oak Park Community Handbook and Business Directory*.

CITY/STATE: Oak Park, Illinois
POPULATION: 62,511 1960-70 change: +2.3 %
1.2 % non-white. 16.3 % over 65.
REAL ESTATE: Median value, $26,200. 19 less than $10,000, 4,103 $10,000 to $25,000, 4,865 $25,000 and over. Median gross rent, $145. 1,089 less than $100, 5,419. $100 to $150, 5,280 $150 and over.
EDUCATION: Median school years completed, 12.8.
73.0 % high school graduates.
INCOME: Median family income, $13,823. 4,429 less than $10,000, 9,642 $10,000 to $25,000, 2,058 $25,000 and over.
EMPLOYMENT: 28,018 in labor force, 19.9 % in manufacturing, 2.3 % unemployed.

44 SCHENECTADY, New York

Founded in 1661 by Dutch settlers, the little village of "Shinnectady" (or "Schanhechtade"—early spellings vary) received its first notoriety in a most unfortunate manner. French troops, supported by hostile Indians, descended on the settlement at 11 o'clock on a Saturday night in 1690, massacring most of the population. As recorded by Albany Mayor Peter Schuyler, they "murther'd Sixty men women and Children most Barbarously, Burning ye Place and Carried 27 along with them Prisoners. . . . The Cruelties Committed at sd Place no Penn can write nor Tongue Expresse, ye women bigg with Childe Rip'd up and ye Children alive throwne into ye flames, and there hads Dash'd in Pieces against the Doors and windows."

From the ruins of that infamous Massacre of 1690, the first battle of the French and Indian Wars, Schenectady grew again and prospered as a stopping place for traders and settlers making their way west on the Mohawk River. Later, with the opening of the Erie Canal and the railroad, Schenectady became a thriving "Gateway to the West."

Schenectady's economy today is dominated by the General Electric Company, whose Schenectady Works is the original GE plant, where the genius of Steinmetz discovered alternating current and changed the face of our nation and most of the world. Employing thousands of area residents, it constitutes the largest electrical manufacturing facility in the world.

Other important industries include Alco Products (a major producer of locomotives), the Electrical Products Division of Minnesota Mining and Manufacturing Company, Sealtest Division of National Dairy Products Corporation, Schenectady Chemicals, and Consolidated Diesel Electric Corporation.

Housing in Schenectady ranges from the old Stockade area, where the homes date from the early 1700s, to modern garden apartments and developments in the city and surrounding towns. New middle-income and luxury apartments are being built. The average rent for middle-income apartments is $150 a month, and for luxury apartments from $175 to $325 a month. And if you're handy with a hammer, the surrounding area abounds with rural homes suitable for renovation.

Schenectady's public school system consists of 21 elementary schools, a middle school (in new facilities that opened in 1973), and two high schools. Also in the city is Union College, a men's college with the oldest planned campus in the United States. The nation's first social fraternity, Kappa Alpha, was founded at Union, as were five other fraternities and the first New York chapter of Phi Beta Kappa. Many other colleges are located in the Albany-Schenectady-Utica section of central New York State.

Schenectady has easy access to both the New York Thruway and the Northway. Limousine service is available for air travelers who arrive through the Albany County Airport, only 11 miles away.

On the cultural side, Schenectady has its own symphony orchestra, several choruses, a light opera company, and a civic playhouse producing both classical and modern drama. With more scientists and engineers than practically any other community of its size in the country, Schenectady has local chapters of 27 professional organizations. A visit to the Schenectady Museum will provide you with fascinating insights on local history, American Indian lore, and the natural sciences. On the campus of Union College are the Jackson Gardens, with annuals and perennials in bloom throughout the spring and fall, and 15-sided Nott Memorial Hall, which features an extensive collection of the letters of George Washington. Schenectady's most prominent attraction, however, is the Stockade area of town— with 66 historic homes and buildings built between 1700 and 1850. Each building is now marked with the name of its original owner and the date of construction. Before leaving the Stockade area, visit the museum of the Schenectady Historical Society.

The city's recreational program is extensive, with a budget of nearly $500,000 annually. Five golf courses are in the immediate area, as well as plenty of facilities for bowling, skiing, tennis, swimming, and picnicking. Major attractions are nearby in all directions, too— Lake George (55 miles), Lake Champlain and Fort Ticonderoga (75 miles), the Saratoga Performing Arts Center and Raceway (22 miles), the Baseball Hall of Fame at Cooperstown (50 miles), the Tanglewood Music Festival (50 miles), and many other attractions in the Adirondacks, Catskills, and Berkshires.

FOR FURTHER INFORMATION Write to the Schenectady County Chamber of Commerce, Inc., 101 State Street, Schenectady, N.Y. 12305, and ask for their folders, *Schenectady: Drive It-Yourself Tour*, *Welcome to Historic Schenectady*, and *Schenectady . . . As Interesting As It Is Friendly!* Also available from the chamber, at $5 each, are an *Industrial List* (with information on 164 firms in the area) and an *Organization List* (with data on 273 civic, fraternal, welfare, and cultural organizations).

CITY/STATE: ___Schenectady, New York___
POPULATION: __77,859__1960-70 change: __-4.7__%
__4.7__% non-white. __15.0__% over 65.
REAL ESTATE: Median value, $__15,000__. __1,530__less than $10,000, __6,446__$10,000 to $25,000, __794__$25,000 and over. Median gross rent, $__79__. __9,618__less than $100, __3,250__. $100 to $150, __583__$150 and over.
EDUCATION: Median school years completed, __12.1__. __52.7__% high school graduates.
INCOME: Median family income, $__9,318__. __11,032__less than $10,000, __8,517__$10,000 to $25,000, __650__$25,000 and over.
EMPLOYMENT: __31,235__in labor force, __27.0__% in manufacturing, __3.7__% unemployed.

45 ELMHURST, Illinois

Elmhurst portrays itself as "a suburban town with a metropolitan atmosphere." With fine homes and good shops, its residents find that a pleasant and accurate description.

Three business areas will be found in the city—the downtown business district; a commercial area on the west side of town, consisting of an older shopping area and a newer shopping center; and a shopping center located on Route 83. Three industrial parks, consisting of some 800 acres zoned for light industry, are in the process of development at the north end of the city.

Housing in Elmhurst ranges from the excellent sections of all custom-built homes around Elmhurst College, and on the south and southwest sides of the city, to the solidly built large frame-houses in the rest of the city. Seventy percent of the homes were built since World War II. A new planned development covering 27 acres is locating luxury condominiums and town houses on the south end of the city. Homes range from $20,000 to $140,000, with new homes starting at $30,000. Some lots are still available, and rents for an estimated 2,000 rental units range from $150 to $360 per month.

Elmhurst has a police force with 67 regular personnel and 25 auxiliary personnel, and equipped with 14 radio squad cars and a rescue wagon. William T. Payne, Chief of Police, told me of various ways in which "the citizens of Elmhurst stand behind their police department in its efforts to enforce the law," and credits these as contributing factors to the low crime-rate. "This was shown," he says, "by the fact that a referendum to increase salaries for the police officers was passed by a four-to-one vote. Support like this is a great incentive to the officers to give that little extra effort which is so necessary today.

"Another reason," he adds, "is the way the city government has provided the department with the tools it needs to do the job. New and improved equipment is a great morale booster and when it is provided, the Chief can expect the men to produce.

"The final, but not the least important factor," he concludes, "is desire on the part of the men in the field. Prevention is best provided by good aggressive patrol. The city has been receptive to their requests for salaries and fringe benefits, and in return they feel a responsibility to give the best performance possible."

Public schools include a high school, two junior highs, and 14 elementary schools. Elmhurst has three Catholic elementary schools and a coed Catholic high school. There is also a Lutheran elementary school, and a Lutheran junior high and high school are being constructed. Elmhurst College, a four-year liberal arts college founded in 1871, has a day enrollment of 1,700 and a night enrollment of 1,200. Adult education and training courses are offered by the high school, the college, and the YMCA.

Memorial Hospital of DuPage County, located in Elmhurst, has 451 beds, a laboratory, an outpatient clinic, and emergency-room facilities. An estimated 70 doctors and 47 dentists practice in the city.

The average mean temperature is 24.9 degrees in January, 74.6 degrees in July. The elevation is 681 feet, and the normal annual precipitation is 32.72 inches.

Chicago's Loop is reached in approximately 40 minutes by automobile, taking the Eisenhower Expressway, or in 32 minutes by Chicago & Northwestern trains—25 minutes on the express runs. O'Hare International Airport is six miles north on Interstate 294, and DuPage County Airport is 16 miles west on Illinois highway 64. In addition to a twice-weekly local newspaper and an FM radio station broadcasting from Elmhurst College, there is full newspaper, radio, and television coverage from Chicago.

Elmhurst's recreational system includes 16 parks with facilities for swimming, ice skating, softball, arts and crafts instruction, tennis, and music. Mayor Charles Weigel, Jr., reports that improvements to the park system costing approximately $4 million are under construction, including indoor tennis courts on the west side of town. More than 100 organizations are active in Elmhurst, and cultural attractions include the activities of the Children's Theater, the Artists' Guild, the Symphony Orchestra, the Public Library, and the Historical Commission. The Lizzadro Museum of Lapidary Art, the nation's only museum devoted exclusively to the lapidary arts, displays gems, minerals, and objets d'art made of gem materials. A lapidary school and material shop, tours, a gift shop, lectures, and television demonstrations of gem cutting are among its programs.

FOR FURTHER INFORMATION Write to the Elmhurst Chamber of Commerce, 111 South York Street, Elmhurst, Ill. 60126, for its Elmhurst brochure, a map of the city, and a folder on the Lizzadro Museum of Lapidary Art.

CITY/STATE: Elmhurst, Illinois
POPULATION: 50,547   1960-70 change: +36.6 %
0.8 % non-white.   8.1 % over 65.
REAL ESTATE: Median value, $28,600. 56 less than $10,000, 4,263 $10,000 to $25,000, 7,582 $25,000 and over. Median gross rent, $153. 211 less than $100, 785. $100 to $150, 1,065 $150 and over.
EDUCATION: Median school years completed, 12.7. 73.4 % high school graduates.
INCOME: Median family income, $14,955. 2,283 less than $10,000, 8,672 $10,000 to $25,000, 1,949 $25,000 and over.
EMPLOYMENT: 20,783 in labor force, 27.4 % in manufacturing, 1.7 % unemployed.

46 READING, Pennsylvania

Berks County, with its rolling hills and fertile fields, has the dual advantage of retaining plenty of open space and rural atmosphere while being adjacent to the eastern "megalopolis" centers of New York City, Philadelphia, Baltimore, and Washington.

Reading was founded in 1748 by the sons of William Penn, Richard and Thomas, who were so impressed by its beauty that they named it in honor of their home town of Reading and their home county of Berkshire in England. The Schuylkill River flows through the county, and the local topography varies from the Appalachian Valley and ridges in the northern part, the Great Valley in the central portion, the Reading Hills and South Mountain, to the Piedmont lowlands in the southern part. Into this area in the early 1700s came Quakers, French Huguenots and settlers from the Palatinate region of Germany, followed by an inundation of German Amish, Mennonites, and Dunkards that has made this area a center of the "Pennsylvania Dutch" country ever since. The Tulpehocken settlers from Schoharie, New York, led by friendly Indians down the Susquehanna River and then eastward, began their settlements about 1723. Conrad Weiser, who later became Indian agent for the Penns, arrived in 1729. The Schwenkfelders, who founded their settlements in Hereford Township in 1734, are another distinct group with great cultural influence.

Modern Berks County still has plenty of farms—2,821 in all—but it is also a manufacturing center with 647 diversified industrial establishments employing 57,600 persons. Located in Reading are the largest full-fashioned hosiery mills in the world, the largest single-unit foundry under one roof in the world, the largest brick-burning kiln in the world, the largest locomotive and car shops in the world, the largest paint-manufacturing plant in the world, and the largest pretzel-baking plant in the world (giving it the nickname of "Pretzel City").

In the 16-year period 1956 through 1971, the county lost 69 industries, which had provided 5,434 jobs. But it gained 158 new ones, which provided 6,154 jobs, and gained 8,025 jobs by the expansion of 280 existing industries, for a net gain of 8,745 jobs.

The largest employer, the Textile Machine Works (knitting machines), has a work force of about 4,000. Other major employers are Berkshire International Corporation (ladies' hosiery), Parish Pressed Steel (auto frames), Western Electric (electronic components), Carpenter Steel Company (stainless steel), Luden's (candy and cough drops), Caloric Corporation (gas stoves), and Bethlehem Steel (iron ore). Also made in Berks County are such items as industrial plastics, batteries, spark plugs, ribbons and braided goods, copper products, paints, optical lenses, wearing apparel, upholstered furniture, pressure boilers, building brick, paper coating, truck bodies, dyestuffs, hardware specialties, even light metals for use in space vehicles.

In the 1960s, more than 3,000 new homes were built. Apartment construction has been booming, too, with rents ranging from $100 to $250. About 70 percent of Berks County homes are owner-occupied.

With a favorable AAA fire-insurance rating, Reading is the only city of its size in the United States with a volunteer fire fighting system. Rainbow Fire Company, one of 14 in the city, is 195 years old. Predating the Declaration of Independence, it is the oldest volunteer fire company in the nation.

Bernard J. Dobinsky, Chief of Police, pointed out to me that serious crimes in Reading *decreased* 9 percent in 1972 over 1971. "During the past three years," he told me, "personnel of the Police Department have been attending Pennsylvania State University to earn an Associate Degree in law enforcement. Our own accredited Police Academy trains all trainees for a period of 12 weeks, in addition to brush-up subjects to other personnel. Officers attend seminars offered by the State Police, FBI, and Southern Police Institute. We have one FBI Academy graduate and two men graduated from Redstone Arsenal for the Bomb Squad. Administrative personnel are placed by Civil Service tests. Raises in salary to the amount of $1,500 have been given during the last two years. I feel that all these changes have resulted in more efficient police services, thereby reducing the crime rate."

At the elementary level, Berks County has 125 public schools and 10 parochial schools; at the secondary level, 26 public high schools and six parochial high schools. At the collegiate level, the county is home to Albright College, Alvernia College, Kutztown State College, the Berks Center of Pennsylvania State University, Temple University Technical Institute, and the Wyomissing Institute of Fine Arts. Miscellaneous educational institutions include three technical-vocational schools, three business colleges, and four specialized facilities.

The three hospitals in the area have a total of 1,300 beds. A rehabilitation center, mental institute, home for the aged and infirm, and the Visiting Nurses Association round out the public health services.

Mean temperatures are 51.4 degrees in the spring, 73.1 in the summer, 53.6 in the autumn, and 33.3 in the winter. Average rainfall is 40 inches annually, with an average annual snowfall of 30 inches. Elevations within the county range from 125 feet to almost 1,700 feet.

Berks County has access to the Pennsylvania Turnpike and Interstates 78 and 176. Reading Municipal Airport is served by Allegheny, Eastern, Suburban, and General airlines. For three days each year it is the busiest airport in the nation, exceeding even O'Hare International Airport in Chicago. During those three days it hosts the Reading Air Show, perhaps the largest general aviation show in the country.

The city has two daily newspapers, the *Times* (mornings) and the *Eagle* (afternoons and Sundays). Three AM radio stations and two FM stations broadcast from the county. Three companies provide up to 12 UHF and VHF television channels by cable, in addition to a local cable channel.

Parks cover over 2,000 acres in Reading, and over 11,000 acres in the county. Also here are French Creek State Park; Hopewell Village, an early American iron-making village that is now a national historical site; and Daniel Boone's homestead. The county is also a Pennsylvania Dutch tourist mecca, with numerous annual festivals. Among them are a Mennonite Sale, a Colonial American Fair, antique flea markets, the Berks Art Festival, Patriot Days at the Daniel Boone Homestead, something called Establishment Day at Hopewell Village, the Pennsylvania Dutch Farm Festival, several Bavarian Festivals, and the nationally famous Kutztown Folk Festival.

FOR FURTHER INFORMATION Write to the Chamber of Commerce of Reading and Berks County, Box 1698, Reading, Pa. 19603, and ask for *Partners in Progress* (a 48-page illustrated color booklet), *Welcome to Pennsylvania Dutch Land!* (a brochure), *Facts about Reading and Berks County,* and its printed six-page letter of information about the city and the county.

CITY/STATE: Reading, Pennsylvania
POPULATION: 87,643   1960–70 change: -10.7 %
6.8 % non-white. 15.8 % over 65.
REAL ESTATE: Median value, $ 8,500 . 11,252 less than $10,000, 4,537 $10,000 to $25,000, 673 $25,000 and over. Median gross rent, $ 66 . 11,379 less than $100, 1,185 . $100 to $150, 407 $150 and over.
EDUCATION: Median school years completed, 10.1 . 34.8 % high school graduates.
INCOME: Median family income, $ 8,786 . 13,669 less than $10,000, 8,487 $10,000 to $25,000, 471 $25,000 and over.
EMPLOYMENT: 38,023 in labor force, 44.5 % in manufacturing, 3.3 % unemployed.

47 INDEPENDENCE, Missouri

While Independence is best known today as the home town of former President Harry S. Truman, it once was important as the only city of consequence west of the Mississippi. Known as the "Queen City of the Trails," it was here that early homesteaders and pioneers started their westward treks to unknown territories and the great California gold rush on the Santa Fe, California, and Oregon trails.

Present-day reminders of that colorful past include the old city jail, temporary residence of Frank James and of border outlaw Quantrill, who staged a spectacular escape. Fort Osage, first outpost of the United States in the Louisiana Purchase, has been restored, and—reflecting more recent times—the Harry S. Truman Library and Museum houses the late President's personal papers and mementos. Interest in local history is intense, and the Jackson County Historical Society is the largest local history society in the nation, with over 2,500 members.

Often considered a suburb of Kansas City, which it adjoins, Independence is a county seat and business center on its own. An Allis-Chalmers plant manufactures Gleaner combines and employs nearly 1,000. The Sugar Creek Refinery of American Oil Company employs more than 500, and Remington Arms has a small-arms plant nearby.

Agriculture is also important in the rich farmland surrounding Independence. Corn is the leading crop, but wheat, oats, and soybeans are also important. Beef cattle, hogs, chickens, and sheep are abundant, and there is a thriving dairy business. Other local crops are tomatoes, vegetables, apples, peaches, and concord grapes.

More than 75 percent of the homes in Independence are owner-occupied. Most new homes are selling in the $25,000 category, but you can also find less expensive homes and luxury residences priced up to $100,000. Many top executives of the metropolitan area live here, and there seems to be a good supply of apartments, town houses, homes, and land available for building.

The public school system consists of 27 elementary schools, four junior highs, and three senior high schools. In addition, there are a Lutheran elementary school, three Catholic elementary schools, and a Catholic high school. The University of Missouri Extension Center and the Central Missouri State University Residence Center are in Independence. Many colleges and universities are located in the two Kansas Cities (Missouri and Kansas), and in the surrounding area.

Medical facilities include two hospitals, with 362 beds and bassinets; an underground civil defense hospital; a chiropractic clinic; and five animal hospitals. Seventy-one physicians and surgeons, 33 osteopaths, 46 chiropractors, 63 dentists, nine optometrists, and 16 veterinarians practice in Independence, with many more available in nearby Kansas City.

The climate features mild winters with plenty of sunshine and moderate snowfall (an average of 14.4 inches), early springs, and long Indian summers. The average temperature in July is 83.4 degrees. Average precipitation is 27.21 inches. Independence is 1,048 feet above sea level.

Transportation facilities include access to Interstates 70 and 435, and the two Kansas City airports, served by eight commercial airlines. Independence has a daily newspaper, a weekly, and a radio station, in addition to the *Kansas City Star & Times*, 19 radio stations in the area, and six metropolitan-area television channels.

More than 100 churches represent virtually every denomination. Independence is the world headquarters of the Reorganized Church of Jesus Christ of Latter-Day Saints, which holds its world conference here every two years and has constructed an ultramodern visitors center. Nearby, Unity School of Christianity and the Church of the Nazarene have their headquarters.

Independence has extensive recreational programs and facilities, and just outside the city limits are Kansas City's twin stadiums— Arrowhead, home of the world-champion K.C. Chiefs, and the Royals baseball stadium. Kansas City also has professional basketball, a soccer team, and an ice hockey team. Slightly to the southeast is Lake Jacomo, with many outdoor activities. And in addition to the many organizations and cultural activities in Independence, including a Community Theater, there is ready access to Kansas City's nationally known Starlight Theater, the Lyric Theater, the William Rockhill Nelson Gallery of Art, the Mary Atkins Museum of Fine Arts, the Kansas City Museum of Natural History and Science, and the Kansas City Philharmonic Orchestra.

FOR FURTHER INFORMATION Write to the Independence Chamber of Commerce, P.O. Box 147, Independence, Mo. 64051, and ask for its 36-page color booklet, *Some Facts About Our City;* also available are *Industries in Independence,* the mimeographed historical-sheet, *Independence, Missouri—Where the West Began* and other mimeographed materials on the Truman Library and Museum, the trails, the old county jail, and Fort Osage.

CITY/STATE: Independence, Missouri

POPULATION: 111,662   1960–70 change: +79.2 %
   1.0   % non-white.   8.1   % over 65.

REAL ESTATE: Median value, $ 16,400 .   3,476 less than $10,000, 18,262 $10,000 to $25,000, 2,830 $25,000 and over. Median gross rent, $ 89   .   5,681 less than $100,   3,074 . $100 to $150,   543 $150 and over.

EDUCATION: Median school years completed,   12.2   .
   59.3 % high school graduates.

INCOME: Median family income, $ 10,787 .   13,282 less than $10,000, 16,596 $10,000 to $25,000,   826 $25,000 and over.

EMPLOYMENT: 47,946 in labor force, 29.5   % in manufacturing,   2.6   % unemployed.

48 LAKEWOOD, California

Crime is rampant in California, far above national levels, but there is a city in the southern half of the state that qualifies as one of America's 50 safest cities. Lakewood is a young city, incorporated in 1954; it is situated in the midst of a vast metropolitan area— Los Angeles to its north, booming Orange County to the south. With freeways leading in every direction, Southern California's attractions are unusually convenient—the Los Angeles Civic Center is 21 miles from Lakewood, and the Pacific Ocean beaches are only 15 minutes away.

Lakewood is primarily a residential community, but it does serve as a center for research and development firms. The Purex Corporation has its modern world administrative headquarters here, and in the surrounding area are such major manufacturing plants and industrial centers as the McDonnell Douglas Aircraft Company, the North American-Rockwell Corporation, Aerojet General, and the Long Beach Naval Shipyard. The business centers of both Los Angeles and Orange County are within easy commuting distance.

Most of the homes here range in price from $18,000 to $28,000. Several residential areas, however, reflect considerably higher price brackets.

Police protection is provided by the Los Angeles County Sheriff's Department, and the more than 200 personnel at the Lakewood Sheriff's Station serve Lakewood and five neighboring communities. Their equipment is modern and effective—under Project Sky Knight, for example, Lakewood became a showcase city for the use of patrol helicopters to increase mobility.

The modern educational system includes 17 elementary schools, two junior highs, two high schools, and two parochial schools. Long Beach City College has a Lakewood campus, and in the surrounding towns are its Business and Technical Campus, California State College at Long Beach, Cerritos College in Norwalk, Compton Junior College, and Whittier College. Still within easy commuting distance are the University of Southern California, UCLA, Loyola University of Los Angeles, Pepperdine College, Occidental College, California State College at Los Angeles, the Claremont Colleges, and the University of California's beautiful new campus at Irvine.

Medical facilities include the 75-bed Woodruff Gables Hospital, with six more hospitals in the immediate area making a total of more than 600 beds.

The climate is typical of Southern California—an average high of 72.0 degrees and an average low of 52.8 degrees, with rainfall averaging 12.36 inches and coming mostly in the winter.

Being in the midst of the Los Angeles-Orange County metropolitan area, newspaper, radio, and television coverage is complete. Lakewood is surrounded by freeways—the Long Beach, Santa Ana, San Diego, Garden Grove, San Gabriel River, and Artesia freeways. Passenger air service is available at Long Beach Municipal Airport, adjacent to Lakewood, or 30 minutes away at Los Angeles International Airport. Shopping facilities are deluxe—there are more than 100 specialty shops and retail establishments in the 154-acre Lakewood Center, including branches of five major department stores, and Dutch Village is graced by charming Dutch Provincial architecture.

Lakewood has 21 churches, and a major event each year is the week-long Pan-American Festival, with its sports contests, English- and Spanish-language contests, Latin-style fiesta, beauty contest, and parade. The city's parks are fully equipped with playgrounds, baseball diamonds, tot-lots, a youth center, and swimming pools (you will find three in town). Lakewood Country Club, a county-operated public facility, has an 18-hole golf course and five tennis courts. The city's Park and Recreation Department has a full calendar of activities the year-round, including team sports, teen and preteen dances, crafts and hobby courses, and dramatic productions for children and adults. And heading out in any direction you will find Southern California's most famous attractions—whether the beaches, Disneyland, Marineland, or Knott's Berry Farm.

FOR FURTHER INFORMATION Write to the Greater Lakewood Chamber of Commerce, 5787 South Street, Lakewood, Calif. 90713, and ask for its illustrated booklet on the city.

CITY/STATE: Lakewood, California
POPULATION: 82,973   1960-70 change: +23.6 %
   1.5 % non-white. 4.4 % over 65.
REAL ESTATE: Median value, $ 22,300 . 47 less than $10,000, 14,748 $10,000 to $25,000, 4,070 $25,000 and over. Median gross rent, $ 145 . 542 less than $100, 2,011 . $100 to $150, 2,034 $150 and over.
EDUCATION: Median school years completed, 12.3 . 64.2 % high school graduates.
INCOME: Median family income, $ 12,089 . 7,081 less than $10,000, 14,119 $10,000 to $25,000, 835 $25,000 and over.
EMPLOYMENT: 33,535 in labor force, 32.7 % in manufacturing, 5.7 % unemployed.

49 WAUWATOSA, Wisconsin

Wauwatosa is a pleasant, settled, suburban neighbor to Milwaukee. Among the 25 largest cities in Wisconsin, it ranks first in per capita property value and second in per capita income. It is bonded to only a sixth of its legal limit and has the highest Dunn & Bradstreet rating granted to those 25 cities; moreover, its tax rate is in the lower third.

"All of this is highly due to having home rule," says Mayor F.D. Kuckuck. And he warns that "today there is a strong trend and continuous effort by higher levels of government, with their superior financial resources and ·legislative authority, to appropriate the home rule powers which made this present Wauwatosa possible."

No detailed information is available from the local chamber of commerce, but Wauwatosa does have 11 elementary schools, three junior highs, and two high schools in its public school system. Within its boundaries are Booth Memorial, County Emergency, Lakeview, and Milwaukee Psychiatric hospitals, as well as St. Camillus Health Center. Six parks, in addition to the football and track stadium, include facilities for golf and swimming.

John P. Howard, the Chief of Police, is a member of the Uniform Crime Reporting Committee of the International Association of Chiefs of Police, the Wisconsin Council on Criminal Justice, and the Citizens Study Committee on Judicial Organization. He is also a part-time instructor in the criminal justice program at the University of Wisconsin—Milwaukee. Here is how he analyses the crime situation in Wauwatosa and the metropolitan area:

"Historically this metropolitan area and Milwaukee, its central city, have enjoyed the lowest crime rates of any of the major metropolitan areas and major cities in the United States. The reasons for this distinction are difficult to assess. In my opinion, they are related to such factors as the following:

"1. Relatively low unemployment rates together with high employment rates.

"2. Median per capita income which is relatively very high for major cities and metropolitan areas.

"3. Very high per capita expenditures for welfare services.

"4. A relatively low percentage of substandard housing.

"5. A relatively high percentage of owner-occupied dwellings.

"6. A tradition of good government.

"7. A high degree of citizen support and cooperation in the law enforcement function.

"8. A very strong tax base to support high levels of municipal and county public services.

"9. A tradition of integrity, professionalism and cooperation among local law enforcement officers.

"10. Court dockets which are less overloaded than those of most major metropolitan counties.

"11. A relatively small transient population.

"12. A good educational system.

"13. A state statute which empowers police officers to arrest on probable cause to believe that a crime has been committed. Many jurisdictions limit an officer's probable cause arrest powers to felonies only.

"14. A relatively small number of hard narcotics addicts, although I can *not* document this statistically with data presently at hand.

"15. *Relative* freedom from the influence of syndicated crime.

"The above listed factors apply to all the communities, individually and collectively, which comprise our metropolitan area. With regard to Wauwatosa specifically, three facts seem important to me:

"1. Our citizens are urged to report crimes and suspicious occurrences promptly to the police. Annually, our officers investigate over 1,600 reports of suspicious persons, cars or incidents, and many of these result in arrests or the aborting of crimes. We have excellent support from the news media and citizen organizations for dissemination of crime warnings and crime prevention information.

"2. Our police department has developed eight excellent citizen information programs which are presented to thousands of citizens in organized groups. These programs cover such topics as burglary prevention, self-defense for women, drug abuse, the police role in the community, and shoplifting. A fulltime Community Support Officer is in charge of these and other programs.

"3. A very active, trained 120-man Police Reserve unit which augments the regular force of 95 officers and 17 civilian employees.

"I should also point out that our city, like most Wisconsin cities, is experiencing crime rates which are rising from a relatively low base. Burglary is our number one Index Crime problem at this time. All segments of the criminal justice system in Wisconsin are trying to combat rising crime rates by many federal and state funded projects, some of which are based on the recommendations of various statewide study committees."

CITY/STATE: Wauwatosa, Wisconsin
POPULATION: __58,676__ 1960-70 change: __+3.1__ %
__1.0__ % non-white. __14.5__ % over 65.
REAL ESTATE: Median value, $__26,600__ __58__ less than $10,000, __5,221__ $10,000 to $25,000, __6,653__ $25,000 and over. Median gross rent, $__130__ . __938__ less than $100, __2,052__ . $100 to $150, __1,396__ $150 and over.
EDUCATION: Median school years completed, __12.6__ . __70.1__ % high school graduates.
INCOME: Median family income, $__13,432__ . __4,091__ less than $10,000, __9,002__ $10,000 to $25,000, __1,710__ $25,000 and over.
EMPLOYMENT: __22,970__ in labor force, __25.9__ % in manufacturing, __2.0__ % unemployed.

50 FARGO, North Dakota

Fargo and its sister city of Moorhead, Minnesota, first flourished when farming became established in the area and set their future as wholesale and distribution centers for the upper Midwest. The two towns were the southern boundary for steamboats carrying cargoes of grain, hides, and furs to and from Winnepeg on the Red River of the North. When the Great Northern Railway selected their location as a crossing site over the Red River, their future was secured. Indeed, Fargo and Moorhead were named for William G. Fargo, a founder of Wells-Fargo Express, and William G. Moorhead, both of whom were directors of the Northern Pacific.

Agriculture is still the backbone of the area's economy, and the stability of the population reflects its strong attachment to the soil. (North Dakota, of all states in the nation, is second-lowest in terms of percentage of population on welfare—only Wyoming is lower.) Well over 95 percent of the land in Cass and Clay counties is farmed. Small grains, potatoes, sunflowers, soybeans, and sugarbeets are the main crops. Truck farms produce onions, tomatoes, cabbages, pumpkins, squash, and other vegetables. Dairy and beef cattle are the chief livestock.

Farm-related industries and businesses in the Fargo area include Steiger Tractor, West Fargo Manufacturing, and Frontier, Inc.—all farm equipment manufacturers, Union Stockyards at West Fargo, the Sioux Land Dressed Beef Company, Cass-Clay Creameries, Kraft Foods, the American Crystal Sugar Company refinery north of Moorhead, and the edible oil sunflower-seed processing plant of Dahlgren & Company in Fargo. Other major employers in the city are Northwestern Bell, the *Fargo Forum* (newspaper), Fargo Foundry (fabricated steel products), Northern States Power, and Branick Manufacturing (auto- and tire-repair equipment).

The average purchase price for houses in Fargo is $16,750 for a two-bedroom home and $24,200 for three bedrooms. Average monthly rentals are $125 to $160 for two bedrooms, $150 to $210 for three bedrooms. Shopping facilities include West Acres, the largest shopping center in the north between the Twin Cities and the West Coast.

Edwin R. Anderson, Chief of Police, gave me five reasons for the relatively low crime-rate:

"1. Fargo is made up of a very stable population, quite conservative in nature.

"2. We do not have any 'ghettos' as such, nor do we have any depressed or 'Skid-Row' area.

"3. Minority group problems are generally minor in nature.

"4. Fargo, while it is the largest city in the state, is still small enough in nature so that people think of each other as neighbors and are concerned with their neighbors and their problems. They are concerned with the crime problem and insist on good law enforcement.

"5. Our Police Department can rank with the most progressive in the country. We have instituted a training program which I feel is second to none. We have taken advantage of every means available to provide our officers with the best in equipment, education and training. Our salaries are such that we attract the best applicants. The Department is basically a young, vigorous and vital Department."

Fargo's public school system enrolls 10,500 students and consists of 13 elementary schools, two junior highs, and two senior highs. Ten Lutheran and Catholic schools, including two high schools, enroll 2,550 students. North Dakota State University has 6,700 students, and Moorhead is home to two more colleges—Moorhead State College and Concordia College.

Practicing in Fargo are 121 physicians and surgeons, 30 dentists, eight optometrists, and nine chiropractors. The city has four hospitals (including a Veterans Administration hospital) and five clinics, with a total of 1,086 beds. In addition there is the West Fargo Medical Center and, in Moorhead, another hospital and an adjacent center with practicing physicians.

The average temperature is 7.3 in January, 42 in April, 71.4 in July, and 46.5 in October. Average annual precipitation is 18.45 inches.

Fargo has access to Interstates 94 and 29, and both rail and air passenger service. Amtrak, the national railroad passenger service, has two trains east and two west daily. Hector Airport has 15 flights daily on Northwest and North Central airlines.

Fargo also has a Pulitzer Prize-winning daily newspaper, the *Forum,* and five AM and four FM radio stations. The two cities have three network-affiliated television stations and an educational TV station, with cable television on the way.

Religiously, Lutherans and Catholics are predominant, and the area has 50 Protestant congregations, a dozen Catholic parishes, and two Jewish synagogues. The three colleges and universities are a cultural boon—with the Center for the Arts at Moorhead State, and its Series for the Performing Arts and Straw Hat Players; the Community Choir, Little Country Theater, and Oratorio Society at North Dakota State; the Moorhead State College Opera; and the a capella choirs of Concordia and North Dakota State. Community cultural groups include the Fargo-Moorhead Community Theater, the Fargo-Moorhead Symphony, the Fargo-Moorhead Civic Opera Company, and the Ambassador Chorus. For artistic activities and courses, there is the Island Park Art Festival and the Rourke Galleries and Red River Art Center.

Recreation facilities include 850 acres of parks, five swimming pools, 41 softball fields, 16 tennis courts, 14 skating rinks, theaters and bowling alleys, three gun clubs with firing ranges, an outdoor archery area, and a number of golf courses. College and professional sports include football, basketball, track, wrestling, swimming, golf, gymnastics, tennis, and baseball. Dog obedience schools and competitions are available. Nature trails skirt the Red River, and you are just an hour's drive from the famous lake country of Minnesota.

FOR FURTHER INFORMATION Write to the Fargo-Cass County Industrial Development Corporation, P.O. Box 2443, Fargo, N. Dak. 58102, and ask for its 52-page illustrated color booklet, *"Inside" Fargo/Moorhead,* as well as *North Dakota Community Data for Industry* (a report on Fargo), a *Community Data Sheet,* and three color brochures: *Fargo at the Water's Edge, Your Life in the Fargo Area,* and *Education for You . . . In the Fargo Area.*

CITY/STATE: ____Fargo, North Dakota____
POPULATION: __53,365____1960-70 change: __+14.4__%
__0.8__% non-white. __9.5__% over 65.
REAL ESTATE: Median value, $__19,600__. __566__less than $10,000, __5,171__$10,000 to $25,000, __2,121__$25,000 and over. Median gross rent, $__93__. __4,135__less than $100, __2,281__. $100 to $150, __989__$150 and over.
EDUCATION: Median school years completed, __12.6__. __68.7__% high school graduates.
INCOME: Median family income, $__10,175__. __5,904__less than $10,000, __5,685__$10,000 to $25,000, __554__$25,000 and over.
EMPLOYMENT: __21,937__in labor force, __5.8__% in manufacturing, __4.2__% unemployed.

Table 1
Index of Crime, United States, 1970

Area	Population [1]	Total crime index	Violent [2] crime	Property [2] crime	Murder and non-negligent man-slaughter	Forcible rape	Robbery	Aggra-vated assault	Burglary	Larceny $50 and over	Auto theft
United States Total	203,184,772	5,568,197	731,402	4,836,795	15,812	37,273	348,380	329,937	2,169,322	1,746,107	921,366
Rate per 100,000 inhabitants		2,740.5	360.0	2,380.5	7.8	18.3	171.5	162.4	1,067.7	859.4	453.5
Standard Metropolitan Statistical Area.	140,226,949										
Area actually reporting [3]	97.2%	4,691,725	634,446	4,057,279	12,093	30,847	331,819	259,687	1,797,699	1,420,012	839,568
Estimated total	100.0%	4,762,638	641,078	4,121,560	12,265	31,302	333,810	263,701	1,825,851	1,446,224	849,485
Rate per 100,000 inhabitants		3,396.4	457.2	2,939.2	8.7	22.3	238.0	188.1	1,302.1	1,031.3	605.8
Other Cities.	24,092,789										
Area actually reporting	87.8%	396,450	37,895	358,555	906	1,877	8,149	26,963	155,296	163,380	39,879
Estimated total	100.0%	445,129	43,695	401,434	1,070	2,124	9,098	31,403	174,775	182,246	44,413
Rate per 100,000 inhabitants		1,847.6	181.4	1,666.2	4.4	8.8	37.8	130.3	725.4	756.4	184.3
Rural.	38,865,034										
Area actually reporting	71.3%	267,388	28,735	238,653	1,534	2,614	3,639	20,948	129,021	88,702	20,930
Estimated total	100.0%	360,430	46,629	313,801	2,477	3,847	5,472	34,833	168,696	117,637	27,468
Rate per 100,000 inhabitants		927.4	120.0	807.4	6.4	9.9	14.1	89.6	434.1	302.7	70.7

[1] Population is Bureau of the Census decennial census, 1970.

[2] Violent crime is offenses of murder, forcible rape, robbery and aggravated assault; property crime is offenses of burglary, larceny $50 and over and auto theft.

[3] The percentage representing area actually reporting will not coincide with the ratio between reported and estimated crime totals since these data represent the sum of the calculations for individual states which have varying populations, portions reporting and crime rates.

Source: Federal Bureau of Investigation, U.S. Department of Justice, *Crime in the United States, Uniform Crime Reports—1970* (Washington: U.S. Government Printing Office, 1971).

Table 2
Index of Crime, United States, 1971

Area	Population[1]	Total Crime Index	Violent[2] crime	Property[2] crime	Murder and non-negligent man-slaughter	Forcible rape	Robbery	Aggra-vated assault	Burglary	Larceny $50 and over	Auto theft
United States Total	206,256,000	5,995,211	810,018	5,185,193	17,627	41,888	385,908	364,595	2,368,423	1,875,194	941,876
Rate per 100,000 inhabitants		2,906.7	392.7	2,514.0	8.5	20.3	187.1	176.8	1,148.3	909.2	456.5
Standard Metropolitan Statistical Area	145,878,000										
Area actually reporting[3]	97.6%	5,106,494	709,246	4,397,248	13,675	35,106	370,643	289,822	1,988,830	1,542,374	866,044
Estimated total	100.0%	5,173,916	715,731	4,458,185	13,845	35,575	372,486	293,825	2,015,759	1,666,824	875,602
Rate per 100,000 inhabitants		3,546.7	490.6	3,056.1	9.5	24.4	255.3	201.4	1,381.8	1,074.1	600.2
Other Cities	23,068,000										
Area actually reporting	89.1%	393,215	39,332	353,883	1,026	1,965	7,083	29,258	154,562	163,293	36,028
Estimated total	100.0%	436,145	44,522	391,623	1,192	2,177	7,874	33,279	171,744	179,867	40,012
Rate per 100,000 inhabitants		1,890.7	193.0	1,697.7	5.2	9.4	34.1	144.3	744.5	779.7	173.5
Rural	37,309,000										
Area actually reporting	74.8%	304,206	33,089	271,117	1,705	3,044	4,068	24,272	146,321	103,926	20,870
Estimated total	100.0%	385,150	49,765	335,385	2,590	4,136	5,548	37,491	180,920	128,503	25,962
Rate per 100,000 inhabitants		1,032.3	133.4	898.9	6.9	11.1	14.9	100.5	484.9	344.4	69.6

[1] Population is Bureau of the Census provisional estimate as of July 1, 1971.

[2] Violent crime is offenses of murder, forcible rape, robbery and aggravated assault; property crime is offenses of burglary, larceny $50 and over and auto theft.

[3] The percentage representing area actually reporting will not coincide with the ratio between reported and estimated crime totals since these data represent the sum of the calculations for individual states which have varying populations, portions reporting and crime rates.

Source: Federal Bureau of Investigation, U.S. Department of Justice, *Crime in the United States, Uniform Crime Reports—1971* (Washington: U.S. Government Printing Office, 1972).

Table 3
City Crime-Rankings
(The Cities Listed Alphabetically)

CRIME RANK

CITY	STATE	RANK
ABILENE	TEXAS	61
AKRON	OHIO	298
ALAMEDA	CALIFORNIA	118
ALBANY	GEORGIA	17
ALBANY	NEW YORK	150
ALBUQUERQUE	NEW MEXICO	355
ALEXANDRIA	VIRGINIA	317
ALHAMBRA	CALIFORNIA	225
ALLENTOWN	PENNSYLVANIA	112
ALTOONA	PENNSYLVANIA	27
AMARILLO	TEXAS	165
ANAHEIM	CALIFORNIA	299
ANDERSON	INDIANA	42
ANN ARBOR	MICHIGAN	360
APPLETON	WISCONSIN	16
ARLINGTON	MASSACHUSETTS	11
ARLINGTON	TEXAS	214
ARLINGTON	VIRGINIA	142
ARLINGTON HEIGHTS	ILLINOIS	15
ASHEVILLE	NORTH CAROLINA	179
ATLANTA	GEORGIA	343
AUGUSTA	GEORGIA	78
AURORA	COLORADO	227
AURORA	ILLINOIS	108
AUSTIN	TEXAS	139
BAKERSFIELD	CALIFORNIA	341
BALTIMORE	MARYLAND	361
BATON ROUGE	LOUISIANA	325
BAYONNE	NEW JERSEY	22
BEAUMONT	TEXAS	172
BELLEVUE	WASHINGTON	152
BELLFLOWER	CALIFORNIA	101
BERKELEY	CALIFORNIA	344
BERWYN	ILLINOIS	39
BETHLEHEM	PENNSYLVANIA	66
BILLINGS	MONTANA	189
BINGHAMTON	NEW YORK	72
BIRMINGHAM	ALABAMA	293
BLOOMFIELD	NEW JERSEY	58
BLOOMINGTON	MINNESOTA	90
BOISE	IDAHO	124
BOSTON	MASSACHUSETTS	362
BOULDER	COLORADO	96
BRIDGEPORT	CONNECTICUT	377
BRISTOL	CONNECTICUT	14
BROCKTON	MASSACHUSETTS	127
BROOKLINE	MASSACHUSETTS	370
BROWNSVILLE	TEXAS	126
BUENA PARK	CALIFORNIA	135

CRIME RANK

CITY	STATE	RANK
BUFFALO	NEW YORK	263
BURBANK	CALIFORNIA	117
CAMBRIDGE	MASSACHUSETTS	386
CAMDEN	NEW JERSEY	379
CANTON	OHIO	188
CARSON	CALIFORNIA	116
CEDAR RAPIDS	IOWA	31
CHAMPAIGN	ILLINOIS	226
CHARLESTON	SOUTH CAROLINA	334
CHARLESTON	WEST VIRGINIA	265
CHARLOTTE	NORTH CAROLINA	315
CHATTANOOGA	TENNESSEE	270
CHESAPEAKE	VIRGINIA	98
CHESTER	PENNSYLVANIA	374
CHICAGO	ILLINOIS	231
CHICOPEE	MASSACHUSETTS	59
CHULA VISTA	CALIFORNIA	136
CICERO	ILLINOIS	35
CINCINNATI	OHIO	277
CLEARWATER	FLORIDA	250
CLEVELAND	OHIO	351
CLEVELAND HEIGHTS	OHIO	93
CLIFTON	NEW JERSEY	20
COLORADO SPRINGS	COLORADO	264
COLUMBIA	MISSOURI	76
COLUMBIA	SOUTH CAROLINA	297
COLUMBUS	OHIO	308
COLUMBUS	GEORGIA	84
COMPTON	CALIFORNIA	393
CONCORD	CALIFORNIA	278
CORPUS CHRISTI	TEXAS	301
COSTA MESA	CALIFORNIA	294
COUNCIL BLUFFS	IOWA	251
COVINGTON	KENTUCKY	300
CRANSTON	RHODE ISLAND	86
DALLAS	TEXAS	342
DALY CITY	CALIFORNIA	170
DANBURY	CONNECTICUT	75
DAVENPORT	IOWA	132
DAYTON	OHIO	359
DEARBORN	MICHIGAN	182
DEARBORN HEIGHTS	MICHIGAN	119
DECATUR	ILLINOIS	106
DENVER	COLORADO	385
DES MOINES	IOWA	186
DES PLAINES	ILLINOIS	80
DETROIT	MICHIGAN	391
DOWNEY	CALIFORNIA	243
DUBUQUE	IOWA	85
DULUTH	MINNESOTA	97

CRIME RANK

CITY	STATE	RANK
DURHAM	NORTH CAROLINA	204
EAST HARTFORD	CONNECTICUT	21
EAST ORANGE	NEW JERSEY	310
EAST ST. LOUIS	ILLINOIS	369
EL CAJON	CALIFORNIA	121
EL MONTE	CALIFORNIA	161
EL PASO	TEXAS	205
ELGIN	ILLINOIS	104
ELIZABETH	NEW JERSEY	291
ELMHURST	ILLINOIS	45
ELYRIA	OHIO	91
ERIE	PENNSYLVANIA	88
EUCLID	OHIO	6
EUGENE	OREGON	321
EVANSTON	ILLINOIS	95
EVANSVILLE	INDIANA	256
EVERETT	WASHINGTON	273
FAIRFIELD	CONNECTICUT	151
FALL RIVER	MASSACHUSETTS	340
FARGO	NORTH DAKOTA	50
FAYETTEVILLE	NORTH CAROLINA	275
FLINT	MICHIGAN	337
FLORISSANT	MISSOURI	9
FORT LAUDERDALE	FLORIDA	353
FORT SMITH	ARKANSAS	41
FORT WAYNE	INDIANA	255
FORT WORTH	TEXAS	229
FRAMINGHAM	MASSACHUSETTS	123
FREMONT	CALIFORNIA	178
FRESNO	CALIFORNIA	356
FULLERTON	CALIFORNIA	211
GADSDEN	ALABAMA	94
GAINESVILLE	FLORIDA	339
GALVESTON	TEXAS	368
GARDEN GROVE	CALIFORNIA	274
GARLAND	TEXAS	92
GARY	INDIANA	373
GLENDALE	CALIFORNIA	168
GRAND PRAIRIE	TEXAS	155
GRAND RAPIDS	MICHIGAN	213
GREAT FALLS	MONTANA	115
GREEN BAY	WISCONSIN	13
GREENSBORO	NORTH CAROLINA	222
GREENVILLE	SOUTH CAROLINA	364
GREENWICH	CONNECTICUT	8
HAMILTON	OHIO	183
HAMMOND	INDIANA	280
HAMPTON	VIRGINIA	83
HARRISBURG	PENNSYLVANIA	267
HARTFORD	CONNECTICUT	336

CRIME RANK

CITY	STATE	RANK
HAWTHORNE	CALIFORNIA	276
HAYWARD	CALIFORNIA	331
HIALEAH	FLORIDA	281
HIGH POINT	NORTH CAROLINA	143
HOLLYWOOD	FLORIDA	314
HOLYOKE	MASSACHUSETTS	296
HONOLULU	HAWAII	311
HOUSTON	TEXAS	305
HUNTINGTON	WEST VIRGINIA	216
HUNTINGTON BEACH	CALIFORNIA	238
HUNTSVILLE	ALABAMA	235
INDEPENDENCE	MISSOURI	47
INDIANAPOLIS	INDIANA	174
INGLEWOOD	CALIFORNIA	357
IRVING	TEXAS	99
IRVINGTON	NEW JERSEY	154
JACKSON	MISSISSIPPI	113
JACKSONVILLE	FLORIDA	295
JERSEY CITY	NEW JERSEY	219
JOLIET	ILLINOIS	177
KALAMAZOO	MICHIGAN	324
KANSAS CITY	MISSOURI	338
KANSAS CITY	KANSAS	289
KENOSHA	WISCONSIN	103
KETTERING	OHIO	19
KNOXVILLE	TENNESSEE	164
LA CROSSE	WISCONSIN	30
LAFAYETTE	LOUISIANA	195
LAKE CHARLES	LOUISIANA	63
LAKEWOOD	CALIFORNIA	48
LAKEWOOD	COLORADO	82
LAKEWOOD	OHIO	1
LANCASTER	PENNSYLVANIA	79
LANSING	MICHIGAN	358
LAREDO	TEXAS	55
LAS VEGAS	NEVADA	215
LAWRENCE	MASSACHUSETTS	212
LAWTON	OKLAHOMA	279
LEXINGTON	KENTUCKY	307
LIMA	OHIO	206
LINCOLN	NEBRASKA	57
LINCOLN PARK	MICHIGAN	232
LITTLE ROCK	ARKANSAS	330
LIVONIA	MICHIGAN	129
LONG BEACH	CALIFORNIA	292
LORAIN	OHIO	184
LOS ANGELES	CALIFORNIA	365
LOUISVILLE	KENTUCKY	319
LOWELL	MASSACHUSETTS	153
LUBBOCK	TEXAS	244

CRIME RANK

CITY	STATE	RANK
LYNCHBURG	VIRGINIA	37
LYNN	MASSACHUSETTS	304
MACON	GEORGIA	306
MADISON	WISCONSIN	138
MALDEN	MASSACHUSETTS	51
MANCHESTER	NEW HAMPSHIRE	23
MANSFIELD	OHIO	181
MEDFORD	MASSACHUSETTS	32
MEMPHIS	TENNESSEE	221
MERIDEN	CONNECTICUT	105
MESA	ARIZONA	158
MESQUITE	TEXAS	71
MIAMI	FLORIDA	383
MIAMI BEACH	FLORIDA	194
MIDLAND	TEXAS	24
MILFORD	CONNECTICUT	228
MILWAUKEE	WISCONSIN	134
MINNEAPOLIS	MINNESOTA	332
MOBILE	ALABAMA	302
MODESTO	CALIFORNIA	347
MONROE	LOUISIANA	53
MONTGOMERY	ALABAMA	175
MOUNT VERNON	NEW YORK	141
MOUNTAIN VIEW	CALIFORNIA	149
MUNCIE	INDIANA	209
NASHUA	NEW HAMPSHIRE	5
NASHVILLE	TENNESSEE	271
NEW BEDFORD	MASSACHUSETTS	316
NEW BRITAIN	CONNECTICUT	201
NEW HAVEN	CONNECTICUT	348
NEW ORLEANS	LOUISIANA	349
NEW ROCHELLE	NEW YORK	114
NEW YORK CITY	NEW YORK	375
NEWARK	NEW JERSEY	392
NEWPORT NEWS	VIRGINIA	131
NEWTON	MASSACHUSETTS	166
NIAGARA FALLS	NEW YORK	266
NORFOLK	VIRGINIA	283
NORMAN	OKLAHOMA	107
NORTH LITTLE ROCK	ARKANSAS	160
NORWALK	CONNECTICUT	185
NORWALK	CALIFORNIA	62
OAK LAWN	ILLINOIS	18
OAK PARK	ILLINOIS	43
OAKLAND	CALIFORNIA	387
ODESSA	TEXAS	33
OGDEN	UTAH	169
OKLAHOMA CITY	OKLAHOMA	187
OMAHA	NEBRASKA	193
ONTARIO	CALIFORNIA	282

CRIME RANK

CITY	STATE	RANK
ORANGE	CALIFORNIA	218
ORLANDO	FLORIDA	346
OSHKOSH	WISCONSIN	38
OVERLAND PARK	KANSAS	67
OWENSBORO	KENTUCKY	70
OXNARD	CALIFORNIA	318
PALO ALTO	CALIFORNIA	272
PARMA	OHIO	34
PASADENA	CALIFORNIA	376
PASADENA	TEXAS	56
PASSAIC	NEW JERSEY	290
PATERSON	NEW JERSEY	328
PAWTUCKET	RHODE ISLAND	69
PENSACOLA	FLORIDA	240
PEORIA	ILLINOIS	288
PHILADELPHIA	PENNSYLVANIA	122
PHOENIX	ARIZONA	323
PICO RIVERA	CALIFORNIA	65
PINE BLUFF	ARKANSAS	171
PITTSBURGH	PENNSYLVANIA	326
PITTSFIELD	MASSACHUSETTS	40
POMONA	CALIFORNIA	286
PONTIAC	MICHIGAN	390
PORT ARTHUR	TEXAS	217
PORTLAND	MAINE	87
PORTLAND	OREGON	371
PORTSMOUTH	VIRGINIA	260
PROVIDENCE	RHODE ISLAND	367
PROVO	UTAH	7
PUEBLO	COLORADO	140
QUINCY	MASSACHUSETTS	242
RACINE	WISCONSIN	202
RALEIGH	NORTH CAROLINA	234
READING	PENNSYLVANIA	46
REDONDO BEACH	CALIFORNIA	345
REDWOOD CITY	CALIFORNIA	224
RENO	NEVADA	284
RICHMOND	CALIFORNIA	380
RICHMOND	VIRGINIA	352
RIVERSIDE	CALIFORNIA	350
ROANOKE	VIRGINIA	253
ROCHESTER	NEW YORK	252
ROCHESTER	MINNESOTA	29
ROCK ISLAND	ILLINOIS	207
ROCKFORD	ILLINOIS	109
ROME	NEW YORK	2
ROSEVILLE	MICHIGAN	144
ROYAL OAK	MICHIGAN	163
SACRAMENTO	CALIFORNIA	309
SAGINAW	MICHIGAN	329

CRIME RANK

CITY	STATE	RANK
SALEM	OREGON	133
SALINAS	CALIFORNIA	259
SALT LAKE CITY	UTAH	354
SAN ANGELO	TEXAS	81
SAN ANTONIO	TEXAS	258
SAN BERNARINO	CALIFORNIA	372
SAN DIEGO	CALIFORNIA	208
SAN FRANCISCO	CALIFORNIA	389
SAN JOSE	CALIFORNIA	220
SAN LEANDRO	CALIFORNIA	249
SAN MATEO	CALIFORNIA	239
SANTA ANA	CALIFORNIA	247
SANTA BARBARA	CALIFORNIA	196
SANTA CLARA	CALIFORNIA	145
SANTA MONICA	CALIFORNIA	366
SANTA ROSA	CALIFORNIA	312
SAVANNAH	GEORGIA	327
SCHENECTADY	NEW YORK	44
SCOTTSDALE	ARIZONA	200
SCRANTON	PENNSYLVANIA	60
SEATTLE	WASHINGTON	333
SHREVEPORT	LOUISIANA	125
SIOUX CITY	IOWA	100
SIOUX FALLS	SOUTH DAKOTA	28
SKOKIE	ILLINOIS	110
SOMERVILLE	MASSACHUSETTS	148
SOUTH BEND	INDIANA	257
SOUTH GATE	CALIFORNIA	287
SOUTHFIELD	MICHIGAN	262
SPOKANE	WASHINGTON	197
SPRINGFIELD	OHIO	68
SPRINGFIELD	MISSOURI	162
SPRINGFIELD	ILLINOIS	111
SPRINGFIELD	MASSACHUSETTS	335
ST. CLAIR SHORES	MICHIGAN	120
ST. JOSEPH	MISSOURI	128
ST. LOUIS	MISSOURI	381
ST. PAUL	MINNESOTA	303
ST. PETERSBURG	FLORIDA	233
STAMFORD	CONNECTICUT	199
STERLING HEIGHTS	MICHIGAN	146
STOCKTON	CALIFORNIA	363
SUNNYVALE	CALIFORNIA	52
SYRACUSE	NEW YORK	198
TACOMA	WASHINGTON	241
TALLAHASSEE	FLORIDA	180
TAMPA	FLORIDA	313
TAYLOR	MICHIGAN	54
TEMPE	ARIZONA	269
TERRE HAUTE	INDIANA	156

CRIME RANK

CITY	STATE	RANK
TOLEDO	OHIO	210
TOPEKA	KANSAS	223
TORRANCE	CALIFORNIA	268
TRENTON	NEW JERSEY	382
TROY	NEW YORK	77
TUCSON	ARIZONA	173
TULSA	OKLAHOMA	230
TUSCALOOSA	ALABAMA	147
TYLER	TEXAS	137
UNION CITY	NEW JERSEY	130
UTICA	NEW YORK	4
VALLEJO	CALIFORNIA	320
VENTURA(SAN BUENAVENTURA)	CALIFORNIA	285
VIRGINIA BEACH	VIRGINIA	102
WACO	TEXAS	261
WALTHAM	MASSACHUSETTS	74
WARREN	OHIO	167
WARREN	MICHIGAN	157
WARWICK	RHODE ISLAND	192
WASHINGTON	D.C.	384
WATERBURY	CONNECTICUT	190
WATERLOO	IOWA	89
WAUKEGAN	ILLINOIS	246
WAUWATOSA	WISCONSIN	49
WEST ALLIS	WISCONSIN	25
WEST COVINA	CALIFORNIA	237
WEST HARTFORD	CONNECTICUT	12
WEST HAVEN	CONNECTICUT	64
WEST PALM BEACH	FLORIDA	322
WESTLAND	MICHIGAN	10
WESTMINSTER	CALIFORNIA	236
WEYMOUTH	MASSACHUSETTS	3
WHITE PLAINS	NEW YORK	203
WHITTIER	CALIFORNIA	176
WICHITA	KANSAS	248
WICHITA FALLS	TEXAS	36
WILKES-BARRE	PENNSYLVANIA	26
WILMINGTON	DELAWARE	388
WINSTON-SALEM	NORTH CAROLINA	254
WORCESTER	MASSACHUSETTS	378
WYOMING	MICHIGAN	73
YONKERS	NEW YORK	191
YORK	PENNSYLVANIA	159
YOUNGSTOWN	OHIO	245

Table 4
City Crime-Rankings
(The Cities Listed in Descending Order of Safety)

CRIME RANK

CITY	STATE	RANK
LAKEWOOD	OHIO	1
ROME	NEW YORK	2
WEYMOUTH	MASSACHUSETTS	3
UTICA	NEW YORK	4
NASHUA	NEW HAMPSHIRE	5
EUCLID	OHIO	6
PROVO	UTAH	7
GREENWICH	CONNECTICUT	8
FLORISSANT	MISSOURI	9
WESTLAND	MICHIGAN	10
ARLINGTON	MASSACHUSETTS	11
WEST HARTFORD	CONNECTICUT	12
GREEN BAY	WISCONSIN	13
BRISTOL	CONNECTICUT	14
ARLINGTON HEIGHTS	ILLINOIS	15
APPLETON	WISCONSIN	16
ALBANY	GEORGIA	17
OAK LAWN	ILLINOIS	18
KETTERING	OHIO	19
CLIFTON	NEW JERSEY	20
EAST HARTFORD	CONNECTICUT	21
BAYONNE	NEW JERSEY	22
MANCHESTER	NEW HAMPSHIRE	23
MIDLAND	TEXAS	24
WEST ALLIS	WISCONSIN	25
WILKES-BARRE	PENNSYLVANIA	26
ALTOONA	PENNSYLVANIA	27
SIOUX FALLS	SOUTH DAKOTA	28
ROCHESTER	MINNESOTA	29
LA CROSSE	WISCONSIN	30
CEDAR RAPIDS	IOWA	31
MEDFORD	MASSACHUSETTS	32
ODESSA	TEXAS	33
PARMA	OHIO	34
CICERO	ILLINOIS	35
WICHITA FALLS	TEXAS	36
LYNCHBURG	VIRGINIA	37
OSHKOSH	WISCONSIN	38
BERWYN	ILLINOIS	39
PITTSFIELD	MASSACHUSETTS	40
FORT SMITH	ARKANSAS	41
ANDERSON	INDIANA	42
OAK PARK	ILLINOIS	43
SCHENECTADY	NEW YORK	44
ELMHURST	ILLINOIS	45
READING	PENNSYLVANIA	46
INDEPENDENCE	MISSOURI	47
LAKEWOOD	CALIFORNIA	48
WAUWATOSA	WISCONSIN	49

CRIME RANK

CITY	STATE	RANK
FARGO	NORTH DAKOTA	50
MALDEN	MASSACHUSETTS	51
SUNNYVALE	CALIFORNIA	52
MONROE	LOUISIANA	53
TAYLOR	MICHIGAN	54
LAREDO	TEXAS	55
PASADENA	TEXAS	56
LINCOLN	NEBRASKA	57
BLOOMFIELD	NEW JERSEY	58
CHICOPEE	MASSACHUSETTS	59
SCRANTON	PENNSYLVANIA	60
ABILENE	TEXAS	61
NORWALK	CALIFORNIA	62
LAKE CHARLES	LOUISIANA	63
WEST HAVEN	CONNECTICUT	64
PICO RIVERA	CALIFORNIA	65
BETHLEHEM	PENNSYLVANIA	66
OVERLAND PARK	KANSAS	67
SPRINGFIELD	OHIO	68
PAWTUCKET	RHODE ISLAND	69
OWENSBORO	KENTUCKY	70
MESQUITE	TEXAS	71
BINGHAMTON	NEW YORK	72
WYOMING	MICHIGAN	73
WALTHAM	MASSACHUSETTS	74
DANBURY	CONNECTICUT	75
COLUMBIA	MISSOURI	76
TROY	NEW YORK	77
AUGUSTA	GEORGIA	78
LANCASTER	PENNSYLVANIA	79
DES PLAINES	ILLINOIS	80
SAN ANGELO	TEXAS	81
LAKEWOOD	COLORADO	82
HAMPTON	VIRGINIA	83
COLUMBUS	GEORGIA	84
DUBUQUE	IOWA	85
CRANSTON	RHODE ISLAND	86
PORTLAND	MAINE	87
ERIE	PENNSYLVANIA	88
WATERLOO	IOWA	89
BLOOMINGTON	MINNESOTA	90
ELYRIA	OHIO	91
GARLAND	TEXAS	92
CLEVELAND HEIGHTS	OHIO	93
GADSDEN	ALABAMA	94
EVANSTON	ILLINOIS	95
BOULDER	COLORADO	96
DULUTH	MINNESOTA	97
CHESAPEAKE	VIRGINIA	98
IRVING	TEXAS	99

CRIME RANK

CITY	STATE	RANK
SIOUX CITY	IOWA	100
BELLFLOWER	CALIFORNIA	101
VIRGINIA BEACH	VIRGINIA	102
KENOSHA	WISCONSIN	103
ELGIN	ILLINOIS	104
MERIDEN	CONNECTICUT	105
DECATUR	ILLINOIS	106
NORMAN	OKLAHOMA	107
AURORA	ILLINOIS	108
ROCKFORD	ILLINOIS	109
SKOKIE	ILLINOIS	110
SPRINGFIELD	ILLINOIS	111
ALLENTOWN	PENNSYLVANIA	112
JACKSON	MISSISSIPPI	113
NEW ROCHELLE	NEW YORK	114
GREAT FALLS	MONTANA	115
CARSON	CALIFORNIA	116
BURBANK	CALIFORNIA	117
ALAMEDA	CALIFORNIA	118
DEARBORN HEIGHTS	MICHIGAN	119
ST. CLAIR SHORES	MICHIGAN	120
EL CAJON	CALIFORNIA	121
PHILADELPHIA	PENNSYLVANIA	122
FRAMINGHAM	MASSACHUSETTS	123
BOISE	IDAHO	124
SHREVEPORT	LOUISIANA	125
BROWNSVILLE	TEXAS	126
BROCKTON	MASSACHUSETTS	127
ST. JOSEPH	MISSOURI	128
LIVONIA	MICHIGAN	129
UNION CITY	NEW JERSEY	130
NEWPORT NEWS	VIRGINIA	131
DAVENPORT	IOWA	132
SALEM	OREGON	133
MILWAUKEE	WISCONSIN	134
BUENA PARK	CALIFORNIA	135
CHULA VISTA	CALIFORNIA	136
TYLER	TEXAS	137
MADISON	WISCONSIN	138
AUSTIN	TEXAS	139
PUEBLO	COLORADO	140
MOUNT VERNON	NEW YORK	141
ARLINGTON	VIRGINIA	142
HIGH POINT	NORTH CAROLINA	143
ROSEVILLE	MICHIGAN	144
SANTA CLARA	CALIFORNIA	145
STERLING HEIGHTS	MICHIGAN	146
TUSCALOOSA	ALABAMA	147
SOMERVILLE	MASSACHUSETTS	148
MOUNTAIN VIEW	CALIFORNIA	149

CRIME RANK

CITY	STATE	RANK
ALBANY	NEW YORK	150
FAIRFIELD	CONNECTICUT	151
BELLEVUE	WASHINGTON	152
LOWELL	MASSACHUSETTS	153
IRVINGTON	NEW JERSEY	154
GRAND PRAIRIE	TEXAS	155
TERRE HAUTE	INDIANA	156
WARREN	MICHIGAN	157
MESA	ARIZONA	158
YORK	PENNSYLVANIA	159
NORTH LITTLE ROCK	ARKANSAS	160
EL MONTE	CALIFORNIA	161
SPRINGFIELD	MISSOURI	162
ROYAL OAK	MICHIGAN	163
KNOXVILLE	TENNESSEE	164
AMARILLO	TEXAS	165
NEWTON	MASSACHUSETTS	166
WARREN	OHIO	167
GLENDALE	CALIFORNIA	168
OGDEN	UTAH	169
DALY CITY	CALIFORNIA	170
PINE BLUFF	ARKANSAS	171
BEAUMONT	TEXAS	172
TUCSON	ARIZONA	173
INDIANAPOLIS	INDIANA	174
MONTGOMERY	ALABAMA	175
WHITTIER	CALIFORNIA	176
JOLIET	ILLINOIS	177
FREMONT	CALIFORNIA	178
ASHEVILLE	NORTH CAROLINA	179
TALLAHASSEE	FLORIDA	180
MANSFIELD	OHIO	181
DEARBORN	MICHIGAN	182
HAMILTON	OHIO	183
LORAIN	OHIO	184
NORWALK	CONNECTICUT	185
DES MOINES	IOWA	186
OKLAHOMA CITY	OKLAHOMA	187
CANTON	OHIO	188
BILLINGS	MONTANA	189
WATERBURY	CONNECTICUT	190
YONKERS	NEW YORK	191
WARWICK	RHODE ISLAND	192
OMAHA	NEBRASKA	193
MIAMI BEACH	FLORIDA	194
LAFAYETTE	LOUISIANA	195
SANTA BARBARA	CALIFORNIA	196
SPOKANE	WASHINGTON	197
SYRACUSE	NEW YORK	198
STAMFORD	CONNECTICUT	199

CRIME RANK

CITY	STATE	RANK
SCOTTSDALE	ARIZONA	200
NEW BRITAIN	CONNECTICUT	201
RACINE	WISCONSIN	202
WHITE PLAINS	NEW YORK	203
DURHAM	NORTH CAROLINA	204
EL PASO	TEXAS	205
LIMA	OHIO	206
ROCK ISLAND	ILLINOIS	207
SAN DIEGO	CALIFORNIA	208
MUNCIE	INDIANA	209
TOLEDO	OHIO	210
FULLERTON	CALIFORNIA	211
LAWRENCE	MASSACHUSETTS	212
GRAND RAPIDS	MICHIGAN	213
ARLINGTON	TEXAS	214
LAS VEGAS	NEVADA	215
HUNTINGTON	WEST VIRGINIA	216
PORT ARTHUR	TEXAS	217
ORANGE	CALIFORNIA	218
JERSEY CITY	NEW JERSEY	219
SAN JOSE	CALIFORNIA	220
MEMPHIS	TENNESSEE	221
GREENSBORO	NORTH CAROLINA	222
TOPEKA	KANSAS	223
REDWOOD CITY	CALIFORNIA	224
ALHAMBRA	CALIFORNIA	225
CHAMPAIGN	ILLINOIS	226
AURORA	COLORADO	227
MILFORD	CONNECTICUT	228
FORT WORTH	TEXAS	229
TULSA	OKLAHOMA	230
CHICAGO	ILLINOIS	231
LINCOLN PARK	MICHIGAN	232
ST. PETERSBURG	FLORIDA	233
RALEIGH	NORTH CAROLINA	234
HUNTSVILLE	ALABAMA	235
WESTMINSTER	CALIFORNIA	236
WEST COVINA	CALIFORNIA	237
HUNTINGTON BEACH	CALIFORNIA	238
SAN MATEO	CALIFORNIA	239
PENSACOLA	FLORIDA	240
TACOMA	WASHINGTON	241
QUINCY	MASSACHUSETTS	242
DOWNEY	CALIFORNIA	243
LUBBOCK	TEXAS	244
YOUNGSTOWN	OHIO	245
WAUKEGAN	ILLINOIS	246
SANTA ANA	CALIFORNIA	247
WICHITA	KANSAS	248
SAN LEANDRO	CALIFORNIA	249

CRIME RANK

CITY	STATE	RANK
CLEARWATER	FLORIDA	250
COUNCIL BLUFFS	IOWA	251
ROCHESTER	NEW YORK	252
ROANOKE	VIRGINIA	253
WINSTON-SALEM	NORTH CAROLINA	254
FORT WAYNE	INDIANA	255
EVANSVILLE	INDIANA	256
SOUTH BEND	INDIANA	257
SAN ANTONIO	TEXAS	258
SALINAS	CALIFORNIA	259
PORTSMOUTH	VIRGINIA	260
WACO	TEXAS	261
SOUTHFIELD	MICHIGAN	262
BUFFALO	NEW YORK	263
COLORADO SPRINGS	COLORADO	264
CHARLESTON	WEST VIRGINIA	265
NIAGARA FALLS	NEW YORK	266
HARRISBURG	PENNSYLVANIA	267
TORRANCE	CALIFORNIA	268
TEMPE	ARIZONA	269
CHATTANOOGA	TENNESSEE	270
NASHVILLE	TENNESSEE	271
PALO ALTO	CALIFORNIA	272
EVERETT	WASHINGTON	273
GARDEN GROVE	CALIFORNIA	274
FAYETTEVILLE	NORTH CAROLINA	275
HAWTHORNE	CALIFORNIA	276
CINCINNATI	OHIO	277
CONCORD	CALIFORNIA	278
LAWTON	OKLAHOMA	279
HAMMOND	INDIANA	280
HIALEAH	FLORIDA	281
ONTARIO	CALIFORNIA	282
NORFOLK	VIRGINIA	283
RENO	NEVADA	284
VENTURA(SAN BUENAVENTURA)	CALIFORNIA	285
POMONA	CALIFORNIA	286
SOUTH GATE	CALIFORNIA	287
PEORIA	ILLINOIS	288
KANSAS CITY	KANSAS	289
PASSAIC	NEW JERSEY	290
ELIZABETH	NEW JERSEY	291
LONG BEACH	CALIFORNIA	292
BIRMINGHAM	ALABAMA	293
COSTA MESA	CALIFORNIA	294
JACKSONVILLE	FLORIDA	295
HOLYOKE	MASSACHUSETTS	296
COLUMBIA	SOUTH CAROLINA	297
AKRON	OHIO	298
ANAHEIM	CALIFORNIA	299

CRIME RANK

CITY	STATE	RANK
COVINGTON	KENTUCKY	300
CORPUS CHRISTI	TEXAS	301
MOBILE	ALABAMA	302
ST. PAUL	MINNESOTA	303
LYNN	MASSACHUSETTS	304
HOUSTON	TEXAS	305
MACON	GEORGIA	306
LEXINGTON	KENTUCKY	307
COLUMBUS	OHIO	308
SACRAMENTO	CALIFORNIA	309
EAST ORANGE	NEW JERSEY	310
HONOLULU	HAWAII	311
SANTA ROSA	CALIFORNIA	312
TAMPA	FLORIDA	313
HOLLYWOOD	FLORIDA	314
CHARLOTTE	NORTH CAROLINA	315
NEW BEDFORD	MASSACHUSETTS	316
ALEXANDRIA	VIRGINIA	317
OXNARD	CALIFORNIA	318
LOUISVILLE	KENTUCKY	319
VALLEJO	CALIFORNIA	320
EUGENE	OREGON	321
WEST PALM BEACH	FLORIDA	322
PHOENIX	ARIZONA	323
KALAMAZOO	MICHIGAN	324
BATON ROUGE	LOUISIANA	325
PITTSBURGH	PENNSYLVANIA	326
SAVANNAH	GEORGIA	327
PATERSON	NEW JERSEY	328
SAGINAW	MICHIGAN	329
LITTLE ROCK	ARKANSAS	330
HAYWARD	CALIFORNIA	331
MINNEAPOLIS	MINNESOTA	332
SEATTLE	WASHINGTON	333
CHARLESTON	SOUTH CAROLINA	334
SPRINGFIELD	MASSACHUSETTS	335
HARTFORD	CONNECTICUT	336
FLINT	MICHIGAN	337
KANSAS CITY	MISSOURI	338
GAINESVILLE	FLORIDA	339
FALL RIVER	MASSACHUSETTS	340
BAKERSFIELD	CALIFORNIA	341
DALLAS	TEXAS	342
ATLANTA	GEORGIA	343
BERKELEY	CALIFORNIA	344
REDONDO BEACH	CALIFORNIA	345
ORLANDO	FLORIDA	346
MODESTO	CALIFORNIA	347
NEW HAVEN	CONNECTICUT	348
NEW ORLEANS	LOUISIANA	349

CRIME RANK

CITY	STATE	RANK
RIVERSIDE	CALIFORNIA	350
CLEVELAND	OHIO	351
RICHMOND	VIRGINIA	352
FORT LAUDERDALE	FLORIDA	353
SALT LAKE CITY	UTAH	354
ALBUQUERQUE	NEW MEXICO	355
FRESNO	CALIFORNIA	356
INGLEWOOD	CALIFORNIA	357
LANSING	MICHIGAN	358
DAYTON	OHIO	359
ANN ARBOR	MICHIGAN	360
BALTIMORE	MARYLAND	361
BOSTON	MASSACHUSETTS	362
STOCKTON	CALIFORNIA	363
GREENVILLE	SOUTH CAROLINA	364
LOS ANGELES	CALIFORNIA	365
SANTA MONICA	CALIFORNIA	366
PROVIDENCE	RHODE ISLAND	367
GALVESTON	TEXAS	368
EAST ST. LOUIS	ILLINOIS	369
BROOKLINE	MASSACHUSETTS	370
PORTLAND	OREGON	371
SAN BERNARINO	CALIFORNIA	372
GARY	INDIANA	373
CHESTER	PENNSYLVANIA	374
NEW YORK CITY	NEW YORK	375
PASADENA	CALIFORNIA	376
BRIDGEPORT	CONNECTICUT	377
WORCESTER	MASSACHUSETTS	378
CAMDEN	NEW JERSEY	379
RICHMOND	CALIFORNIA	380
ST. LOUIS	MISSOURI	381
TRENTON	NEW JERSEY	382
MIAMI	FLORIDA	383
WASHINGTON	D.C.	384
DENVER	COLORADO	385
CAMBRIDGE	MASSACHUSETTS	386
OAKLAND	CALIFORNIA	387
WILMINGTON	DELAWARE	388
SAN FRANCISCO	CALIFORNIA	389
PONTIAC	MICHIGAN	390
DETROIT	MICHIGAN	391
NEWARK	NEW JERSEY	392
COMPTON	CALIFORNIA	393

Table 5
City Crime Tables
(The Cities Listed Alphabetically)

ABILENE,TEXAS

POPULATION   89,653

	MURDER	FORCED RAPE	ROB-BERY	AGGRYTD ASSAULT	BUR-GLARY	LARCENY +$50	AUTO THEFT
70 CRIMES	10	11	35	30	768	749	145
RATE PER 100,000	11.2	12.3	39.0	33.5	856.6	835.4	161.7
71 CRIMES	7	10	31	47	801	702	115
RATE PER 100,000	7.8	11.2	34.6	52.4	893.4	783.0	128.3

RATIO FOR 2 YEAR PERIOD   1 CRIME PER   51.8 PEOPLE

RANKING   61

AKRON,OHIO

POPULATION   275,425

	MURDER	FORCED RAPE	ROB-BERY	AGGRYTD ASSAULT	BUR-GLARY	LARCENY +$50	AUTO THEFT
70 CRIMES	25	106	716	463	4,080	4,773	3,089
RATE PER 100,000	9.1	38.5	260.0	168.1	1481.3	1733.0	1121.5
71 CRIMES	38	100	772	362	4,386	4,102	2,910
RATE PER 100,000	13.8	36.3	280.3	131.4	1592.4	1489.3	1056.5

RATIO FOR 2 YEAR PERIOD   1 CRIME PER   21.2 PEOPLE

RANKING   298

ALAMEDA,CALIFORNIA

POPULATION   70,968

	MURDER	FORCED RAPE	ROB-BERY	AGGRYTD ASSAULT	BUR-GLARY	LARCENY +$50	AUTO THEFT
70 CRIMES	3	11	58	38	620	258	283
RATE PER 100,000	4.2	15.5	81.7	53.5	873.6	363.5	398.8
71 CRIMES	3	7	64	41	715	1,450	310
RATE PER 100,000	4.2	9.9	90.2	57.8	1007.5	2043.2	436.8

RATIO FOR 2 YEAR PERIOD   1 CRIME PER   36.7 PEOPLE

RANKING   118

ALBANY,GEORGIA

POPULATION   72,623

	MURDER	FORCED RAPE	ROB- BERY	AGGRYTD ASSAULT	BUR- GLARY	LARCENY +$50	AUTO THEFT
70 CRIMES	6	21	56	76	514	93	135
RATE PER 100,000	8.3	28.9	77.1	104.7	707.8	128.1	185.9
71 CRIMES	15	15	80	77	649	119	159
RATE PER 100,000	20.7	20.7	110.2	106.0	893.7	163.9	218.9

RATIO FOR 2 YEAR PERIOD   1 CRIME PER   72.0 PEOPLE

RANKING   17

ALBANY,NEW YORK

POPULATION   114,873

	MURDER	FORCED RAPE	ROB- BERY	AGGRYTD ASSAULT	BUR- GLARY	LARCENY +$50	AUTO THEFT
70 CRIMES	6	10	191	88	1,529	530	1,004
RATE PER 100,000	5.2	8.7	166.3	76.6	1331.0	461.4	874.0
71 CRIMES	6	17	282	111	2,012	390	860
RATE PER 100,000	5.2	14.8	245.5	96.6	1751.5	339.5	748.7

RATIO FOR 2 YEAR PERIOD   1 CRIME PER   32.6 PEOPLE

RANKING   150

ALBUQUERQUE,NEW MEXICO

POPULATION   243,751

	MURDER	FORCED RAPE	ROB- BERY	AGGRYTD ASSAULT	BUR- GLARY	LARCENY +$50	AUTO THEFT
70 CRIMES	19	95	433	893	5,235	4,856	1,832
RATE PER 100,000	7.8	39.0	177.6	366.4	2147.7	1992.2	751.6
71 CRIMES	31	103	667	988	6,232	6,531	1,988
RATE PER 100,000	12.7	42.3	273.6	405.3	2556.7	2679.4	815.6

RATIO FOR 2 YEAR PERIOD   1 CRIME PER   16.3 PEOPLE

RANKING   355

ALEXANDRIA,VIRGINIA

POPULATION   110,938

	MURDER	FORCED RAPE	ROB- BERY	AGGRYTD ASSAULT	BUR- GLARY	LARCENY +$50	AUTO THEFT
70 CRIMES	14	31	518	371	1,663	1,936	823
RATE PER 100,000	12.6	27.9	466.9	334.4	1499.0	1745.1	741.9
71 CRIMES	9	51	490	424	1,864	2,186	875
RATE PER 100,000	8.1	46.0	441.7	382.2	1680.2	1970.5	788.7

RATIO FOR 2 YEAR PERIOD   1 CRIME PER   19.7 PEOPLE

RANKING   317

ALHAMBRA,CALIFORNIA

POPULATION   62,125

	MURDER	FORCED RAPE	ROB- BERY	AGGRYTD ASSAULT	BUR- GLARY	LARCENY +$50	AUTO THEFT
70 CRIMES	2	17	75	73	861	781	319
RATE PER 100,000	3.2	27.4	120.7	117.5	1385.9	1257.1	513.5
71 CRIMES	1	17	105	69	972	935	397
RATE PER 100,000	1.6	27.4	169.0	111.1	1564.6	1505.0	639.0

RATIO FOR 2 YEAR PERIOD   1 CRIME PER   26.8 PEOPLE

RANKING   225

ALLENTOWN,PENNSYLVANIA

POPULATION   109,527

	MURDER	FORCED RAPE	ROB- BERY	AGGRYTD ASSAULT	BUR- GLARY	LARCENY +$50	AUTO THEFT
70 CRIMES	1	12	52	148	841	1,324	289
RATE PER 100,000	0.9	11.0	47.5	135.1	767.8	1208.8	263.9
71 CRIMES	5	22	137	178	1,238	1,252	302
RATE PER 100,000	4.6	20.1	125.1	162.5	1130.3	1143.1	275.7

RATIO FOR 2 YEAR PERIOD   1 CRIME PER   37.7 PEOPLE

RANKING   112

ALTOONA,PENNSYLVANIA

POPULATION   62,900

70 CRIMES	MURDER 4	FORCED RAPE 4	ROB- BERY 13	AGGRYTD ASSAULT 37	BUR- GLARY 431	LARCENY +$50 203	AUTO THEFT 139
RATE PER 100,000	6.4	6.4	20.7	58.8	685.2	322.7	221.0
71 CRIMES	1	8	22	33	702	189	134
RATE PER 100,000	1.6	12.7	35.0	52.5	1116.1	300.5	213.0

RATIO FOR 2 YEAR PERIOD   1 CRIME PER   65.5 PEOPLE

RANKING   27

AMARILLO,TEXAS

POPULATION   127,010

70 CRIMES	MURDER 13	FORCED RAPE 16	ROB- BERY 97	AGGRYTD ASSAULT 156	BUR- GLARY 1,697	LARCENY +$50 1,561	AUTO THEFT 451
RATE PER 100,000	10.2	12.6	76.4	122.8	1336.1	1229.0	355.1
71 CRIMES	9	18	91	174	1,664	1,752	421
RATE PER 100,000	7.1	14.2	71.6	137.0	1310.1	1379.4	331.5

RATIO FOR 2 YEAR PERIOD   1 CRIME PER   31.2 PEOPLE

RANKING   165

ANAHEIM,CALIFORNIA

POPULATION   166,701

70 CRIMES	MURDER 3	FORCED RAPE 37	ROB- BERY 248	AGGRYTD ASSAULT 139	BUR- GLARY 3,390	LARCENY +$50 2,559	AUTO THEFT 849
RATE PER 100,000	1.8	22.2	148.8	83.4	2033.6	1535.1	509.3
71 CRIMES	5	56	223	165	4,118	3,097	855
RATE PER 100,000	3.0	33.6	133.8	99.0	2470.3	1857.8	512.9

RATIO FOR 2 YEAR PERIOD   1 CRIME PER   21.1 PEOPLE

RANKING   299

ANDERSON,INDIANA

POPULATION   70,787

	MURDER	FORCED RAPE	ROB-BERY	AGGRVTD ASSAULT	BUR-GLARY	LARCENY +$50	AUTO THEFT
70 CRIMES	3	15	37	69	496	225	143
RATE PER 100,000	4.2	21.2	52.3	97.5	700.7	317.9	202.0
71 CRIMES	4	24	47	118	463	682	137
RATE PER 100,000	5.7	33.9	66.4	166.7	654.1	963.5	193.5

RATIO FOR 2 YEAR PERIOD   1 CRIME PER   57.4 PEOPLE

RANKING   42

ANN ARBOR,MICHIGAN

POPULATION   99,797

	MURDER	FORCED RAPE	ROB-BERY	AGGRVTD ASSAULT	BUR-GLARY	LARCENY +$50	AUTO THEFT
70 CRIMES	1	20	213	159	2,734	2,248	388
RATE PER 100,000	1.0	20.0	213.4	159.3	2739.6	2252.6	388.8
71 CRIMES	3	26	224	227	3,154	2,677	331
RATE PER 100,000	3.0	26.1	224.5	227.5	3160.4	2682.4	331.7

RATIO FOR 2 YEAR PERIOD   1 CRIME PER   16.0 PEOPLE

RANKING   360

APPLETON,WISCONSIN

POPULATION   57,143

	MURDER	FORCED RAPE	ROB-BERY	AGGRVTD ASSAULT	BUR-GLARY	LARCENY +$50	AUTO THEFT
70 CRIMES			8	6	318	259	67
RATE PER 100,000	0.0	0.0	14.0	10.5	556.5	453.2	117.2
71 CRIMES		2	4	11	476	358	62
RATE PER 100,000	0.0	3.5	7.0	19.2	833.0	626.5	108.5

RATIO FOR 2 YEAR PERIOD   1 CRIME PER   72.7 PEOPLE

RANKING   16

ARLINGTON,MASSACHUSETTS

POPULATION   53,524

	MURDER	FORCED RAPE	ROB-BERY	AGGRYTD ASSAULT	BUR-GLARY	LARCENY +$50	AUTO THEFT
70 CRIMES		3	14	27	276	103	146
RATE PER 100,000	0.0	5.6	26.2	50.4	515.7	192.4	272.8
71 CRIMES	1		22	31	382	145	237
RATE PER 100,000	1.9	0.0	41.1	57.9	713.7	270.9	442.8

RATIO FOR 2 YEAR PERIOD   1 CRIME PER   77.1 PEOPLE

RANKING   11

ARLINGTON,TEXAS

POPULATION   90,643

	MURDER	FORCED RAPE	ROB-BERY	AGGRYTD ASSAULT	BUR-GLARY	LARCENY +$50	AUTO THEFT
70 CRIMES	4	13	35	83	739	1,934	424
RATE PER 100,000	4.4	14.3	38.6	91.6	815.3	2133.6	467.8
71 CRIMES	2	12	38	115	837	1,811	448
RATE PER 100,000	2.2	13.2	41.9	126.9	923.4	1997.9	494.2

RATIO FOR 2 YEAR PERIOD   1 CRIME PER   27.9 PEOPLE

RANKING   214

ARLINGTON,VIRGINIA

POPULATION   174,284

	MURDER	FORCED RAPE	ROB-BERY	AGGRYTD ASSAULT	BUR-GLARY	LARCENY +$50	AUTO THEFT
70 CRIMES	8	33	211	86	1,493	2,473	1,061
RATE PER 100,000	4.6	18.9	121.1	49.3	856.6	1418.9	608.8
71 CRIMES	7	45	245	101	1,468	2,431	830
RATE PER 100,000	4.0	25.8	140.6	58.0	842.3	1394.8	476.2

RATIO FOR 2 YEAR PERIOD   1 CRIME PER   33.2 PEOPLE

RANKING   142

ARLINGTON HEIGHTS, ILLINOIS

POPULATION   64,884

	MURDER	FORCED RAPE	ROB- BERY	AGGRYTD ASSAULT	BUR- GLARY	LARCENY +$50	AUTO THEFT
70 CRIMES			6	17	343	399	68
RATE PER 100,000	0.0	0.0	9.2	26.2	528.6	614.9	104.8
71 CRIMES	2	2	12	28	368	411	99
RATE PER 100,000	3.1	3.1	18.5	43.2	567.2	633.4	152.6

RATIO FOR 2 YEAR PERIOD   1 CRIME   PER   73.9 PEOPLE

RANKING   15

ASHEVILLE, NORTH CAROLINA

POPULATION   57,681

	MURDER	FORCED RAPE	ROB- BERY	AGGRYTD ASSAULT	BUR- GLARY	LARCENY +$50	AUTO THEFT
70 CRIMES	14	4	40	75	587	770	322
RATE PER 100,000	24.3	6.9	69.3	130.0	1017.7	1334.9	558.2
71 CRIMES	9	13	46	63	536	986	324
RATE PER 100,000	15.6	22.5	79.7	109.2	929.2	1709.4	561.7

RATIO FOR 2 YEAR PERIOD   1 CRIME   PER   30.4 PEOPLE

RANKING   179

ATLANTA, GEORGIA

POPULATION   496,973

	MURDER	FORCED RAPE	ROB- BERY	AGGRYTD ASSAULT	BUR- GLARY	LARCENY +$50	AUTO THEFT
70 CRIMES	242	202	2,126	1,304	11,529	7,251	4,724
RATE PER 100,000	48.7	40.6	427.8	262.4	2319.8	1459.0	950.6
71 CRIMES	230	268	2,207	1,935	13,726	7,656	4,034
RATE PER 100,000	46.3	53.9	444.1	389.4	2761.9	1540.5	811.7

RATIO FOR 2 YEAR PERIOD   1 CRIME   PER   17.3 PEOPLE

RANKING   343

178

AUGUSTA,GEORGIA

POPULATION   59,864

	MURDER	FORCED RAPE	ROB- BERY	AGGRYTD ASSAULT	BUR- GLARY	LARCENY +$50	AUTO THEFT
70 CRIMES	35	3	95	248	414	121	342
RATE PER 100,000	58.5	5.0	158.7	414.3	691.6	202.1	571.3
71 CRIMES	22	6	110	214	523	128	247
RATE PER 100,000	36.7	10.0	183.7	357.5	873.6	213.8	412.6

RATIO FOR 2 YEAR PERIOD   1 CRIME PER   47.7 PEOPLE

RANKING   78

AURORA,COLORADO

POPULATION   74,974

	MURDER	FORCED RAPE	ROB- BERY	AGGRYTD ASSAULT	BUR- GLARY	LARCENY +$50	AUTO THEFT
70 CRIMES	1	16	54	180	950	1,205	323
RATE PER 100,000	1.3	21.3	72.0	240.1	1267.1	1607.2	430.8
71 CRIMES	1	19	75	126	1,093	1,248	332
RATE PER 100,000	1.3	25.3	100.0	168.1	1457.8	1664.6	442.8

RATIO FOR 2 YEAR PERIOD   1 CRIME PER   26.6 PEOPLE

RANKING   227

AURORA,ILLINOIS

POPULATION   74,182

	MURDER	FORCED RAPE	ROB- BERY	AGGRYTD ASSAULT	BUR- GLARY	LARCENY +$50	AUTO THEFT
70 CRIMES	9	7	74	171	407	796	214
RATE PER 100,000	12.1	9.4	99.8	230.5	548.7	1073.0	288.5
71 CRIMES	5	9	92	215	594	1,018	232
RATE PER 100,000	6.7	12.1	124.0	289.8	800.7	1372.3	312.7

RATIO FOR 2 YEAR PERIOD   1 CRIME PER   38.6 PEOPLE

RANKING   108

AUSTIN, TEXAS

POPULATION   251,808

	MURDER	FORCED RAPE	ROB- BERY	AGGRYTD ASSAULT	BUR- GLARY	LARCENY +$50	AUTO THEFT
70 CRIMES	22	76	215	931	3,515	952	1,083
RATE PER 100,000	8.7	30.2	85.4	369.7	1395.9	378.1	430.1
71 CRIMES	27	66	372	1,119	4,334	1,336	1,053
RATE PER 100,000	10.7	26.2	147.7	444.4	1721.2	530.6	418.2

RATIO FOR 2 YEAR PERIOD   1 CRIME PER   33.3 PEOPLE

RANKING   139

BAKERSFIELD, CALIFORNIA

POPULATION   69,515

	MURDER	FORCED RAPE	ROB- BERY	AGGRYTD ASSAULT	BUR- GLARY	LARCENY +$50	AUTO THEFT
70 CRIMES	11	11	151	98	1,318	1,387	571
RATE PER 100,000	15.8	15.8	217.2	141.0	1896.0	1995.3	821.4
71 CRIMES	10	16	222	140	1,817	1,593	614
RATE PER 100,000	14.4	23.0	319.4	201.4	2613.8	2291.6	883.3

RATIO FOR 2 YEAR PERIOD   1 CRIME PER   17.4 PEOPLE

RANKING   341

BALTIMORE, MARYLAND

POPULATION   935,759

	MURDER	FORCED RAPE	ROB- BERY	AGGRYTD ASSAULT	BUR- GLARY	LARCENY +$50	AUTO THEFT
70 CRIMES	231	555	10,965	7,159	19,041	13,866	10,333
RATE PER 100,000	24.7	59.3	1171.8	765.0	2034.8	1481.8	1104.2
71 CRIMES	323	537	9,480	6,556	18,481	10,134	8,938
RATE PER 100,000	34.5	57.4	1013.1	700.6	1975.0	1083.0	955.2

RATIO FOR 2 YEAR PERIOD   1 CRIME PER   16.0 PEOPLE

RANKING   361

180

BATON ROUGE,LOUISIANA

POPULATION   165,963

	MURDER	FORCED RAPE	ROB- BERY	AGGRYTD ASSAULT	BUR- GLARY	LARCENY +$50	AUTO THEFT
70 CRIMES	15	58	316	664	3,783	2,324	1,217
RATE PER 100,000	9.0	34.9	190.4	400.1	2279.4	1400.3	733.3
71 CRIMES	22	46	301	767	3,769	2,692	1,457
RATE PER 100,000	13.3	27.7	181.4	462.2	2271.0	1622.0	877.9

RATIO FOR 2 YEAR PERIOD   1 CRIME PER   19.0 PEOPLE

RANKING   325

BAYONNE,NEW JERSEY

POPULATION   72,743

	MURDER	FORCED RAPE	ROB- BERY	AGGRYTD ASSAULT	BUR- GLARY	LARCENY +$50	AUTO THEFT
70 CRIMES	2	2	27	13	349	270	312
RATE PER 100,000	2.7	2.7	37.1	17.9	479.8	371.2	428.9
71 CRIMES	3	2	44	19	421	369	338
RATE PER 100,000	4.1	2.7	60.5	26.1	578.7	507.3	464.6

RATIO FOR 2 YEAR PERIOD   1 CRIME PER   67.0 PEOPLE

RANKING   22

BEAUMONT,TEXAS

POPULATION   115,919

	MURDER	FORCED RAPE	ROB- BERY	AGGRYTD ASSAULT	BUR- GLARY	LARCENY +$50	AUTO THEFT
70 CRIMES	18	15	168	537	1,751	644	317
RATE PER 100,000	15.5	12.9	144.9	463.3	1510.5	555.6	273.5
71 CRIMES	20	6	207	617	1,886	1,018	288
RATE PER 100,000	17.3	5.2	178.6	532.3	1627.0	878.2	248.4

RATIO FOR 2 YEAR PERIOD   1 CRIME PER   30.9 PEOPLE

RANKING   172

BELLEVUE,WASHINGTON

POPULATION   61,102

	MURDER	FORCED RAPE	ROB-BERY	AGGRYTD ASSAULT	BUR-GLARY	LARCENY +$50	AUTO THEFT
70 CRIMES	1	12	16	82	804	776	107
RATE PER 100,000	1.6	19.6	26.2	134.2	1315.8	1270.0	175.1
71 CRIMES	2	4	15	136	671	983	141
RATE PER 100,000	3.3	6.5	24.5	222.6	1098.2	1608.8	230.8

RATIO FOR 2 YEAR PERIOD   1 CRIME PER   32.5 PEOPLE

RANKING   152

BELLFLOWER,CALIFORNIA

POPULATION   51,454

	MURDER	FORCED RAPE	ROB-BERY	AGGRYTD ASSAULT	BUR-GLARY	LARCENY +$50	AUTO THEFT
70 CRIMES							
RATE PER 100,000							
71 CRIMES	7	10	108	146	1,009	796	486
RATE PER 100,000	13.6	19.4	209.9	283.7	1961.0	1547.0	944.5

RATIO FOR 2 YEAR PERIOD   1 CRIME PER   40.1 PEOPLE

RANKING   101

BERKELEY,CALIFORNIA

POPULATION   116,716

	MURDER	FORCED RAPE	ROB-BERY	AGGRYTD ASSAULT	BUR-GLARY	LARCENY +$50	AUTO THEFT
70 CRIMES	12	116	369	235	3,846	787	1,077
RATE PER 100,000	10.3	99.4	316.2	201.3	3295.2	674.3	922.8
71 CRIMES	11	78	528	256	4,147	886	1,232
RATE PER 100,000	9.4	66.8	452.4	219.3	3553.1	759.1	1055.6

RATIO FOR 2 YEAR PERIOD   1 CRIME PER   17.1 PEOPLE

RANKING   344

BERWYN,ILLINOIS

POPULATION   52,502

	MURDER	FORCED RAPE	ROB- BERY	AGGRYTD ASSAULT	BUR- GLARY	LARCENY +$50	AUTO THEFT
70 CRIMES	1	2	22	11	276	235	224
RATE PER 100,000	1.9	3.8	41.9	21.0	525.7	447.6	426.7
71 CRIMES		2	26	12	343	359	260
RATE PER 100,000	0.0	3.8	49.5	22.9	653.3	683.8	495.2

RATIO FOR 2 YEAR PERIOD   1 CRIME   PER   59.2 PEOPLE

RANKING   39

BETHLEHEM,PENNSYLVANIA

POPULATION   72,686

	MURDER	FORCED RAPE	ROB- BERY	AGGRYTD ASSAULT	BUR- GLARY	LARCENY +$50	AUTO THEFT
70 CRIMES	4	6	34	68	441	558	167
RATE PER 100,000	5.5	8.3	46.8	93.6	606.7	767.7	229.8
71 CRIMES	2	2	59	99	544	685	209
RATE PER 100,000	2.8	2.8	81.2	136.2	748.4	942.4	287.5

RATIO FOR 2 YEAR PERIOD   1 CRIME   PER   50.5 PEOPLE

RANKING   66

BILLINGS,MONTANA

POPULATION   61,581

	MURDER	FORCED RAPE	ROB- BERY	AGGRYTD ASSAULT	BUR- GLARY	LARCENY +$50	AUTO THEFT
70 CRIMES	3	4	44	30	677	1,034	280
RATE PER 100,000	4.9	6.5	71.5	48.7	1099.4	1679.1	454.7
71 CRIMES	7	5	40	36	621	1,065	259
RATE PER 100,000	11.4	8.1	65.0	58.5	1008.4	1729.4	420.6

RATIO FOR 2 YEAR PERIOD   1 CRIME   PER   30.0 PEOPLE

RANKING   189

BINGHAMTON,NEW YORK

POPULATION   64,123

	MURDER	FORCED RAPE	ROB-BERY	AGGRYTD ASSAULT	BUR-GLARY	LARCENY +$50	AUTO THEFT
70 CRIMES	2	8	30	82	649	450	148
RATE PER 100,000	3.1	12.5	46.8	127.9	1012.1	701.8	230.8
71 CRIMES	2	6	28	39	477	496	179
RATE PER 100,000	3.1	9.4	43.7	60.8	743.9	773.5	279.2

RATIO FOR 2 YEAR PERIOD   1 CRIME PER   49.4 PEOPLE

RANKING   72

BIRMINGHAM,ALABAMA

POPULATION   300,910

	MURDER	FORCED RAPE	ROB-BERY	AGGRYTD ASSAULT	BUR-GLARY	LARCENY +$50	AUTO THEFT
70 CRIMES	63	86	328	1,509	4,365	4,267	2,744
RATE PER 100,000	20.9	28.6	109.0	501.5	1450.6	1418.0	911.9
71 CRIMES	82	98	465	1,470	4,857	4,286	2,894
RATE PER 100,000	27.3	32.6	154.5	488.5	1614.1	1424.3	961.7

RATIO FOR 2 YEAR PERIOD   1 CRIME PER   21.8 PEOPLE

RANKING   293

BLOOMFIELD,NEW JERSEY

POPULATION   52,029

	MURDER	FORCED RAPE	ROB-BERY	AGGRYTD ASSAULT	BUR-GLARY	LARCENY +$50	AUTO THEFT
70 CRIMES	1	2	24	4	411	421	136
RATE PER 100,000	1.9	3.8	46.1	7.7	789.9	809.2	261.4
71 CRIMES	4	1	27	18	465	374	106
RATE PER 100,000	7.7	1.9	51.9	34.6	893.7	718.8	203.7

RATIO FOR 2 YEAR PERIOD   1 CRIME PER   52.1 PEOPLE

RANKING   58

184

BLOOMINGTON, MINNESOTA

POPULATION 81,970

	MURDER	FORCED RAPE	ROB-BERY	AGGRYTD ASSAULT	BUR-GLARY	LARCENY +$50	AUTO THEFT
70 CRIMES		2	15	42	372	1,139	222
RATE PER 100,000	0.0	2.4	18.3	51.2	453.8	1389.5	270.8
71 CRIMES		2	23	42	402	1,248	196
RATE PER 100,000	0.0	2.4	28.1	51.2	490.4	1522.5	239.1

RATIO FOR 2 YEAR PERIOD   1 CRIME PER   44.2 PEOPLE

RANKING   90

BOISE, IDAHO

POPULATION 74,990

	MURDER	FORCED RAPE	ROB-BERY	AGGRYTD ASSAULT	BUR-GLARY	LARCENY +$50	AUTO THEFT
70 CRIMES	6	14	33	105	592	969	239
RATE PER 100,000	8.0	18.7	44.0	140.0	789.4	1292.2	318.7
71 CRIMES	4	17	33	105	724	1,069	255
RATE PER 100,000	5.3	22.7	44.0	140.0	965.5	1425.5	340.0

RATIO FOR 2 YEAR PERIOD   1 CRIME PER   36.0 PEOPLE

RANKING   124

BOSTON, MASSACHUSETTS

POPULATION 641,071

	MURDER	FORCED RAPE	ROB-BERY	AGGRYTD ASSAULT	BUR-GLARY	LARCENY +$50	AUTO THEFT
70 CRIMES	114	303	3,371	1,627	10,002	7,543	15,334
RATE PER 100,000	17.8	47.3	525.8	253.8	1560.2	1176.6	2391.9
71 CRIMES	116	235	4,735	1,907	12,439	7,055	16,027
RATE PER 100,000	18.1	36.7	738.6	297.5	1940.3	1100.5	2500.0

RATIO FOR 2 YEAR PERIOD   1 CRIME PER   15.8 PEOPLE

RANKING   362

BOULDER,COLORADO

POPULATION   66,870

	MURDER	FORCED RAPE	ROB- BERY	AGGRYTD ASSAULT	BUR- GLARY	LARCENY +$50	AUTO THEFT
70 CRIMES	2	10	41	264	565	1,996	331
RATE PER 100,000	3.0	15.0	61.3	394.8	844.9	2984.9	495.0
71 CRIMES							
RATE PER 100,000							

RATIO FOR 2 YEAR PERIOD   1 CRIME PER   41.6 PEOPLE

RANKING   96

BRIDGEPORT,CONNECTICUT

POPULATION   156,542

	MURDER	FORCED RAPE	ROB- BERY	AGGRYTD ASSAULT	BUR- GLARY	LARCENY +$50	AUTO THEFT
70 CRIMES	27	21	502	234	2,993	3,341	2,804
RATE PER 100,000	17.2	13.4	320.7	149.5	1911.9	2134.3	1791.2
71 CRIMES	18	20	572	207	3,494	3,101	3,742
RATE PER 100,000	11.5	12.8	365.4	132.2	2232.0	1980.9	2390.4

RATIO FOR 2 YEAR PERIOD   1 CRIME PER   14.8 PEOPLE

RANKING   377

BRISTOL,CONNECTICUT

POPULATION   55,487

	MURDER	FORCED RAPE	ROB- BERY	AGGRYTD ASSAULT	BUR- GLARY	LARCENY +$50	AUTO THEFT
70 CRIMES	2	17	3	73	314	379	65
RATE PER 100,000	3.6	30.6	5.4	131.6	565.9	683.0	117.1
71 CRIMES		10	4	95	228	284	24
RATE PER 100,000	0.0	18.0	7.2	171.2	410.9	511.8	43.3

RATIO FOR 2 YEAR PERIOD   1 CRIME PER   74.0 PEOPLE

RANKING   14

186

BROCKTON,MASSACHUSETTS

POPULATION 89,040

	MURDER	FORCED RAPE	ROB- BERY	AGGRYTD ASSAULT	BUR- GLARY	LARCENY +$50	AUTO THEFT
70 CRIMES	2	19	41	124	789	640	500
RATE PER 100,000	2.2	21.3	46.0	139.3	886.1	718.8	561.5
71 CRIMES	2	31	66	109	1,203	683	872
RATE PER 100,000	2.2	34.8	74.1	122.4	1351.1	767.1	979.3

RATIO FOR 2 YEAR PERIOD 1 CRIME PER 35.0 PEOPLE

RANKING 127

BROOKLINE,MASSACHUSETTS

POPULATION 58,886

	MURDER	FORCED RAPE	ROB- BERY	AGGRYTD ASSAULT	BUR- GLARY	LARCENY +$50	AUTO THEFT
70 CRIMES	1	21	59	31	1,161	1,334	952
RATE PER 100,000	1.7	35.7	100.2	52.6	1971.6	2265.4	1616.7
71 CRIMES	1	12	62	24	1,412	1,386	1,146
RATE PER 100,000	1.7	20.4	105.3	40.8	2397.9	2353.7	1946.1

RATIO FOR 2 YEAR PERIOD 1 CRIME PER 15.4 PEOPLE

RANKING 370

BROWNSVILLE,TEXAS

POPULATION 52,522

	MURDER	FORCED RAPE	ROB- BERY	AGGRYTD ASSAULT	BUR- GLARY	LARCENY +$50	AUTO THEFT
70 CRIMES	3		2	31	962	459	214
RATE PER 100,000	5.7	0.0	3.8	59.0	1831.6	873.9	407.4
71 CRIMES	3	2	3	26	723	344	198
RATE PER 100,000	5.7	3.8	5.7	49.5	1376.6	655.0	377.0

RATIO FOR 2 YEAR PERIOD 1 CRIME PER 35.3 PEOPLE

RANKING 126

BUENA PARK,CALIFORNIA

POPULATION   63,646

	MURDER	FORCED RAPE	ROB-BERY	AGGRYTD ASSAULT	BUR-GLARY	LARCENY +$50	AUTO THEFT
70 CRIMES	1	1	54	45	812	539	275
RATE PER 100,000	1.6	1.6	84.8	70.7	1275.8	846.9	432.1
71 CRIMES	2	9	64	57	1,113	489	291
RATE PER 100,000	3.1	14.1	100.6	89.6	1748.7	768.3	457.2

RATIO FOR 2 YEAR PERIOD   1 CRIME PER   33.9 PEOPLE

RANKING   135

BUFFALO,NEW YORK

POPULATION   462,768

	MURDER	FORCED RAPE	ROB-BERY	AGGRYTD ASSAULT	BUR-GLARY	LARCENY +$50	AUTO THEFT
70 CRIMES	57	151	1,497	896	5,959	5,405	4,319
RATE PER 100,000	12.3	32.6	323.5	193.6	1287.7	1168.0	933.3
71 CRIMES	76	134	2,207	812	6,287	6,016	4,694
RATE PER 100,000	16.4	29.0	476.9	175.5	1358.6	1300.0	1014.3

RATIO FOR 2 YEAR PERIOD   1 CRIME PER   24.0 PEOPLE

RANKING   263

BURBANK,CALIFORNIA

POPULATION   88,871

	MURDER	FORCED RAPE	ROB-BERY	AGGRYTD ASSAULT	BUR-GLARY	LARCENY +$50	AUTO THEFT
70 CRIMES	3	5	86	100	1,075	654	531
RATE PER 100,000	3.4	5.6	96.8	112.5	1209.6	735.9	597.5
71 CRIMES	1	10	111	80	1,078	541	508
RATE PER 100,000	1.1	11.3	124.9	90.0	1213.0	608.7	571.6

RATIO FOR 2 YEAR PERIOD   1 CRIME PER   37.1 PEOPLE

RANKING   117

CAMBRIDGE,MASSACHUSETTS

POPULATION   100,361

	MURDER	FORCED RAPE	ROB- BERY	AGGRYTD ASSAULT	BUR- GLARY	LARCENY +$50	AUTO THEFT
70 CRIMES	1	41	256	276	2,181	1,448	3,360
RATE PER 100,000	1.0	40.9	255.1	275.0	2173.2	1442.8	3347.9
71 CRIMES	5	42	355	243	1,978	1,315	3,239
RATE PER 100,000	5.0	41.8	353.7	242.1	1970.9	1310.3	3227.3

RATIO FOR 2 YEAR PERIOD   1 CRIME PER   13.6 PEOPLE

RANKING   386

CAMDEN,NEW JERSEY

POPULATION   102,551

	MURDER	FORCED RAPE	ROB- BERY	AGGRYTD ASSAULT	BUR- GLARY	LARCENY +$50	AUTO THEFT
70 CRIMES	27	41	684	266	2,726	1,046	2,214
RATE PER 100,000	26.3	40.0	667.0	259.4	2658.2	1020.0	2158.9
71 CRIMES	15	57	682	413	2,958	986	2,122
RATE PER 100,000	14.6	55.6	665.0	402.7	2884.4	961.5	2069.2

RATIO FOR 2 YEAR PERIOD   1 CRIME PER   14.4 PEOPLE

RANKING   379

CANTON,OHIO

POPULATION   110,053

	MURDER	FORCED RAPE	ROB- BERY	AGGRYTD ASSAULT	BUR- GLARY	LARCENY +$50	AUTO THEFT
70 CRIMES	5	21	287	130	861	1,570	544
RATE PER 100,000	4.5	19.1	260.8	118.1	782.4	1426.6	494.3
71 CRIMES	11	15	327	137	1,265	1,582	565
RATE PER 100,000	10.0	13.6	297.1	124.5	1149.4	1437.5	513.4

RATIO FOR 2 YEAR PERIOD   1 CRIME PER   30.0 PEOPLE

RANKING   188

CARSON,CALIFORNIA

POPULATION   71,150

	MURDER	FORCED RAPE	ROB- BERY	AGGRYTD ASSAULT	BUR- GLARY	LARCENY +$50	AUTO THEFT
70 CRIMES							
RATE PER 100,000							
71 CRIMES	6	34	141	269	1,781	898	697
RATE PER 100,000	8.4	47.8	198.2	378.1	2503.2	1262.1	979.6

RATIO FOR 2 YEAR PERIOD   1 CRIME PER   37.1 PEOPLE

RANKING   116

CEDAR RAPIDS,IOWA

POPULATION   110,642

	MURDER	FORCED RAPE	ROB- BERY	AGGRYTD ASSAULT	BUR- GLARY	LARCENY +$50	AUTO THEFT
70 CRIMES	3	6	18	22	572	606	310
RATE PER 100,000	2.7	5.4	16.3	19.9	517.0	547.7	280.2
71 CRIMES	5	10	34	15	683	842	343
RATE PER 100,000	4.5	9.0	30.7	13.6	617.3	761.0	310.0

RATIO FOR 2 YEAR PERIOD   1 CRIME PER   63.7 PEOPLE

RANKING   31

CHAMPAIGN,ILLINOIS

POPULATION   56,532

	MURDER	FORCED RAPE	ROB- BERY	AGGRYTD ASSAULT	BUR- GLARY	LARCENY +$50	AUTO THEFT
70 CRIMES	2	24	119	253	853	477	170
RATE PER 100,000	3.5	42.5	210.5	447.5	1508.9	843.8	300.7
71 CRIMES	4	19	121	269	1,099	647	159
RATE PER 100,000	7.1	33.6	214.0	475.8	1944.0	1144.5	281.3

RATIO FOR 2 YEAR PERIOD   1 CRIME PER   26.8 PEOPLE

RANKING   226

CHARLESTON,SOUTH CAROLINA

POPULATION   66,945

	MURDER	FORCED RAPE	ROB- BERY	AGGRYTD ASSAULT	BUR- GLARY	LARCENY +$50	AUTO THEFT
70 CRIMES	9	37	176	273	1,349	1,260	318
RATE PER 100,000	13.4	55.3	262.9	407.8	2015.1	1882.1	475.0
71 CRIMES	14	28	265	277	1,686	1,294	367
RATE PER 100,000	20.9	41.8	395.8	413.8	2518.5	1932.9	548.2

RATIO FOR 2 YEAR PERIOD   1 CRIME PER   18.2 PEOPLE

RANKING   334

CHARLESTON,WEST VIRGINIA

POPULATION   71,505

	MURDER	FORCED RAPE	ROB- BERY	AGGRYTD ASSAULT	BUR- GLARY	LARCENY +$50	AUTO THEFT
70 CRIMES	6	11	163	184	892	1,210	352
RATE PER 100,000	8.4	15.4	228.0	257.3	1247.5	1692.2	492.3
71 CRIMES	13	5	195	189	875	1,557	328
RATE PER 100,000	18.2	7.0	272.7	264.3	1223.7	2177.5	458.7

RATIO FOR 2 YEAR PERIOD   1 CRIME PER   23.9 PEOPLE

RANKING   265

CHARLOTTE,NORTH CAROLINA

POPULATION   241,178

	MURDER	FORCED RAPE	ROB- BERY	AGGRYTD ASSAULT	BUR- GLARY	LARCENY +$50	AUTO THEFT
70 CRIMES	79	66	488	1,417	5,430	4,135	1,367
RATE PER 100,000	32.8	27.4	202.3	587.5	2251.4	1714.5	566.8
71 CRIMES	54	98	573	1,246	4,938	3,276	1,086
RATE PER 100,000	22.4	40.6	237.6	516.6	2047.5	1358.3	450.3

RATIO FOR 2 YEAR PERIOD   1 CRIME PER   19.8 PEOPLE

RANKING   315

CHATTANOOGA, TENNESSEE

POPULATION   119,082

	MURDER	FORCED RAPE	ROB- BERY	AGGRYTD ASSAULT	BUR- GLARY	LARCENY +$50	AUTO THEFT
70 CRIMES	26	26	431	171	2,756	482	1,240
RATE PER 100,000	21.8	21.8	361.9	143.6	2314.4	404.8	1041.3
71 CRIMES	38	24	365	161	2,463	760	1,218
RATE PER 100,000	31.9	20.2	306.5	135.2	2068.3	638.2	1022.8

RATIO FOR 2 YEAR PERIOD   1 CRIME PER   23.4 PEOPLE

RANKING   270

CHESAPEAKE, VIRGINIA

POPULATION   89,580

	MURDER	FORCED RAPE	ROB- BERY	AGGRYTD ASSAULT	BUR- GLARY	LARCENY +$50	AUTO THEFT
70 CRIMES	9	24	71	177	935	604	244
RATE PER 100,000	10.0	26.8	79.3	197.6	1043.8	674.3	272.4
71 CRIMES	7	39	58	288	985	702	184
RATE PER 100,000	7.8	43.5	64.7	321.5	1099.6	783.7	205.4

RATIO FOR 2 YEAR PERIOD   1 CRIME PER   41.4 PEOPLE

RANKING   98

CHESTER, PENNSYLVANIA

POPULATION   56,331

	MURDER	FORCED RAPE	ROB- BERY	AGGRYTD ASSAULT	BUR- GLARY	LARCENY +$50	AUTO THEFT
70 CRIMES	14	29	379	420	1,039	408	1,127
RATE PER 100,000	24.9	51.5	672.8	745.6	1844.5	724.3	2000.7
71 CRIMES	18	31	495	545	1,501	496	955
RATE PER 100,000	32.0	55.0	878.7	967.5	2664.6	880.5	1695.3

RATIO FOR 2 YEAR PERIOD   1 CRIME PER   15.1 PEOPLE

RANKING   374

CHICAGO,ILLINOIS

POPULATION   3,366,957

	MURDER	FORCED RAPE	ROB- BERY	AGGRYTD ASSAULT	BUR- GLARY	LARCENY +$50	AUTO THEFT
70 CRIMES	810	1,405	23,198	11,667	35,190	16,479	39,268
RATE PER 100,000	24.1	41.7	689.0	346.5	1045.2	489.4	1166.3
71 CRIMES	824	1,549	24,012	11,285	38,385	15,593	35,206
RATE PER 100,000	24.5	46.0	713.2	335.2	1140.1	463.1	1045.6

RATIO FOR 2 YEAR PERIOD   1 CRIME   PER   26.4 PEOPLE

RANKING   231

CHICOPEE,MASSACHUSETTS

POPULATION   66,676

	MURDER	FORCED RAPE	ROB- BERY	AGGRYTD ASSAULT	BUR- GLARY	LARCENY +$50	AUTO THEFT
70 CRIMES	1		11	38	398	404	366
RATE PER 100,000	1.5	0.0	16.5	57.0	596.9	605.9	548.9
71 CRIMES	5	1	13	33	454	453	382
RATE PER 100,000	7.5	1.5	19.5	49.5	680.9	679.4	572.9

RATIO FOR 2 YEAR PERIOD   1 CRIME   PER   52.1 PEOPLE

RANKING   59

CHULA VISTA,CALIFORNIA

POPULATION   67,901

	MURDER	FORCED RAPE	ROB- BERY	AGGRYTD ASSAULT	BUR- GLARY	LARCENY +$50	AUTO THEFT
70 CRIMES	2	14	40	60	796	720	231
RATE PER 100,000	2.9	20.6	58.9	88.4	1172.3	1060.4	340.2
71 CRIMES	2	8	54	71	1,024	764	229
RATE PER 100,000	2.9	11.8	79.5	104.6	1508.1	1125.2	337.3

RATIO FOR 2 YEAR PERIOD   1 CRIME   PER   33.8 PEOPLE

RANKING   136

CICERO,ILLINOIS

		FORCED	ROB-	AGGRYTD	BUR-	LARCENY	AUTO
	MURDER	RAPE	BERY	ASSAULT	GLARY	+$50	THEFT

POPULATION   67,058

	MURDER	FORCED RAPE	ROB-BERY	AGGRYTD ASSAULT	BUR-GLARY	LARCENY +$50	AUTO THEFT
70 CRIMES	3	5	90	47	202	234	460
RATE PER 100,000	4.5	7.5	134.2	70.1	301.2	349.0	686.0
71 CRIMES	5	6	74	56	234	261	523
RATE PER 100,000	7.5	8.9	110.4	83.5	349.0	389.2	779.9

RATIO FOR 2 YEAR PERIOD   1 CRIME PER   60.9 PEOPLE

RANKING   35

CINCINNATI,OHIO

POPULATION   452,524

	MURDER	FORCED RAPE	ROB-BERY	AGGRYTD ASSAULT	BUR-GLARY	LARCENY +$50	AUTO THEFT
70 CRIMES	59	170	1,236	790	6,395	6,118	2,627
RATE PER 100,000	13.0	37.6	273.1	174.6	1413.2	1352.0	580.5
71 CRIMES	79	189	1,749	819	9,751	6,144	3,149
RATE PER 100,000	17.5	41.8	386.5	181.0	2154.8	1357.7	695.9

RATIO FOR 2 YEAR PERIOD   1 CRIME PER   23.0 PEOPLE

RANKING   277

CLEARWATER,FLORIDA

POPULATION   52,074

	MURDER	FORCED RAPE	ROB-BERY	AGGRYTD ASSAULT	BUR-GLARY	LARCENY +$50	AUTO THEFT
70 CRIMES	4	10	49	94	747	751	158
RATE PER 100,000	7.7	19.2	94.1	180.5	1434.5	1442.2	303.4
71 CRIMES	4	12	64	142	853	1,056	179
RATE PER 100,000	7.7	23.0	122.9	272.7	1638.1	2027.9	343.7

RATIO FOR 2 YEAR PERIOD   1 CRIME PER   25.2 PEOPLE

RANKING   250

194

CLEVELAND,OHIO

POPULATION   750,903

	MURDER	FORCED RAPE	ROB- BERY	AGGRYTD ASSAULT	BUR- GLARY	LARCENY +$50	AUTO THEFT
70 CRIMES	271	307	5,475	1,909	10,765	6,234	19,603
RATE PER 100,000	36.1	40.9	729.1	254.2	1433.6	830.2	2610.6
71 CRIMES	270	428	5,987	2,004	11,780	5,971	19,855
RATE PER 100,000	36.0	57.0	797.3	266.9	1568.8	795.2	2644.1

RATIO FOR 2 YEAR PERIOD   1 CRIME PER   16.5 PEOPLE

RANKING   351

CLEVELAND HEIGHTS,OHIO

POPULATION   60,767

	MURDER	FORCED RAPE	ROB- BERY	AGGRYTD ASSAULT	BUR- GLARY	LARCENY +$50	AUTO THEFT
70 CRIMES		15	38	48	338	447	400
RATE PER 100,000	0.0	24.7	62.5	79.0	556.2	735.6	658.3
71 CRIMES	3	12	68	49	418	347	603
RATE PER 100,000	4.9	19.7	111.9	80.6	687.9	571.0	992.3

RATIO FOR 2 YEAR PERIOD   1 CRIME PER   43.6 PEOPLE

RANKING   93

CLIFTON,NEW JERSEY

POPULATION   82,437

	MURDER	FORCED RAPE	ROB- BERY	AGGRYTD ASSAULT	BUR- GLARY	LARCENY +$50	AUTO THEFT
70 CRIMES		1	34	19	392	393	361
RATE PER 100,000	0.0	1.2	41.2	23.0	475.5	476.7	437.9
71 CRIMES	1	2	59	38	392	368	364
RATE PER 100,000	1.2	2.4	71.6	46.1	475.5	446.4	441.5

RATIO FOR 2 YEAR PERIOD   1 CRIME PER   68.0 PEOPLE

RANKING   20

COLORADO SPRINGS,COLORADO

POPULATION   135,060

	MURDER	FORCED RAPE	ROB- BERY	AGGRYTD ASSAULT	BUR- GLARY	LARCENY +$50	AUTO THEFT
70 CRIMES	9	45	285	211	1,925	2,286	629
RATE PER 100,000	6.7	33.3	211.0	156.2	1425.3	1692.6	465.7
71 CRIMES	9	70	183	198	2,183	2,558	694
RATE PER 100,000	6.7	51.8	135.5	146.6	1616.3	1894.0	513.8

RATIO FOR 2 YEAR PERIOD   1 CRIME PER   23.9 PEOPLE

RANKING   264

COLUMBIA,MISSOURI

POPULATION   58,804

	MURDER	FORCED RAPE	ROB- BERY	AGGRYTD ASSAULT	BUR- GLARY	LARCENY +$50	AUTO THEFT
70 CRIMES	4	15	31	74	407	618	94
RATE PER 100,000	6.8	25.5	52.7	125.8	692.1	1050.9	159.9
71 CRIMES	2	4	42	45	367	621	112
RATE PER 100,000	3.4	6.8	71.4	76.5	624.1	1056.1	190.5

RATIO FOR 2 YEAR PERIOD   1 CRIME PER   48.2 PEOPLE

RANKING   76

COLUMBIA,SOUTH CAROLINA

POPULATION   113,542

	MURDER	FORCED RAPE	ROB- BERY	AGGRYTD ASSAULT	BUR- GLARY	LARCENY +$50	AUTO THEFT
70 CRIMES	18	18	233	338	2,406	1,342	854
RATE PER 100,000	15.9	15.9	205.2	297.7	2119.0	1181.9	752.1
71 CRIMES	32	37	264	353	2,650	1,490	630
RATE PER 100,000	28.2	32.6	232.5	310.9	2333.9	1312.3	554.9

RATIO FOR 2 YEAR PERIOD   1 CRIME PER   21.2 PEOPLE

RANKING   297

COLUMBUS,GEORGIA

POPULATION   154,168

	MURDER	FORCED RAPE	ROB- BERY	AGGRYTD ASSAULT	BUR- GLARY	LARCENY +$50	AUTO THEFT
70 CRIMES	17	11	103	95	1,056	676	715
RATE PER 100,000	11.0	7.1	66.8	61.6	685.0	438.5	463.8
71 CRIMES	22	14	200	158	1,779	1,167	685
RATE PER 100,000	14.3	9.1	129.7	102.5	1153.9	757.0	444.3

RATIO FOR 2 YEAR PERIOD   1 CRIME PER   46.0 PEOPLE

RANKING   84

COLUMBUS,OHIO

POPULATION   539,677

	MURDER	FORCED RAPE	ROB- BERY	AGGRYTD ASSAULT	BUR- GLARY	LARCENY +$50	AUTO THEFT
70 CRIMES	47	263	1,682	922	9,095	8,558	5,217
RATE PER 100,000	8.7	48.7	311.7	170.8	1685.3	1585.8	966.7
71 CRIMES	69	269	1,873	943	10,023	8,176	5,226
RATE PER 100,000	12.8	49.8	347.1	174.7	1857.2	1515.0	968.4

RATIO FOR 2 YEAR PERIOD   1 CRIME PER   20.6 PEOPLE

RANKING   308

COMPTON,CALIFORNIA

POPULATION   78,611

	MURDER	FORCED RAPE	ROB- BERY	AGGRYTD ASSAULT	BUR- GLARY	LARCENY +$50	AUTO THEFT
70 CRIMES	22	118	660	791	3,329	1,459	3,713
RATE PER 100,000	28.0	150.1	839.6	1006.2	4234.8	1856.0	4723.3
71 CRIMES	20	98	802	916	4,792	1,284	3,567
RATE PER 100,000	25.4	124.7	1020.2	1165.2	6095.8	1633.4	4537.5

RATIO FOR 2 YEAR PERIOD   1 CRIME PER   7.2 PEOPLE

RANKING   393

CONCORD,CALIFORNIA

POPULATION   85,164

	MURDER	FORCED RAPE	ROB-BERY	AGGRVTD ASSAULT	BUR-GLARY	LARCENY +$50	AUTO THEFT
70 CRIMES	1	9	52	50	1,408	1,633	374
RATE PER 100,000	1.2	10.6	61.1	58.7	1653.3	1917.5	439.2
71 CRIMES	2	17	61	56	1,447	1,927	364
RATE PER 100,000	2.3	20.0	71.6	65.8	1699.1	2262.7	427.4

RATIO FOR 2 YEAR PERIOD   1 CRIME PER   23.0 PEOPLE

RANKING   278

CORPUS CHRISTI,TEXAS

POPULATION   204,525

	MURDER	FORCED RAPE	ROB-BERY	AGGRVTD ASSAULT	BUR-GLARY	LARCENY +$50	AUTO THEFT
70 CRIMES	32	55	346	947	3,905	3,328	1,093
RATE PER 100,000	15.6	26.9	169.2	463.0	1909.3	1627.2	534.4
71 CRIMES	33	59	256	872	3,970	3,355	1,108
RATE PER 100,000	16.1	28.8	125.2	426.4	1941.1	1640.4	541.7

RATIO FOR 2 YEAR PERIOD   1 CRIME PER   21.1 PEOPLE

RANKING   301

COSTA MESA,CALIFORNIA

POPULATION   72,660

	MURDER	FORCED RAPE	ROB-BERY	AGGRVTD ASSAULT	BUR-GLARY	LARCENY +$50	AUTO THEFT
70 CRIMES	5	18	66	71	1,327	1,288	282
RATE PER 100,000	6.9	24.8	90.8	97.7	1826.3	1772.6	388.1
71 CRIMES	1	27	58	74	1,548	1,535	346
RATE PER 100,000	1.4	37.2	79.8	101.8	2130.5	2112.6	476.2

RATIO FOR 2 YEAR PERIOD   1 CRIME PER   21.8 PEOPLE

RANKING   294

COUNCIL BLUFFS, IOWA

POPULATION   60,348

70 CRIMES	MURDER	FORCED RAPE	ROB- BERY	AGGRYTD ASSAULT	BUR- GLARY	LARCENY +$50	AUTO THEFT
70 CRIMES	2	11	44	58	702	1,161	404
RATE PER 100,000	3.3	18.2	72.9	96.1	1163.3	1923.8	669.5
71 CRIMES	3	11	50	46	748	1,103	437
RATE PER 100,000	5.0	18.2	82.9	76.2	1239.5	1827.7	724.1

RATIO FOR 2 YEAR PERIOD   1 CRIME PER   25.2 PEOPLE

RANKING   251

COVINGTON, KENTUCKY

POPULATION   52,535

70 CRIMES	MURDER	FORCED RAPE	ROB- BERY	AGGRYTD ASSAULT	BUR- GLARY	LARCENY +$50	AUTO THEFT
70 CRIMES	5	7	129	104	842	686	516
RATE PER 100,000	9.5	13.3	245.6	198.0	1602.7	1305.8	982.2
71 CRIMES	6	11	162	126	1,046	708	617
RATE PER 100,000	11.4	20.9	308.4	239.8	1991.1	1347.7	1174.5

RATIO FOR 2 YEAR PERIOD   1 CRIME PER   21.1 PEOPLE

RANKING   300

CRANSTON, RHODE ISLAND

POPULATION   73,037

70 CRIMES	MURDER	FORCED RAPE	ROB- BERY	AGGRYTD ASSAULT	BUR- GLARY	LARCENY +$50	AUTO THEFT
70 CRIMES	3	2	21	45	550	580	287
RATE PER 100,000	4.1	2.7	28.8	61.6	753.0	794.1	393.0
71 CRIMES		4	18	32	642	681	385
RATE PER 100,000	0.0	5.5	24.6	43.8	879.0	932.4	527.1

RATIO FOR 2 YEAR PERIOD   1 CRIME PER   44.9 PEOPLE

RANKING   86

DALLAS,TEXAS

POPULATION   844,401

	MURDER	FORCED RAPE	ROB-BERY	AGGRYTD ASSAULT	BUR-GLARY	LARCENY +$50	AUTO THEFT
70 CRIMES	242	552	2,964	4,399	19,510	15,069	7,655
RATE PER 100,000	28.7	65.4	351.0	521.0	2310.5	1784.6	906.6
71 CRIMES	207	585	2,861	5,282	18,322	12,229	6,914
RATE PER 100,000	24.5	69.3	338.8	625.5	2169.8	1448.2	818.8

RATIO FOR 2 YEAR PERIOD   1 CRIME PER   17.4 PEOPLE

RANKING   342

DALY CITY,CALIFORNIA

POPULATION   66,922

	MURDER	FORCED RAPE	ROB-BERY	AGGRYTD ASSAULT	BUR-GLARY	LARCENY +$50	AUTO THEFT
70 CRIMES	2	14	104	51	847	669	498
RATE PER 100,000	3.0	20.9	155.4	76.2	1265.7	999.7	744.1
71 CRIMES	4	17	97	41	766	726	466
RATE PER 100,000	6.0	25.4	144.9	61.3	1144.6	1084.8	696.3

RATIO FOR 2 YEAR PERIOD   1 CRIME PER   31.1 PEOPLE

RANKING   170

DANBURY,CONNECTICUT

POPULATION   50,781

	MURDER	FORCED RAPE	ROB-BERY	AGGRYTD ASSAULT	BUR-GLARY	LARCENY +$50	AUTO THEFT
70 CRIMES		2	9	17	285	428	166
RATE PER 100,000	0.0	3.9	17.7	33.5	561.2	842.8	326.9
71 CRIMES	1	4	15	15	477	468	196
RATE PER 100,000	2.0	7.9	29.5	29.5	939.3	921.6	386.0

RATIO FOR 2 YEAR PERIOD   1 CRIME PER   48.7 PEOPLE

RANKING   75

DAVENPORT, IOWA

POPULATION   98,469

70 CRIMES	MURDER	FORCED RAPE	ROB- BERY	AGGRYTD ASSAULT	BUR- GLARY	LARCENY +$50	AUTO THEFT
70 CRIMES	5	18	143	116	1,119	780	544
RATE PER 100,000	5.1	18.3	145.2	117.8	1136.4	792.1	552.5
71 CRIMES	3	23	111	440	1,327	736	406
RATE PER 100,000	3.0	23.4	112.7	446.8	1347.6	747.4	412.3

RATIO FOR 2 YEAR PERIOD   1 CRIME PER   34.1 PEOPLE

RANKING   132

DAYTON, OHIO

POPULATION   243,601

70 CRIMES	MURDER	FORCED RAPE	ROB- BERY	AGGRYTD ASSAULT	BUR- GLARY	LARCENY +$50	AUTO THEFT
70 CRIMES	57	95	1,752	972	6,813	4,138	2,270
RATE PER 100,000	23.4	39.0	719.2	399.0	2796.8	1698.7	931.9
71 CRIMES	89	96	1,778	1,013	6,285	3,003	1,875
RATE PER 100,000	36.5	39.4	729.9	415.8	2580.0	1232.8	769.7

RATIO FOR 2 YEAR PERIOD   1 CRIME PER   16.1 PEOPLE

RANKING   359

DEARBORN, MICHIGAN

POPULATION   104,199

70 CRIMES	MURDER	FORCED RAPE	ROB- BERY	AGGRYTD ASSAULT	BUR- GLARY	LARCENY +$50	AUTO THEFT
70 CRIMES	4	14	152	60	1,075	1,545	668
RATE PER 100,000	3.8	13.4	145.9	57.6	1031.7	1482.7	641.1
71 CRIMES	8	13	148	73	1,090	1,310	718
RATE PER 100,000	7.7	12.5	142.0	70.1	1046.1	1257.2	689.1

RATIO FOR 2 YEAR PERIOD   1 CRIME PER   30.2 PEOPLE

RANKING   182

DEARBORN HEIGHTS,MICHIGAN

POPULATION   80,069

	MURDER	FORCED RAPE	ROB- BERY	AGGRYTD ASSAULT	BUR- GLARY	LARCENY +$50	AUTO THEFT
70 CRIMES		10	102	112	832	766	217
RATE PER 100,000	0.0	12.5	127.4	139.9	1039.1	956.7	271.0
71 CRIMES	1	11	113	109	919	859	305
RATE PER 100,000	1.2	13.7	141.1	136.1	1147.8	1072.8	380.9

RATIO FOR 2 YEAR PERIOD   1 CRIME PER   36.7 PEOPLE

RANKING   119

DECATUR,ILLINOIS

POPULATION   90,397

	MURDER	FORCED RAPE	ROB- BERY	AGGRYTD ASSAULT	BUR- GLARY	LARCENY +$50	AUTO THEFT
70 CRIMES	3	3	130	198	1,004	790	248
RATE PER 100,000	3.3	3.3	143.8	219.0	1110.7	873.9	274.3
71 CRIMES	6	14	103	195	1,034	692	228
RATE PER 100,000	6.6	15.5	113.9	215.7	1143.8	765.5	252.2

RATIO FOR 2 YEAR PERIOD   1 CRIME PER   38.8 PEOPLE

RANKING   106

DENVER,COLORADO

POPULATION   514,678

	MURDER	FORCED RAPE	ROB- BERY	AGGRYTD ASSAULT	BUR- GLARY	LARCENY +$50	AUTO THEFT
70 CRIMES	74	474	1,980	1,685	15,111	10,569	7,942
RATE PER 100,000	14.4	92.1	384.7	327.4	2936.0	2053.5	1543.1
71 CRIMES	82	434	2,167	2,050	15,228	10,657	7,088
RATE PER 100,000	15.9	84.3	421.0	398.3	2958.7	2070.6	1377.2

RATIO FOR 2 YEAR PERIOD   1 CRIME PER   13.6 PEOPLE

RANKING   385

DES MOINES,IOWA

POPULATION   200,587

	MURDER	FORCED RAPE	ROB- BERY	AGGRYTD ASSAULT	BUR- GLARY	LARCENY +$50	AUTO THEFT
70 CRIMES	11	35	340	87	1,963	3,157	1,160
RATE PER 100,000	5.5	17.4	169.5	43.4	978.6	1573.9	578.3
71 CRIMES	11	66	361	159	1,885	3,301	778
RATE PER 100,000	5.5	32.9	180.0	79.3	939.7	1645.7	387.9

RATIO FOR 2 YEAR PERIOD   1 CRIME PER   30.1 PEOPLE

RANKING   186

DES PLAINES,ILLINOIS

POPULATION   57,239

	MURDER	FORCED RAPE	ROB- BERY	AGGRYTD ASSAULT	BUR- GLARY	LARCENY +$50	AUTO THEFT
70 CRIMES	1	2	18	31	404	562	149
RATE PER 100,000	1.7	3.5	31.4	54.2	705.8	981.8	260.3
71 CRIMES		3	18	68	433	588	130
RATE PER 100,000	0.0	5.2	31.4	118.8	756.5	1027.3	227.1

RATIO FOR 2 YEAR PERIOD   1 CRIME PER   47.5 PEOPLE

RANKING   80

DETROIT,MICHIGAN

POPULATION   1,511,482

	MURDER	FORCED RAPE	ROB- BERY	AGGRYTD ASSAULT	BUR- GLARY	LARCENY +$50	AUTO THEFT
70 CRIMES	495	819	23,038	4,881	50,868	26,665	20,864
RATE PER 100,000	32.7	54.2	1524.2	322.9	3365.4	1764.2	1380.4
71 CRIMES	577	853	20,753	5,400	51,531	25,361	22,770
RATE PER 100,000	38.2	56.4	1373.0	357.3	3409.3	1677.9	1506.5

RATIO FOR 2 YEAR PERIOD   1 CRIME PER   11.8 PEOPLE

RANKING   391

DOWNEY,CALIFORNIA

POPULATION   88,445

	MURDER	FORCED RAPE	ROB- BERY	AGGRYTD ASSAULT	BUR- GLARY	LARCENY +$50	AUTO THEFT
70 CRIMES	1	9	121	69	1,155	1,443	507
RATE PER 100,000	1.1	10.2	136.8	78.0	1305.9	1631.5	573.2
71 CRIMES	4	11	116	88	1,344	1,526	544
RATE PER 100,000	4.5	12.4	131.2	99.5	1519.6	1725.4	615.1

RATIO FOR 2 YEAR PERIOD   1 CRIME PER   25.4 PEOPLE

RANKING   243

DUBUQUE,IOWA

POPULATION   62,309

	MURDER	FORCED RAPE	ROB- BERY	AGGRYTD ASSAULT	BUR- GLARY	LARCENY +$50	AUTO THEFT
70 CRIMES		1	14	17	382	619	229
RATE PER 100,000	0.0	1.6	22.5	27.3	613.1	993.4	367.5
71 CRIMES	1	3	15	13	521	708	201
RATE PER 100,000	1.6	4.8	24.1	20.9	836.2	1136.3	322.6

RATIO FOR 2 YEAR PERIOD   1 CRIME PER   45.7 PEOPLE

RANKING   85

DULUTH,MINNESOTA

POPULATION   100,578

	MURDER	FORCED RAPE	ROB- BERY	AGGRYTD ASSAULT	BUR- GLARY	LARCENY +$50	AUTO THEFT
70 CRIMES	1	9	42	22	755	809	434
RATE PER 100,000	1.0	8.9	41.8	21.9	750.7	804.4	431.5
71 CRIMES	3	14	40	24	1,090	1,081	513
RATE PER 100,000	3.0	13.9	39.8	23.9	1083.7	1074.8	510.1

RATIO FOR 2 YEAR PERIOD   1 CRIME PER   41.5 PEOPLE

RANKING   97

DURHAM,NORTH CAROLINA

POPULATION   95,438

	MURDER	FORCED RAPE	ROB-BERY	AGGRYTD ASSAULT	BUR-GLARY	LARCENY +$50	AUTO THEFT
70 CRIMES	15	18	135	385	1,459	1,141	393
RATE PER 100,000	15.7	18.9	141.5	403.4	1528.7	1195.5	411.8
71 CRIMES	15	26	115	320	1,220	1,170	207
RATE PER 100,000	15.7	27.2	120.5	335.3	1278.3	1225.9	216.9

RATIO FOR 2 YEAR PERIOD   1 CRIME PER   28.8 PEOPLE

RANKING   204

EAST HARTFORD,CONNECTICUT

POPULATION   57,583

	MURDER	FORCED RAPE	ROB-BERY	AGGRYTD ASSAULT	BUR-GLARY	LARCENY +$50	AUTO THEFT
70 CRIMES		3	9	35	367	424	123
RATE PER 100,000	0.0	5.2	15.6	60.8	637.3	736.3	213.6
71 CRIMES	1	1	11	21	267	332	107
RATE PER 100,000	1.7	1.7	19.1	36.5	463.7	576.6	185.8

RATIO FOR 2 YEAR PERIOD   1 CRIME PER   67.7 PEOPLE

RANKING   21

EAST ORANGE,NEW JERSEY

POPULATION   75,471

	MURDER	FORCED RAPE	ROB-BERY	AGGRYTD ASSAULT	BUR-GLARY	LARCENY +$50	AUTO THEFT
70 CRIMES	5	25	371	227	1,270	949	602
RATE PER 100,000	6.6	33.1	491.6	300.8	1682.8	1257.4	797.7
71 CRIMES	7	28	575	186	1,764	940	574
RATE PER 100,000	9.3	37.1	761.9	246.5	2337.3	1245.5	760.6

RATIO FOR 2 YEAR PERIOD   1 CRIME PER   20.0 PEOPLE

RANKING   310

EAST ST. LOUIS,ILLINOIS

POPULATION   69,996

	MURDER	FORCED RAPE	ROB- BERY	AGGRYTD ASSAULT	BUR- GLARY	LARCENY +$50	AUTO THEFT
70 CRIMES	36	80	460	289	1,631	634	1,340
RATE PER 100,000	51.4	114.3	657.2	412.9	2330.1	905.8	1914.4
71 CRIMES	26	68	431	321	2,008	760	936
RATE PER 100,000	37.1	97.1	615.7	458.6	2868.7	1085.8	1337.2

RATIO FOR 2 YEAR PERIOD   1 CRIME PER   15.5 PEOPLE

RANKING   369

EL CAJON,CALIFORNIA

POPULATION   52,273

	MURDER	FORCED RAPE	ROB- BERY	AGGRYTD ASSAULT	BUR- GLARY	LARCENY +$50	AUTO THEFT
70 CRIMES	1	20	24	29	502	615	171
RATE PER 100,000	1.9	38.3	45.9	55.5	960.3	1176.5	327.1
71 CRIMES	2	19	31	34	621	616	184
RATE PER 100,000	3.8	36.3	59.3	65.0	1188.0	1178.4	352.0

RATIO FOR 2 YEAR PERIOD   1 CRIME PER   36.4 PEOPLE

RANKING   121

EL MONTE,CALIFORNIA

POPULATION   69,837

	MURDER	FORCED RAPE	ROB- BERY	AGGRYTD ASSAULT	BUR- GLARY	LARCENY +$50	AUTO THEFT
70 CRIMES	8	31	99	145	772	427	696
RATE PER 100,000	11.5	44.4	141.8	207.6	1105.4	611.4	996.6
71 CRIMES	7	37	118	129	783	531	637
RATE PER 100,000	10.0	53.0	169.0	184.7	1121.2	760.3	912.1

RATIO FOR 2 YEAR PERIOD   1 CRIME PER   31.6 PEOPLE

RANKING   161

EL PASO, TEXAS

POPULATION   322,261

	MURDER	FORCED RAPE	ROB-BERY	AGGRYTD ASSAULT	BUR-GLARY	LARCENY +$50	AUTO THEFT
70 CRIMES	13	43	310	413	4,827	2,146	1,581
RATE PER 100,000	4.0	13.3	96.2	128.2	1497.9	665.9	490.6
71 CRIMES	16	75	398	588	7,621	2,240	2,136
RATE PER 100,000	5.0	23.3	123.5	182.5	2364.9	695.1	662.8

RATIO FOR 2 YEAR PERIOD   1 CRIME PER   28.7 PEOPLE

RANKING   205

ELGIN, ILLINOIS

POPULATION   55,691

	MURDER	FORCED RAPE	ROB-BERY	AGGRYTD ASSAULT	BUR-GLARY	LARCENY +$50	AUTO THEFT
70 CRIMES	1	12	64	114	311	649	119
RATE PER 100,000	1.8	21.5	114.9	204.7	558.4	1165.4	213.7
71 CRIMES	4	11	67	109	426	790	160
RATE PER 100,000	7.2	19.8	120.3	195.7	764.9	1418.5	287.3

RATIO FOR 2 YEAR PERIOD   1 CRIME PER   39.2 PEOPLE

RANKING   104

ELIZABETH, NEW JERSEY

POPULATION   112,654

	MURDER	FORCED RAPE	ROB-BERY	AGGRYTD ASSAULT	BUR-GLARY	LARCENY +$50	AUTO THEFT
70 CRIMES	2	32	279	314	1,764	930	1,406
RATE PER 100,000	1.8	28.4	247.7	278.7	1565.9	825.5	1248.1
71 CRIMES	10	28	475	314	2,067	1,113	1,523
RATE PER 100,000	8.9	24.9	421.6	278.7	1834.8	988.0	1351.9

RATIO FOR 2 YEAR PERIOD   1 CRIME PER   21.9 PEOPLE

RANKING   291

ELMHURST,ILLINOIS

POPULATION   50,547

	MURDER	FORCED RAPE	ROB- BERY	AGGRYTD ASSAULT	BUR- GLARY	LARCENY +$50	AUTO THEFT
70 CRIMES		2	9	32	273	402	96
RATE PER 100,000	0.0	4.0	17.8	63.3	540.1	795.3	189.9
71 CRIMES	2	3	11	40	330	495	96
RATE PER 100,000	4.0	5.9	21.8	79.1	652.9	979.3	189.9

RATIO FOR 2 YEAR PERIOD   1 CRIME PER   56.4 PEOPLE

RANKING   45

ELYRIA,OHIO

POPULATION   53,427

	MURDER	FORCED RAPE	ROB- BERY	AGGRYTD ASSAULT	BUR- GLARY	LARCENY +$50	AUTO THEFT
70 CRIMES	1	8	47	42	422	218	290
RATE PER 100,000	1.9	15.0	88.0	78.6	789.9	408.0	542.8
71 CRIMES	2	8	62	75	612	293	353
RATE PER 100,000	3.7	15.0	116.0	140.4	1145.5	548.4	660.7

RATIO FOR 2 YEAR PERIOD   1 CRIME PER   43.9 PEOPLE

RANKING   91

ERIE,PENNSYLVANIA

POPULATION   129,231

	MURDER	FORCED RAPE	ROB- BERY	AGGRYTD ASSAULT	BUR- GLARY	LARCENY +$50	AUTO THEFT
70 CRIMES	3	30	186	144	949	749	463
RATE PER 100,000	2.3	23.2	143.9	111.4	734.3	579.6	358.3
71 CRIMES	7	21	273	141	1,400	939	467
RATE PER 100,000	5.4	16.2	211.2	109.1	1083.3	726.6	361.4

RATIO FOR 2 YEAR PERIOD   1 CRIME PER   44.7 PEOPLE

RANKING   88

208

EUCLID, OHIO

POPULATION 71,552

	MURDER	FORCED RAPE	ROB-BERY	AGGRYTD ASSAULT	BUR-GLARY	LARCENY +$50	AUTO THEFT
70 CRIMES		2	11	8	164	53	427
RATE PER 100,000	0.0	2.8	15.4	11.2	229.2	74.1	596.8
71 CRIMES	2		26	5	127	36	433
RATE PER 100,000	2.8	0.0	36.3	7.0	177.5	50.3	605.2

RATIO FOR 2 YEAR PERIOD   1 CRIME PER   110.5 PEOPLE

RANKING 6

EUGENE, OREGON

POPULATION 76,346

	MURDER	FORCED RAPE	ROB-BERY	AGGRYTD ASSAULT	BUR-GLARY	LARCENY +$50	AUTO THEFT
70 CRIMES	5	14	52	44	1,030	2,002	251
RATE PER 100,000	6.5	18.3	68.1	57.6	1349.1	2622.3	328.8
71 CRIMES	1	32	80	95	1,609	2,338	310
RATE PER 100,000	1.3	41.9	104.8	124.4	2107.5	3062.4	406.0

RATIO FOR 2 YEAR PERIOD   1 CRIME PER   19.4 PEOPLE

RANKING 321

EVANSTON, ILLINOIS

POPULATION 79,808

	MURDER	FORCED RAPE	ROB-BERY	AGGRYTD ASSAULT	BUR-GLARY	LARCENY +$50	AUTO THEFT
70 CRIMES	5	17	111	113	842	450	453
RATE PER 100,000	6.3	21.3	139.1	141.6	1055.0	563.9	567.6
71 CRIMES	4	18	128	98	716	416	407
RATE PER 100,000	5.0	22.6	160.4	122.8	897.2	521.3	510.0

RATIO FOR 2 YEAR PERIOD   1 CRIME PER   42.2 PEOPLE

RANKING 95

EVANSVILLE,INDIANA

POPULATION   138,764

	MURDER	FORCED RAPE	ROB- BERY	AGGRYTD ASSAULT	BUR- GLARY	LARCENY +$50	AUTO THEFT
70 CRIMES	12	58	211	365	1,922	2,629	701
RATE PER 100,000	8.6	41.8	152.1	263.0	1385.1	1894.6	505.2
71 CRIMES	9	59	261	565	1,980	1,881	704
RATE PER 100,000	6.5	42.5	188.1	407.2	1426.9	1355.5	507.3

RATIO FOR 2 YEAR PERIOD   1 CRIME PER   24.4 PEOPLE

RANKING   256

EVERETT,WASHINGTON

POPULATION   53,622

	MURDER	FORCED RAPE	ROB- BERY	AGGRYTD ASSAULT	BUR- GLARY	LARCENY +$50	AUTO THEFT
70 CRIMES	1	9	34	75	673	1,153	299
RATE PER 100,000	1.9	16.8	63.4	139.9	1255.1	2150.2	557.6
71 CRIMES	1	6	35	115	827	1,115	270
RATE PER 100,000	1.9	11.2	65.3	214.5	1542.3	2079.4	503.5

RATIO FOR 2 YEAR PERIOD   1 CRIME PER   23.2 PEOPLE

RANKING   273

FAIRFIELD,CONNECTICUT

POPULATION   56,487

	MURDER	FORCED RAPE	ROB- BERY	AGGRYTD ASSAULT	BUR- GLARY	LARCENY +$50	AUTO THEFT
70 CRIMES			14	9	562	624	312
RATE PER 100,000	0.0	0.0	24.8	15.9	994.9	1104.7	552.3
71 CRIMES	1	4	23	50	698	935	229
RATE PER 100,000	1.8	7.1	40.7	88.5	1235.7	1655.2	405.4

RATIO FOR 2 YEAR PERIOD   1 CRIME PER   32.6 PEOPLE

RANKING   151

FALL RIVER,MASSACHUSETTS

POPULATION　　　　96,898

	MURDER	FORCED RAPE	ROB-BERY	AGGRYTD ASSAULT	BUR-GLARY	LARCENY +$50	AUTO THEFT
70 CRIMES	2	8	80	68	1,927	965	1,520
RATE PER 100,000	2.1	8.3	82.6	70.2	1988.7	995.9	1568.7
71 CRIMES	3	16	129	108	3,052	1,395	1,751
RATE PER 100,000	3.1	16.5	133.1	111.5	3149.7	1439.7	1807.1

RATIO FOR 2 YEAR PERIOD　　1 CRIME PER　17.5 PEOPLE

RANKING　340

FARGO,NORTH DAKOTA

POPULATION　　　　53,365

	MURDER	FORCED RAPE	ROB-BERY	AGGRYTD ASSAULT	BUR-GLARY	LARCENY +$50	AUTO THEFT
70 CRIMES		5	9	11	176	551	94
RATE PER 100,000	0.0	9.4	16.9	20.6	329.8	1032.5	176.1
71 CRIMES	1	2	11	15	354	574	126
RATE PER 100,000	1.9	3.7	20.6	28.1	663.4	1075.6	236.1

RATIO FOR 2 YEAR PERIOD　　1 CRIME PER　55.3 PEOPLE

RANKING　50

FAYETTEVILLE,NORTH CAROLINA

POPULATION　　　　53,510

	MURDER	FORCED RAPE	ROB-BERY	AGGRYTD ASSAULT	BUR-GLARY	LARCENY +$50	AUTO THEFT
70 CRIMES	8	13	96	687	679	806	238
RATE PER 100,000	15.0	24.3	179.4	1283.9	1268.9	1506.3	444.8
71 CRIMES	9	11	112	344	497	749	379
RATE PER 100,000	16.8	20.6	209.3	642.9	928.8	1399.7	708.3

RATIO FOR 2 YEAR PERIOD　　1 CRIME PER　23.1 PEOPLE

RANKING　275

FLINT,MICHIGAN

POPULATION   193,317

	MURDER	FORCED RAPE	ROB- BERY	AGGRVTD ASSAULT	BUR- GLARY	LARCENY +$50	AUTO THEFT
70 CRIMES	25	63	584	1,288	4,115	3,346	1,092
RATE PER 100,000	12.9	32.6	302.1	666.3	2128.6	1730.8	564.9
71 CRIMES	33	81	635	1,258	4,214	3,517	1,330
RATE PER 100,000	17.1	41.9	328.5	650.7	2179.8	1819.3	688.0

RATIO FOR 2 YEAR PERIOD   1 CRIME PER   17.9 PEOPLE

RANKING   337

FLORISSANT,MISSOURI

POPULATION   65,908

	MURDER	FORCED RAPE	ROB- BERY	AGGRVTD ASSAULT	BUR- GLARY	LARCENY +$50	AUTO THEFT
70 CRIMES	1	1	13	21	279	387	104
RATE PER 100,000	1.5	1.5	19.7	31.9	423.3	587.2	157.8
71 CRIMES		1	6	20	340	347	105
RATE PER 100,000	0.0	1.5	9.1	30.3	515.9	526.5	159.3

RATIO FOR 2 YEAR PERIOD   1 CRIME PER   81.1 PEOPLE

RANKING   9

FORT LAUDERDALE,FLORIDA

POPULATION   139,590

	MURDER	FORCED RAPE	ROB- BERY	AGGRVTD ASSAULT	BUR- GLARY	LARCENY +$5C	AUTO THEFT
70 CRIMES	16	41	402	280	3,315	3,176	1,303
RATE PER 100,000	11.5	29.4	288.0	200.6	2374.8	2275.2	933.4
71 CRIMES	13	53	412	263	3,643	2,902	1,229
RATE PER 100,000	9.3	38.0	295.2	188.4	2609.8	2078.9	880.4

RATIO FOR 2 YEAR PERIOD   1 CRIME PER   16.3 PEOPLE

RANKING   353

FORT SMITH,ARKANSAS

POPULATION   62,802

	MURDER	FORCED RAPE	ROB- BERY	AGGRYTD ASSAULT	BUR- GLARY	LARCENY +$50	AUTO THEFT
70 CRIMES		10	22	63	451	480	162
RATE PER 100,000	0.0	15.9	35.0	100.3	718.1	764.3	258.0
71 CRIMES	6	5	20	64	319	460	116
RATE PER 100,000	9.6	8.0	31.8	101.9	507.9	732.5	184.7

RATIO FOR 2 YEAR PERIOD   1 CRIME PER   57.6 PEOPLE

RANKING   41

FORT WAYNE,INDIANA

POPULATION   177,671

	MURDER	FORCED RAPE	ROB- BERY	AGGRYTD ASSAULT	BUR- GLARY	LARCENY +$50	AUTO THEFT
70 CRIMES	9	42	263	96	2,080	3,624	784
RATE PER 100,000	5.1	23.6	148.0	54.0	1170.7	2039.7	441.3
71 CRIMES	6	46	343	102	2,391	3,876	619
RATE PER 100,000	3.4	25.9	193.1	57.4	1345.7	2181.6	348.4

RATIO FOR 2 YEAR PERIOD   1 CRIME PER   24.8 PEOPLE

RANKING   255

FORT WORTH,TEXAS

POPULATION   393,476

	MURDER	FORCED RAPE	ROB- BERY	AGGRYTD ASSAULT	BUR- GLARY	LARCENY +$50	AUTO THEFT
70 CRIMES	105	72	1,016	589	7,301	3,126	3,443
RATE PER 100,000	26.7	18.3	258.2	149.7	1855.5	794.5	875.0
71 CRIMES	102	88	917	549	6,615	2,816	2,861
RATE PER 100,000	25.9	22.4	233.1	139.5	1681.2	715.7	727.1

RATIO FOR 2 YEAR PERIOD   1 CRIME PER   26.5 PEOPLE

RANKING   229

FRAMINGHAM,MASSACHUSETTS

POPULATION   64,048

70 CRIMES	MURDER	FORCED RAPE	ROB- BERY	AGGRYTD ASSAULT	BUR- GLARY	LARCENY +$50	AUTO THEFT
		3	14	30	456	645	260

| RATE PER 100,000 | 0.0 | 4.7 | 21.9 | 46.8 | 712.0 | 1007.1 | 405.9 |

| 71 CRIMES | | 2 | 19 | 72 | 713 | 929 | 379 |

| RATE PER 100,000 | 0.0 | 3.1 | 29.7 | 112.4 | 1113.2 | 1450.5 | 591.7 |

RATIO FOR 2 YEAR PERIOD   1 CRIME PER   36.3 PEOPLE

RANKING   123

FREMONT,CALIFORNIA

POPULATION   100,869

70 CRIMES	MURDER	FORCED RAPE	ROB- BERY	AGGRYTD ASSAULT	BUR- GLARY	LARCENY +$50	AUTO THEFT
	4	11	42	97	1,525	740	247

| RATE PER 100,000 | 4.0 | 10.9 | 41.6 | 96.2 | 1511.9 | 733.6 | 244.9 |

| 71 CRIMES | 1 | 26 | 56 | 98 | 1,942 | 1,370 | 443 |

| RATE PER 100,000 | 1.0 | 25.8 | 55.5 | 97.2 | 1925.3 | 1358.2 | 439.2 |

RATIO FOR 2 YEAR PERIOD   1 CRIME PER   30.5 PEOPLE

RANKING   178

FRESNO,CALIFORNIA

POPULATION   165,972

70 CRIMES	MURDER	FORCED RAPE	ROB- BERY	AGGRYTD ASSAULT	BUR- GLARY	LARCENY +$50	AUTO THEFT
	23	29	287	185	3,346	3,004	1,980

| RATE PER 100,000 | 13.9 | 17.5 | 172.9 | 111.5 | 2016.0 | 1809.9 | 1193.0 |

| 71 CRIMES | 19 | 35 | 386 | 226 | 4,562 | 4,152 | 2,188 |

| RATE PER 100,000 | 11.4 | 21.1 | 232.6 | 136.2 | 2748.7 | 2501.6 | 1318.3 |

RATIO FOR 2 YEAR PERIOD   1 CRIME PER   16.2 PEOPLE

RANKING   356

214

FULLERTON,CALIFORNIA

POPULATION   85,826

	MURDER	FORCED RAPE	ROB- BERY	AGGRYTD ASSAULT	BUR- GLARY	LARCENY +$50	AUTO THEFT
70 CRIMES	3	10	90	65	640	1,696	328
RATE PER 100,000	3.5	11.7	104.9	75.7	745.7	1976.1	382.2
71 CRIMES	1	23	58	72	772	2,013	316
RATE PER 100,000	1.2	26.8	67.6	83.9	899.5	2345.4	368.2

RATIO FOR 2 YEAR PERIOD   1 CRIME PER   28.1 PEOPLE

RANKING   211

GADSDEN,ALABAMA

POPULATION   53,928

	MURDER	FORCED RAPE	ROB- BERY	AGGRYTD ASSAULT	BUR- GLARY	LARCENY +$50	AUTO THEFT
70 CRIMES	5	5	22	72	649	378	177
RATE PER 100,000	9.3	9.3	40.8	133.5	1203.5	700.9	328.2
71 CRIMES	10	9	51	61	581	357	159
RATE PER 100,000	18.5	16.7	94.6	113.1	1077.4	662.0	294.8

RATIO FOR 2 YEAR PERIOD   1 CRIME PER   42.5 PEOPLE

RANKING   94

GAINESVILLE,FLORIDA

POPULATION   64,510

	MURDER	FORCED RAPE	ROB- BERY	AGGRYTD ASSAULT	BUR- GLARY	LARCENY +$50	AUTO THEFT
70 CRIMES	10	8	119	295	1,298	1,366	264
RATE PER 100,000	15.5	12.4	184.5	457.3	2012.1	2117.5	409.2
71 CRIMES	5	11	110	379	1,426	1,714	274
RATE PER 100,000	7.8	17.1	170.5	587.5	2210.5	2657.0	424.7

RATIO FOR 2 YEAR PERIOD   1 CRIME PER   17.7 PEOPLE

RANKING   339

GALVESTON,TEXAS

POPULATION   61,809

70 CRIMES	MURDER	FORCED RAPE	ROB-BERY	AGGRYTD ASSAULT	BUR-GLARY	LARCENY +$50	AUTO THEFT
	15	21	247	315	1,494	1,478	297
RATE PER 100,000	24.3	34.0	399.6	509.6	2417.1	2391.2	480.5
71 CRIMES	18	26	383	309	1,630	1,419	305
RATE PER 100,000	29.1	42.1	619.7	499.9	2637.2	2295.8	493.5

RATIO FOR 2 YEAR PERIOD   1 CRIME PER   15.5 PEOPLE

RANKING   368

GARDEN GROVE,CALIFORNIA

POPULATION   122,524

70 CRIMES	MURDER	FORCED RAPE	ROB-BERY	AGGRYTD ASSAULT	BUR-GLARY	LARCENY +$50	AUTO THEFT
	3	32	159	108	1,931	2,283	537
RATE PER 100,000	2.4	26.1	129.8	88.1	1576.0	1863.3	438.3
71 CRIMES	3	29	153	113	2,044	2,765	397
RATE PER 100,000	2.4	23.7	124.9	92.2	1668.2	2256.7	324.0

RATIO FOR 2 YEAR PERIOD   1 CRIME PER   23.2 PEOPLE

RANKING   274

GARLAND,TEXAS

POPULATION   81,437

70 CRIMES	MURDER	FORCED RAPE	ROB-BERY	AGGRYTD ASSAULT	BUR-GLARY	LARCENY +$50	AUTO THEFT
	2	8	26	162	639	856	182
RATE PER 100,000	2.5	9.8	31.9	198.9	784.7	1051.1	223.5
71 CRIMES	3	8	29	149	610	898	159
RATE PER 100,000	3.7	9.8	35.6	183.0	749.0	1102.7	195.2

RATIO FOR 2 YEAR PERIOD   1 CRIME PER   43.6 PEOPLE

RANKING   92

GARY,INDIANA

POPULATION   175,415

	MURDER	FORCED RAPE	ROB- BERY	AGGRYTD ASSAULT	BUR- GLARY	LARCENY +$50	AUTO THEFT
70 CRIMES	52	103	929	467	3,412	2,285	4,224
RATE PER 100,000	29.6	58.7	529.6	266.2	1945.1	1302.6	2408.0
71 CRIMES	52	87	1,396	436	4,723	2,040	2,982
RATE PER 100,000	29.6	49.6	795.8	248.6	2692.5	1163.0	1700.0

RATIO FOR 2 YEAR PERIOD   1 CRIME   PER   15.1 PEOPLE

RANKING   373

GLENDALE,CALIFORNIA

POPULATION   132,752

	MURDER	FORCED RAPE	ROB- BERY	AGGRYTD ASSAULT	BUR- GLARY	LARCENY +$50	AUTO THEFT
70 CRIMES	4	22	114	101	1,696	1,274	770
RATE PER 100,000	3.0	16.6	85.9	76.1	1277.6	959.7	580.0
71 CRIMES	1	19	169	116	1,905	1,532	804
RATE PER 100,000	0.8	14.3	127.3	87.4	1435.0	1154.0	605.6

RATIO FOR 2 YEAR PERIOD   1 CRIME   PER   31.1 PEOPLE

RANKING   168

GRAND PRAIRIE,TEXAS

POPULATION   50,904

	MURDER	FORCED RAPE	ROB- BERY	AGGRYTD ASSAULT	BUR- GLARY	LARCENY +$50	AUTO THEFT
70 CRIMES	6	7	33	83	678	681	212
RATE PER 100,000	11.8	13.8	64.8	163.1	1331.9	1337.8	416.5
71 CRIMES	3	19	26	112	546	565	182
RATE PER 100,000	5.9	37.3	51.1	220.0	1072.6	1109.9	357.5

RATIO FOR 2 YEAR PERIOD   1 CRIME   PER   32.2 PEOPLE

RANKING   155

GRAND RAPIDS,MICHIGAN

POPULATION   197,649

	MURDER	FORCED RAPE	ROB-BERY	AGGRYTD ASSAULT	BUR-GLARY	LARCENY +$50	AUTO THEFT
70 CRIMES	14	103	376	471	3,737	1,964	757
RATE PER 100,000	7.1	52.1	190.2	238.3	1890.7	993.7	383.0
71 CRIMES	17	71	262	510	3,601	1,610	592
RATE PER 100,000	8.6	35.9	132.6	258.0	1821.9	814.6	299.5

RATIO FOR 2 YEAR PERIOD   1 CRIME PER   28.0 PEOPLE

RANKING   213

GREAT FALLS,MONTANA

POPULATION   60,091

	MURDER	FORCED RAPE	ROB-BERY	AGGRYTD ASSAULT	BUR-GLARY	LARCENY +$50	AUTO THEFT
70 CRIMES	11	40	58	620	529	315
RATE PER 100,000	0.0	18.3	66.6	96.5	1031.8	880.3	524.2
71 CRIMES	2	8	40	42	720	559	287
RATE PER 100,000	3.3	13.3	66.6	69.9	1198.2	930.3	477.6

RATIO FOR 2 YEAR PERIOD   1 CRIME PER   37.1 PEOPLE

RANKING   115

GREEN BAY,WISCONSIN

POPULATION   87,809

	MURDER	FORCED RAPE	ROB-BERY	AGGRYTD ASSAULT	BUR-GLARY	LARCENY +$50	AUTO THEFT
70 CRIMES			8	5	537	490	156
RATE PER 100,000	0.0	0.0	9.1	5.7	611.6	558.0	177.7
71 CRIMES	1	1	11	7	472	565	101
RATE PER 100,000	1.1	1.1	12.5	8.0	537.5	643.4	115.0

RATIO FOR 2 YEAR PERIOD   1 CRIME PER   74.6 PEOPLE

RANKING   13

GREENSBORO,NORTH CAROLINA

POPULATION 144,076

	MURDER	FORCED RAPE	ROB- BERY	AGGRYTD ASSAULT	BUR- GLARY	LARCENY +$50	AUTO THEFT
70 CRIMES	18	24	200	974	1,906	1,979	522
RATE PER 100,000	12.5	16.7	138.8	676.0	1322.9	1373.6	362.3
71 CRIMES	14	24	166	1,134	1,527	1,642	473
RATE PER 100,000	9.7	16.7	115.2	787.1	1059.9	1139.7	328.3

RATIO FOR 2 YEAR PERIOD 1 CRIME PER 27.1 PEOPLE

RANKING 222

GREENVILLE,SOUTH CAROLINA

POPULATION 61,208

	MURDER	FORCED RAPE	ROB- BERY	AGGRYTD ASSAULT	BUR- GLARY	LARCENY +$50	AUTO THEFT
70 CRIMES	23	25	238	243	1,415	1,359	634
RATE PER 100,000	37.6	40.8	388.8	397.0	2311.8	2220.3	1035.8
71 CRIMES	23	24	179	269	1,412	1,422	541
RATE PER 100,000	37.6	39.2	292.4	439.5	2306.9	2323.2	883.9

RATIO FOR 2 YEAR PERIOD 1 CRIME PER 15.6 PEOPLE

RANKING 364

GREENWICH,CONNECTICUT

POPULATION 59,755

	MURDER	FORCED RAPE	ROB- BERY	AGGRYTD ASSAULT	BUR- GLARY	LARCENY +$50	AUTO THEFT
70 CRIMES		1	12	12	255	250	100
RATE PER 100,000	0.0	1.7	20.1	20.1	426.7	418.4	167.4
71 CRIMES			11	13	245	391	126
RATE PER 100,000	0.0	0.0	18.4	21.8	410.0	654.3	210.9

RATIO FOR 2 YEAR PERIOD 1 CRIME PER 84.3 PEOPLE

RANKING 8

HAMILTON,OHIO

POPULATION   67,865

	MURDER	FORCED RAPE	ROB-BERY	AGGRVTD ASSAULT	BUR-GLARY	LARCENY +$50	AUTO THEFT
70 CRIMES	5	9	71	251	500	1,042	189
RATE PER 100,000	7.4	13.3	104.6	369.9	736.8	1535.4	278.5
71 CRIMES	1	16	113	244	698	1,160	182
RATE PER 100,000	1.5	23.6	166.5	359.5	1028.5	1709.3	268.2

RATIO FOR 2 YEAR PERIOD   1 CRIME PER   30.2 PEOPLE

RANKING   183

HAMMOND,INDIANA

POPULATION   107,790

	MURDER	FORCED RAPE	ROB-BERY	AGGRVTD ASSAULT	BUR-GLARY	LARCENY +$50	AUTO THEFT
70 CRIMES	9	25	223	221	934	1,602	1,423
RATE PER 100,000	8.3	23.2	206.9	205.0	866.5	1486.2	1320.2
71 CRIMES	7	49	298	172	1,044	1,947	1,469
RATE PER 100,000	6.5	45.5	276.5	159.6	968.5	1806.3	1362.8

RATIO FOR 2 YEAR PERIOD   1 CRIME PER   22.8 PEOPLE

RANKING   280

HAMPTON,VIRGINIA

POPULATION   120,779

	MURDER	FORCED RAPE	ROB-BERY	AGGRVTD ASSAULT	BUR-GLARY	LARCENY +$50	AUTO THEFT
70 CRIMES	6	27	94	99	994	1,107	213
RATE PER 100,000	5.0	22.4	77.8	82.0	823.0	916.6	176.4
71 CRIMES	6	20	78	120	1,232	1,004	238
RATE PER 100,000	5.0	16.6	64.6	99.4	1020.0	831.3	197.1

RATIO FOR 2 YEAR PERIOD   1 CRIME PER   46.1 PEOPLE

RANKING   83

HARRISBURG,PENNSYLVANIA

POPULATION   68,061

	MURDER	FORCED RAPE	ROB- BERY	AGGRYTD ASSAULT	BUR- GLARY	LARCENY +$50	AUTO THEFT
70 CRIMES	8	16	273	252	1,212	567	450
RATE PER 100,000	11.8	23.5	401.1	370.3	1780.8	833.1	661.2
71 CRIMES	11	24	308	304	1,000	889	416
RATE PER 100,000	16.2	35.3	452.5	446.7	1469.3	1306.2	611.2

RATIO FOR 2 YEAR PERIOD   1 CRIME PER   23.7 PEOPLE

RANKING   267

HARTFORD,CONNECTICUT

POPULATION   158,017

	MURDER	FORCED RAPE	ROB- BERY	AGGRYTD ASSAULT	BUR- GLARY	LARCENY +$50	AUTO THEFT
70 CRIMES	25	28	553	630	2,885	2,602	2,582
RATE PER 100,000	15.8	17.7	350.0	398.7	1825.8	1646.7	1634.0
71 CRIMES	23	40	574	662	2,507	1,777	2,642
RATE PER 100,000	14.6	25.3	363.3	418.9	1586.5	1124.6	1672.0

RATIO FOR 2 YEAR PERIOD   1 CRIME PER   18.0 PEOPLE

RANKING   336

HAWTHORNE,CALIFORNIA

POPULATION   53,304

	MURDER	FORCED RAPE	ROB- BERY	AGGRYTD ASSAULT	BUR- GLARY	LARCENY +$50	AUTO THEFT
70 CRIMES	1	7	96	54	735	829	471
RATE PER 100,000	1.9	13.1	180.1	101.3	1378.9	1555.2	883.6
71 CRIMES	1	11	157	78	790	888	497
RATE PER 100,000	1.9	20.6	294.5	146.3	1482.1	1665.9	932.4

RATIO FOR 2 YEAR PERIOD   1 CRIME PER   23.1 PEOPLE

RANKING   276

HAYWARD, CALIFORNIA

POPULATION   93,058

	MURDER	FORCED RAPE	ROB- BERY	AGGRVTD ASSAULT	BUR- GLARY	LARCENY +$50	AUTO THEFT
70 CRIMES		18	140	166	1,664	2,284	756
RATE PER 100,000	0.0	19.3	150.4	178.4	1788.1	2454.4	812.4
71 CRIMES	6	14	191	205	1,615	2,083	925
RATE PER 100,000	6.4	15.0	205.2	220.3	1735.5	2238.4	994.0

RATIO FOR 2 YEAR PERIOD   1 CRIME PER   18.4 PEOPLE

RANKING   331

HIALEAH, FLORIDA

POPULATION   102,297

	MURDER	FORCED RAPE	ROB- BERY	AGGRVTD ASSAULT	BUR- GLARY	LARCENY +$50	AUTO THEFT
70 CRIMES	5	9	173	169	1,407	1,941	589
RATE PER 100,000	4.9	8.8	169.1	165.2	1375.4	1897.4	575.8
71 CRIMES	8	12	190	199	1,484	2,126	650
RATE PER 100,000	7.8	11.7	185.7	194.5	1450.7	2078.3	635.4

RATIO FOR 2 YEAR PERIOD   1 CRIME PER   22.8 PEOPLE

RANKING   281

HIGH POINT, NORTH CAROLINA

POPULATION   63,204

	MURDER	FORCED RAPE	ROB- BERY	AGGRVTD ASSAULT	BUR- GLARY	LARCENY +$50	AUTO THEFT
70 CRIMES	10	7	34	49	772	880	139
RATE PER 100,000	15.8	11.1	53.8	77.5	1221.4	1392.3	219.9
71 CRIMES	14	6	35	62	825	803	177
RATE PER 100,000	22.2	9.5	55.4	98.1	1305.3	1270.5	280.0

RATIO FOR 2 YEAR PERIOD   1 CRIME PER   33.1 PEOPLE

RANKING   143

HOLLYWOOD,FLORIDA

POPULATION   106,873

	MURDER	FORCED RAPE	ROB-BERY	AGGRYTD ASSAULT	BUR-GLARY	LARCENY +$50	AUTO THEFT
70 CRIMES	10	18	198	176	2,039	1,697	875
RATE PER 100,000	9.4	16.8	185.3	164.7	1907.9	1587.9	818.7
71 CRIMES	2	23	232	249	2,204	2,105	871
RATE PER 100,000	1.9	21.5	217.1	233.0	2062.3	1969.6	815.0

RATIO FOR 2 YEAR PERIOD   1 CRIME PER   19.9 PEOPLE

RANKING   314

HOLYOKE,MASSACHUSETTS

POPULATION   50,112

	MURDER	FORCED RAPE	ROB-BERY	AGGRYTD ASSAULT	BUR-GLARY	LARCENY +$50	AUTO THEFT
70 CRIMES	3	6	44	37	1,086	595	632
RATE PER 100,000	6.0	12.0	87.8	73.8	2167.1	1187.3	1261.2
71 CRIMES	2	3	50	27	967	649	600
RATE PER 100,000	4.0	6.0	99.8	53.9	1929.7	1295.1	1197.3

RATIO FOR 2 YEAR PERIOD   1 CRIME PER   21.3 PEOPLE

RANKING   296

HONOLULU,HAWAII

POPULATION   324,871

	MURDER	FORCED RAPE	ROB-BERY	AGGRYTD ASSAULT	BUR-GLARY	LARCENY +$50	AUTO THEFT
70 CRIMES	15	55	368	170	6,875	5,463	3,110
RATE PER 100,000	4.6	16.9	113.3	52.3	2116.2	1681.6	957.3
71 CRIMES	19	74	529	251	6,261	6,123	3,095
RATE PER 100,000	5.8	22.8	162.8	77.3	1927.2	1884.7	952.7

RATIO FOR 2 YEAR PERIOD   1 CRIME PER   20.0 PEOPLE

RANKING   311

HOUSTON,TEXAS

POPULATION   1,232,802

	MURDER	FORCED RAPE	ROB-BERY	AGGRYTD ASSAULT	BUR-GLARY	LARCENY +$50	AUTO THEFT
70 CRIMES	289	411	6,405	2,746	25,626	10,833	13,573
RATE PER 100,000	23.4	33.3	519.5	222.7	2078.7	878.7	1101.0
71 CRIMES	303	530	5,127	2,877	26,219	10,993	12,770
RATE PER 100,000	24.6	43.0	415.9	233.4	2126.8	891.7	1035.9

RATIO FOR 2 YEAR PERIOD   1 CRIME PER   20.7 PEOPLE

RANKING   305

HUNTINGTON,WEST VIRGINIA

POPULATION   74,315

	MURDER	FORCED RAPE	ROB-BERY	AGGRYTD ASSAULT	BUR-GLARY	LARCENY +$50	AUTO THEFT
70 CRIMES	3	16	121	229	964	1,149	253
RATE PER 100,000	4.0	21.5	162.8	308.1	1297.2	1546.1	340.4
71 CRIMES	11	10	137	228	933	998	315
RATE PER 100,000	14.8	13.5	184.4	306.8	1255.5	1342.9	423.9

RATIO FOR 2 YEAR PERIOD   1 CRIME PER   27.6 PEOPLE

RANKING   216

HUNTINGTON BEACH,CALIFORNIA

POPULATION   115,960

	MURDER	FORCED RAPE	ROB-BERY	AGGRYTD ASSAULT	BUR-GLARY	LARCENY +$50	AUTO THEFT
70 CRIMES	7	28	58	106	1,623	1,845	406
RATE PER 100,000	6.0	24.1	50.0	91.4	1399.6	1591.1	350.1
71 CRIMES	7	47	83	156	1,867	2,349	424
RATE PER 100,000	6.0	40.5	71.6	134.5	1610.0	2025.7	365.6

RATIO FOR 2 YEAR PERIOD   1 CRIME PER   25.7 PEOPLE

RANKING   238

224

HUNTSVILLE,ALABAMA

POPULATION   137,802

	MURDER	FORCED RAPE	ROB- BERY	AGGRYTD ASSAULT	BUR- GLARY	LARCENY +$50	AUTO THEFT
70 CRIMES	4	32	132	248	2,218	2,241	582
RATE PER 100,000	2.9	23.2	95.8	180.0	1609.6	1626.2	422.3
71 CRIMES	21	27	106	267	2,159	2,007	608
RATE PER 100,000	15.2	19.6	76.9	193.8	1566.7	1456.4	441.2

RATIO FOR 2 YEAR PERIOD   1 CRIME PER   25.8 PEOPLE

RANKING   235

INDEPENDENCE,MISSOURI

POPULATION   111,662

	MURDER	FORCED RAPE	ROB- BERY	AGGRYTD ASSAULT	BUR- GLARY	LARCENY +$50	AUTO THEFT
70 CRIMES	3	15	45	170	801	692	224
RATE PER 100,000	2.7	13.4	40.3	152.2	717.3	619.7	200.6
71 CRIMES	4	15	50	155	868	713	213
RATE PER 100,000	3.6	13.4	44.8	138.8	777.3	638.5	190.8

RATIO FOR 2 YEAR PERIOD   1 CRIME PER   56.2 PEOPLE

RANKING   47

INDIANAPOLIS,INDIANA

POPULATION   744,624

	MURDER	FORCED RAPE	ROB- BERY	AGGRYTD ASSAULT	BUR- GLARY	LARCENY +$50	AUTO THEFT
70 CRIMES	60	253	2,073	1,205	10,309	6,063	5,314
RATE PER 100,000	8.1	34.0	278.4	161.8	1384.5	814.2	713.6
71 CRIMES	60	264	2,109	927	9,480	5,537	4,497
RATE PER 100,000	8.1	35.5	283.2	124.5	1273.1	743.6	603.9

RATIO FOR 2 YEAR PERIOD   1 CRIME PER   30.9 PEOPLE

RANKING   174

INGLEWOOD,CALIFORNIA

POPULATION   89,985

	MURDER	FORCED RAPE	ROB-BERY	AGGRYTD ASSAULT	BUR-GLARY	LARCENY +$50	AUTO THEFT
70 CRIMES	4	19	461	120	1,622	1,681	1,251
RATE PER 100,000	4.4	21.1	512.3	133.4	1802.5	1868.1	1390.2
71 CRIMES	7	33	589	165	1,984	1,684	1,468
RATE PER 100,000	7.8	36.7	654.6	183.4	2204.8	1871.4	1631.4

RATIO FOR 2 YEAR PERIOD   1 CRIME PER   16.2 PEOPLE

RANKING   357

IRVING,TEXAS

POPULATION   97,260

	MURDER	FORCED RAPE	ROB-BERY	AGGRYTD ASSAULT	BUR-GLARY	LARCENY +$50	AUTO THEFT
70 CRIMES	8	15	40	190	799	1,045	316
RATE PER 100,000	8.2	15.4	41.1	195.4	821.5	1074.4	324.9
71 CRIMES	1	18	30	126	863	998	293
RATE PER 100,000	1.0	18.5	30.8	129.5	887.3	1026.1	301.3

RATIO FOR 2 YEAR PERIOD   1 CRIME PER   41.0 PEOPLE

RANKING   99

IRVINGTON,NEW JERSEY

POPULATION   59,743

	MURDER	FORCED RAPE	ROB-BERY	AGGRYTD ASSAULT	BUR-GLARY	LARCENY +$50	AUTO THEFT
70 CRIMES	2	3	114	38	738	491	399
RATE PER 100,000	3.3	5.0	190.8	63.6	1235.3	821.9	667.9
71 CRIMES	5	9	187	59	708	561	382
RATE PER 100,000	8.4	15.1	313.0	98.8	1185.1	939.0	639.4

RATIO FOR 2 YEAR PERIOD   1 CRIME PER   32.3 PEOPLE

RANKING   154

JACKSON,MISSISSIPPI

POPULATION   153,968

	MURDER	FORCED RAPE	ROB-BERY	AGGRVTD ASSAULT	BUR-GLARY	LARCENY +$50	AUTO THEFT
70 CRIMES	29	13	87	138	1,750	1,162	456
RATE PER 100,000	18.8	8.4	56.5	89.6	1136.6	754.7	296.2
71 CRIMES	29	68	185	280	1,998	1,435	640
RATE PER 100,000	18.8	44.2	120.2	181.9	1297.7	932.0	415.7

RATIO FOR 2 YEAR PERIOD   1 CRIME PER   37.2 PEOPLE

RANKING   113

JACKSONVILLE,FLORIDA

POPULATION   528,865

	MURDER	FORCED RAPE	ROB-BERY	AGGRVTD ASSAULT	BUR-GLARY	LARCENY +$50	AUTO THEFT
70 CRIMES	95	296	1,507	2,211	11,568	6,602	2,944
RATE PER 100,000	18.0	56.0	284.9	418.1	2187.3	1248.3	556.7
71 CRIMES	82	254	1,264	1,941	12,035	6,048	2,547
RATE PER 100,000	15.5	48.0	239.0	367.0	2275.6	1143.6	481.6

RATIO FOR 2 YEAR PERIOD   1 CRIME PER   21.4 PEOPLE

RANKING   295

JERSEY CITY,NEW JERSEY

POPULATION   260,545

	MURDER	FORCED RAPE	ROB-BERY	AGGRVTD ASSAULT	BUR-GLARY	LARCENY +$50	AUTO THEFT
70 CRIMES	36	45	866	357	1,815	417	4,154
RATE PER 100,000	13.8	17.3	332.4	137.0	696.6	160.0	1594.4
71 CRIMES	40	51	1,629	442	3,146	803	5,103
RATE PER 100,000	15.4	19.6	625.2	169.6	1207.5	308.2	1958.6

RATIO FOR 2 YEAR PERIOD   1 CRIME PER   27.5 PEOPLE

RANKING   219

JOLIET,ILLINOIS

POPULATION 80,378

	MURDER	FORCED RAPE	ROB- BERY	AGGRYTD ASSAULT	BUR- GLARY	LARCENY +$50	AUTO THEFT
70 CRIMES	7	24	157	143	808	1,084	365
RATE PER 100,000	8.7	29.9	195.3	177.9	1005.3	1348.6	454.1
71 CRIMES	9	18	191	242	910	995	282
RATE PER 100,000	11.2	22.4	237.6	301.1	1132.2	1237.9	350.8

RATIO FOR 2 YEAR PERIOD 1 CRIME PER 30.7 PEOPLE

RANKING 177

KALAMAZOO,MICHIGAN

POPULATION 85,555

	MURDER	FORCED RAPE	ROB- BERY	AGGRYTD ASSAULT	BUR- GLARY	LARCENY +$50	AUTO THEFT
70 CRIMES	5	17	188	618	1,558	1,645	318
RATE PER 100,000	5.8	19.9	219.7	722.3	1821.1	1922.7	371.7
71 CRIMES	3	15	209	617	1,423	2,037	252
RATE PER 100,000	3.5	17.5	244.3	721.2	1663.3	2380.9	294.5

RATIO FOR 2 YEAR PERIOD 1 CRIME PER 19.2 PEOPLE

RANKING 324

KANSAS CITY,KANSAS

POPULATION 168,213

	MURDER	FORCED RAPE	ROB- BERY	AGGRYTD ASSAULT	BUR- GLARY	LARCENY +$50	AUTO THEFT
70 CRIMES	18	104	576	485	3,797	965	1,905
RATE PER 100,000	10.7	61.8	342.4	288.3	2257.3	573.7	1132.5
71 CRIMES	34	85	461	572	3,618	923	1,637
RATE PER 100,000	20.2	50.5	274.1	340.0	2150.8	548.7	973.2

RATIO FOR 2 YEAR PERIOD 1 CRIME PER 22.1 PEOPLE

RANKING 289

KANSAS CITY,MISSOURI

POPULATION   507,087

	MURDER	FORCED RAPE	ROB- BERY	AGGRYTD ASSAULT	BUR- GLARY	LARCENY +$50	AUTO THEFT
70 CRIMES	120	401	2,982	1,921	11,265	6,736	5,570
RATE PER 100,000	23.7	79.1	588.1	378.8	2221.5	1328.4	1098.4
71 CRIMES	103	371	2,473	1,805	11,550	6,154	5,408
RATE PER 100,000	20.3	73.2	487.7	356.0	2277.7	1213.6	1066.5

RATIO FOR 2 YEAR PERIOD   1 CRIME PER   17.8 PEOPLE

RANKING   338

KENOSHA,WISCONSIN

POPULATION   78,805

	MURDER	FORCED RAPE	ROB- BERY	AGGRYTD ASSAULT	BUR- GLARY	LARCENY +$50	AUTO THEFT
70 CRIMES	2	3	97	47	547	664	362
RATE PER 100,000	2.5	3.8	123.1	59.6	694.1	842.6	459.4
71 CRIMES	6	15	92	111	764	782	478
RATE PER 100,000	7.6	19.0	116.7	140.9	969.5	992.3	606.6

RATIO FOR 2 YEAR PERIOD   1 CRIME PER   39.7 PEOPLE

RANKING   103

KETTERING,OHIO

POPULATION   69,599

	MURDER	FORCED RAPE	ROB- BERY	AGGRYTD ASSAULT	BUR- GLARY	LARCENY +$50	AUTO THEFT
70 CRIMES		6	38	35	515	385	139
RATE PER 100,000	0.0	8.6	54.6	50.3	740.0	553.2	199.7
71 CRIMES		1	25	54	416	327	100
RATE PER 100,000	0.0	1.4	35.9	77.6	597.7	469.8	143.7

RATIO FOR 2 YEAR PERIOD   1 CRIME PER   68.2 PEOPLE

RANKING   19

KNOXVILLE,TENNESSEE

POPULATION 174,587

70 CRIMES	MURDER	FORCED RAPE	ROB-BERY	AGGRYTD ASSAULT	BUR-GLARY	LARCENY +$50	AUTO THEFT
70 CRIMES	19	22	194	467	2,347	1,360	1,250
RATE PER 100,000	10.9	12.6	111.1	267.5	1344.3	779.0	716.0
71 CRIMES	28	11	156	298	2,289	1,307	1,353
RATE PER 100,000	16.0	6.3	89.4	170.7	1311.1	748.6	775.0

RATIO FOR 2 YEAR PERIOD   1 CRIME PER   31.4 PEOPLE

RANKING   164

LA CROSSE,WISCONSIN

POPULATION 51,153

70 CRIMES	MURDER	FORCED RAPE	ROB-BERY	AGGRYTD ASSAULT	BUR-GLARY	LARCENY +$50	AUTO THEFT
70 CRIMES			7	2	321	381	110
RATE PER 100,000	0.0	0.0	13.7	3.9	627.5	744.8	215.0
71 CRIMES	2		5	1	302	362	103
RATE PER 100,000	3.9	0.0	9.8	2.0	590.4	707.7	201.4

RATIO FOR 2 YEAR PERIOD   1 CRIME PER   64.1 PEOPLE

RANKING   30

LAFAYETTE,LOUISIANA

POPULATION 68,908

70 CRIMES	MURDER	FORCED RAPE	ROB-BERY	AGGRYTD ASSAULT	BUR-GLARY	LARCENY +$50	AUTO THEFT
70 CRIMES	5	18	93	233	1,214	646	290
RATE PER 100,000	7.3	26.1	135.0	338.1	1761.8	937.5	420.9
71 CRIMES	6	12	92	172	1,120	545	204
RATE PER 100,000	8.7	17.4	133.5	249.6	1625.4	790.9	296.0

RATIO FOR 2 YEAR PERIOD   1 CRIME PER   29.6 PEOPLE

RANKING   195

230

LAKE CHARLES,LOUISIANA

POPULATION   77,998

	MURDER	FORCED RAPE	ROB- BERY	AGGRYTD ASSAULT	BUR- GLARY	LARCENY +$50	AUTO THEFT
70 CRIMES	10	7	54	61	726	498	147
RATE PER 100,000	12.8	9.0	69.2	78.2	930.8	638.5	188.5
71 CRIMES	9	8	45	57	758	527	135
RATE PER 100,000	11.5	10.3	57.7	73.1	971.8	675.7	173.1

RATIO FOR 2 YEAR PERIOD   1 CRIME PER   51.2 PEOPLE

RANKING   63

LAKEWOOD,CALIFORNIA

POPULATION   82,973

	MURDER	FORCED RAPE	ROB- BERY	AGGRYTD ASSAULT	BUR- GLARY	LARCENY +$50	AUTO THEFT
70 CRIMES							
RATE PER 100,000							
71 CRIMES	1	8	107	102	992	1,272	475
RATE PER 100,000	1.2	9.6	129.0	122.9	1195.6	1533.0	572.5

RATIO FOR 2 YEAR PERIOD   1 CRIME PER   56.1 PEOPLE

RANKING   48

LAKEWOOD,COLORADO

POPULATION   92,787

	MURDER	FORCED RAPE	ROB- BERY	AGGRYTD ASSAULT	BUR- GLARY	LARCENY +$50	AUTO THEFT
70 CRIMES							
RATE PER 100,000							
71 CRIMES	1	21	97	100	1,417	1,715	642
RATE PER 100,000	1.1	22.6	104.5	107.8	1527.2	1848.3	691.9

RATIO FOR 2 YEAR PERIOD   1 CRIME PER   46.4 PEOPLE

RANKING   82

LAKEWOOD,OHIO

POPULATION   70,173

	MURDER	FORCED RAPE	ROB- BERY	AGGRYTD ASSAULT	BUR- GLARY	LARCENY +$50	AUTO THEFT
70 CRIMES	1	2	23	21	182	30	241
RATE PER 100,000	1.4	2.9	32.8	29.9	259.4	42.8	343.4
71 CRIMES		1	25	19	149	52	284
RATE PER 100,000	0.0	1.4	35.6	27.1	212.3	74.1	404.7

RATIO FOR 2 YEAR PERIOD   1 CRIME PER   136.2 PEOPLE

RANKING   1

LANCASTER,PENNSYLVANIA

POPULATION   57,690

	MURDER	FORCED RAPE	ROB- BERY	AGGRYTD ASSAULT	BUR- GLARY	LARCENY +$50	AUTO THEFT
70 CRIMES	1	10	54	46	435	433	98
RATE PER 100,000	1.7	17.3	93.6	79.7	754.0	750.6	169.9
71 CRIMES	4	6	90	52	544	524	122
RATE PER 100,000	6.9	10.4	156.0	90.1	943.0	908.3	211.5

RATIO FOR 2 YEAR PERIOD   1 CRIME PER   47.6 PEOPLE

RANKING   79

LANSING,MICHIGAN

POPULATION   131,546

	MURDER	FORCED RAPE	ROB- BERY	AGGRYTD ASSAULT	BUR- GLARY	LARCENY +$50	AUTO THEFT
70 CRIMES	7	29	247	296	3,512	3,217	660
RATE PER 100,000	5.3	22.0	187.8	225.0	2669.8	2445.5	501.7
71 CRIMES	4	33	274	270	3,977	3,074	646
RATE PER 100,000	3.0	25.1	208.3	205.3	3023.3	2336.8	491.1

RATIO FOR 2 YEAR PERIOD   1 CRIME PER   16.1 PEOPLE

RANKING   358

LAREDO, TEXAS

POPULATION 69,024

	MURDER	FORCED RAPE	ROB- BERY	AGGRYTD ASSAULT	BUR- GLARY	LARCENY +$50	AUTO THEFT
70 CRIMES	1	1	14	55	699	398	138
RATE PER 100,000	1.4	1.4	20.3	79.7	1012.7	576.6	199.9
71 CRIMES	1	2	14	46	781	291	155
RATE PER 100,000	1.4	2.9	20.3	66.6	1131.5	421.6	224.6

RATIO FOR 2 YEAR PERIOD   1 CRIME PER   53.1 PEOPLE

RANKING   55

LAS VEGAS, NEVADA

POPULATION 125,787

	MURDER	FORCED RAPE	ROB- BERY	AGGRYTD ASSAULT	BUR- GLARY	LARCENY +$50	AUTO THEFT
70 CRIMES	17	20	311	138	1,971	947	927
RATE PER 100,000	13.5	15.9	247.2	109.7	1566.9	752.9	737.0
71 CRIMES	21	23	326	195	2,140	1,064	928
RATE PER 100,000	16.7	18.3	259.2	155.0	1701.3	845.9	737.8

RATIO FOR 2 YEAR PERIOD   1 CRIME PER   27.8 PEOPLE

RANKING   215

LAWRENCE, MASSACHUSETTS

POPULATION 66,915

	MURDER	FORCED RAPE	ROB- BERY	AGGRYTD ASSAULT	BUR- GLARY	LARCENY +$50	AUTO THEFT
70 CRIMES	2	1	37	35	690	337	860
RATE PER 100,000	3.0	1.5	55.3	52.3	1031.2	503.6	1285.2
71 CRIMES	2	3	30	68	991	410	1,296
RATE PER 100,000	3.0	4.5	44.8	101.6	1481.0	612.7	1936.8

RATIO FOR 2 YEAR PERIOD   1 CRIME PER   28.1 PEOPLE

RANKING   212

LAWTON,OKLAHOMA

POPULATION   74,470

	MURDER	FORCED RAPE	ROB-BERY	AGGRYTD ASSAULT	BUR-GLARY	LARCENY +$50	AUTO THEFT
70 CRIMES	5	32	120	310	1,205	1,239	227
RATE PER 100,000	6.7	43.0	161.1	416.3	1618.1	1663.8	304.8
71 CRIMES	3	54	152	357	1,269	1,191	316
RATE PER 100,000	4.0	72.5	204.1	479.4	1704.0	1599.3	424.3

RATIO FOR 2 YEAR PERIOD   1 CRIME PER   22.9 PEOPLE

RANKING   279

LEXINGTON,KENTUCKY

POPULATION   108,137

	MURDER	FORCED RAPE	ROB-BERY	AGGRYTD ASSAULT	BUR-GLARY	LARCENY +$50	AUTO THEFT
70 CRIMES	13	27	137	205	1,857	2,233	565
RATE PER 100,000	12.0	25.0	126.7	189.6	1717.3	2065.0	522.5
71 CRIMES	16	28	158	293	1,925	2,498	494
RATE PER 100,000	14.8	25.9	146.1	271.0	1780.1	2310.0	456.8

RATIO FOR 2 YEAR PERIOD   1 CRIME PER   20.6 PEOPLE

RANKING   307

LIMA,OHIO

POPULATION   53,734

	MURDER	FORCED RAPE	ROB-BERY	AGGRYTD ASSAULT	BUR-GLARY	LARCENY +$50	AUTO THEFT
70 CRIMES	1	5	140	41	787	784	130
RATE PER 100,000	1.9	9.3	260.5	76.3	1464.6	1459.0	241.9
71 CRIMES	7	2	138	33	889	666	117
RATE PER 100,000	13.0	3.7	256.8	61.4	1654.4	1239.4	217.7

RATIO FOR 2 YEAR PERIOD   1 CRIME PER   28.7 PEOPLE

RANKING   206

234

LINCOLN,NEBRASKA

POPULATION   149,518

	MURDER	FORCED RAPE	ROB- BERY	AGGRYTD ASSAULT	BUR- GLARY	LARCENY +$50	AUTO THEFT
70 CRIMES	1	19	45	256	718	1,515	292
RATE PER 100,000	0.7	12.7	30.1	171.2	480.2	1013.3	195.3
71 CRIMES	3	26	24	198	782	1,576	269
RATE PER 100,000	2.0	17.4	16.1	132.4	523.0	1054.1	179.9

RATIO FOR 2 YEAR PERIOD   1 CRIME PER   52.2 PEOPLE

RANKING   57

LINCOLN PARK,MICHIGAN

POPULATION   52,984

	MURDER	FORCED RAPE	ROB- BERY	AGGRYTD ASSAULT	BUR- GLARY	LARCENY +$50	AUTO THEFT
70 CRIMES	1	13	81	65	440	1,062	361
RATE PER 100,000	1.9	24.5	152.9	122.7	830.4	2004.4	681.3
71 CRIMES	1	11	79	70	517	995	324
RATE PER 100,000	1.9	20.8	149.1	132.1	975.8	1877.9	611.5

RATIO FOR 2 YEAR PERIOD   1 CRIME PER   26.3 PEOPLE

RANKING   232

LITTLE ROCK,ARKANSAS

POPULATION   132,483

	MURDER	FORCED RAPE	ROB- BERY	AGGRYTD ASSAULT	BUR- GLARY	LARCENY +$50	AUTO THEFT
70 CRIMES	38	79	300	702	2,950	2,973	465
RATE PER 100,000	28.7	59.6	226.4	529.9	2226.7	2244.1	351.0
71 CRIMES	36	60	368	634	2,460	2,722	498
RATE PER 100,000	27.2	45.3	277.8	478.6	1856.8	2054.6	375.9

RATIO FOR 2 YEAR PERIOD   1 CRIME PER   18.5 PEOPLE

RANKING   330

LIVONIA,MICHIGAN

POPULATION   110,109

	MURDER	FORCED RAPE	ROB- BERY	AGGRYTD ASSAULT	BUR- GLARY	LARCENY +$50	AUTO THEFT
70 CRIMES	5	19	45	112	1,640	1,074	324
RATE PER 100,000	4.5	17.3	40.9	101.7	1489.4	975.4	294.3
71 CRIMES	2	11	76	108	1,569	1,016	289
RATE PER 100,000	1.8	10.0	69.0	98.1	1425.0	922.7	262.5

RATIO FOR 2 YEAR PERIOD   1 CRIME PER   35.0 PEOPLE

RANKING   129

LONG BEACH,CALIFORNIA

POPULATION   358,633

	MURDER	FORCED RAPE	ROB- BERY	AGGRYTD ASSAULT	BUR- GLARY	LARCENY +$50	AUTO THEFT
70 CRIMES	29	134	1,194	572	6,471	4,118	3,177
RATE PER 100,000	8.1	37.4	332.9	159.5	1804.4	1148.2	885.9
71 CRIMES	31	130	1,480	697	7,223	4,071	3,452
RATE PER 100,000	8.6	36.2	412.7	194.3	2014.0	1135.1	962.5

RATIO FOR 2 YEAR PERIOD   1 CRIME PER   21.8 PEOPLE

RANKING   292

LORAIN,OHIO

POPULATION   78,185

	MURDER	FORCED RAPE	ROB- BERY	AGGRYTD ASSAULT	BUR- GLARY	LARCENY +$50	AUTO THEFT
70 CRIMES	3	22	141	135	835	759	759
RATE PER 100,000	3.8	28.1	180.3	172.7	1068.0	970.8	970.8
71 CRIMES	5	28	112	119	1,028	762	470
RATE PER 100,000	6.4	35.8	143.2	152.2	1314.8	974.6	601.1

RATIO FOR 2 YEAR PERIOD   1 CRIME PER   30.1 PEOPLE

RANKING   184

LOS ANGELES, CALIFORNIA

POPULATION 2,816,061

	MURDER	FORCED RAPE	ROB- BERY	AGGRYTD ASSAULT	BUR- GLARY	LARCENY +$50	AUTO THEFT
70 CRIMES	395	1,988	12,695	14,826	67,993	43,876	33,946
RATE PER 100,000	14.0	70.6	450.8	526.5	2414.5	1558.1	1205.4
71 CRIMES	427	2,062	14,147	14,674	74,812	41,506	36,239
RATE PER 100,000	15.2	73.2	502.4	521.1	2656.6	1473.9	1286.9

RATIO FOR 2 YEAR PERIOD 1 CRIME PER 15.6 PEOPLE

RANKING 365

LOUISVILLE, KENTUCKY

POPULATION 361,472

	MURDER	FORCED RAPE	ROB- BERY	AGGRYTD ASSAULT	BUR- GLARY	LARCENY +$50	AUTO THEFT
70 CRIMES	89	78	1,332	718	5,399	6,024	5,780
RATE PER 100,000	24.6	21.6	368.5	198.6	1493.6	1666.5	1599.0
71 CRIMES	84	85	1,453	527	5,035	4,804	5,579
RATE PER 100,000	23.2	23.5	402.0	145.8	1392.9	1329.0	1543.4

RATIO FOR 2 YEAR PERIOD 1 CRIME PER 19.5 PEOPLE

RANKING 319

LOWELL, MASSACHUSETTS

POPULATION 94,239

	MURDER	FORCED RAPE	ROB- BERY	AGGRYTD ASSAULT	BUR- GLARY	LARCENY +$50	AUTO THEFT
70 CRIMES	3	10	53	56	773	720	1,005
RATE PER 100,000	3.2	10.6	56.2	59.4	820.3	764.0	1066.4
71 CRIMES	4	10	54	53	1,087	638	1,361
RATE PER 100,000	4.2	10.6	57.3	56.2	1153.5	677.0	1444.2

RATIO FOR 2 YEAR PERIOD 1 CRIME PER 32.3 PEOPLE

RANKING 153

LUBBOCK,TEXAS

POPULATION   149,101

	MURDER	FORCED RAPE	ROB- BERY	AGGRYTD ASSAULT	BUR- GLARY	LARCENY +$50	AUTO THEFT
70 CRIMES	13	42	118	571	2,254	2,159	380
RATE PER 100,000	8.7	28.2	79.1	383.0	1511.7	1448.0	254.9
71 CRIMES	28	55	141	565	2,506	2,542	364
RATE PER 100,000	18.8	36.9	94.6	378.9	1680.7	1704.9	244.1

RATIO FOR 2 YEAR PERIOD   1 CRIME PER   25.4 PEOPLE

RANKING   244

LYNCHBURG,VIRGINIA

POPULATION   54,083

	MURDER	FORCED RAPE	ROB- BERY	AGGRYTD ASSAULT	BUR- GLARY	LARCENY +$50	AUTO THEFT
70 CRIMES	8	4	40	66	397	283	45
RATE PER 100,000	14.8	7.4	74.0	122.0	734.1	523.3	83.2
71 CRIMES	4	17	50	48	493	296	54
RATE PER 100,000	7.4	31.4	92.5	88.8	911.6	547.3	99.8

RATIO FOR 2 YEAR PERIOD   1 CRIME PER   59.9 PEOPLE

RANKING   37

LYNN,MASSACHUSETTS

POPULATION   90,294

	MURDER	FORCED RAPE	ROB- BERY	AGGRYTD ASSAULT	BUR- GLARY	LARCENY +$50	AUTO THEFT
70 CRIMES	3	9	146	139	1,992	800	1,199
RATE PER 100,000	3.3	10.0	161.7	153.9	2206.1	886.0	1327.9
71 CRIMES	2	23	142	308	1,825	1,019	1,070
RATE PER 100,000	2.2	25.5	157.3	341.1	2021.2	1128.5	1185.0

RATIO FOR 2 YEAR PERIOD   1 CRIME PER   20.8 PEOPLE

RANKING   304

238

MACON, GEORGIA

POPULATION 122,423

	MURDER	FORCED RAPE	ROB- BERY	AGGRVTD ASSAULT	BUR- GLARY	LARCENY +$50	AUTO THEFT
70 CRIMES	21	28	210	227	2,454	1,887	979
RATE PER 100,000	17.2	22.9	171.5	185.4	2004.5	1541.4	799.7
71 CRIMES	20	31	299	211	2,653	1,758	1,024
RATE PER 100,000	16.3	25.3	244.2	172.4	2167.1	1436.0	836.4

RATIO FOR 2 YEAR PERIOD   1 CRIME PER   20.7 PEOPLE

RANKING   306

MADISON, WISCONSIN

POPULATION 173,258

	MURDER	FORCED RAPE	ROB- BERY	AGGRVTD ASSAULT	BUR- GLARY	LARCENY +$50	AUTO THEFT
70 CRIMES	3	29	86	28	1,723	2,297	454
RATE PER 100,000	1.7	16.7	49.6	16.2	994.5	1325.8	262.0
71 CRIMES	5	31	60	34	2,302	2,724	564
RATE PER 100,000	2.9	17.9	34.6	19.6	1328.7	1572.2	325.5

RATIO FOR 2 YEAR PERIOD   1 CRIME PER   33.5 PEOPLE

RANKING   138

MALDEN, MASSACHUSETTS

POPULATION 56,127

	MURDER	FORCED RAPE	ROB- BERY	AGGRVTD ASSAULT	BUR- GLARY	LARCENY +$50	AUTO THEFT
70 CRIMES		2	25	8	194	267	333
RATE PER 100,000	0.0	3.6	44.5	14.3	345.6	475.7	593.3
71 CRIMES	3		42	32	278	289	606
RATE PER 100,000	5.3	0.0	74.8	57.0	495.3	514.9	1079.7

RATIO FOR 2 YEAR PERIOD   1 CRIME PER   53.9 PEOPLE

RANKING   51

MANCHESTER, NEW HAMPSHIRE

POPULATION   87,754

	MURDER	FORCED RAPE	ROB-BERY	AGGRYTD ASSAULT	BUR-GLARY	LARCENY +$50	AUTO THEFT
70 CRIMES	2	6	25	32	520	553	152
RATE PER 100,000	2.3	6.8	28.5	36.5	592.6	630.2	173.2
71 CRIMES	1	6	29	38	607	498	157
RATE PER 100,000	1.1	6.8	33.0	43.3	691.7	567.5	178.9

RATIO FOR 2 YEAR PERIOD   1 CRIME PER   66.8 PEOPLE

RANKING   23

MANSFIELD, OHIO

POPULATION   55,047

	MURDER	FORCED RAPE	ROB-BERY	AGGRYTD ASSAULT	BUR-GLARY	LARCENY +$50	AUTO THEFT
70 CRIMES	7	9	70	291	571	765	248
RATE PER 100,000	12.7	16.3	127.2	528.6	1037.3	1389.7	450.5
71 CRIMES	2	18	64	178	507	720	178
RATE PER 100,000	3.6	32.7	116.3	323.4	921.0	1308.0	323.4

RATIO FOR 2 YEAR PERIOD   1 CRIME PER   30.3 PEOPLE

RANKING   181

MEDFORD, MASSACHUSETTS

POPULATION   64,397

	MURDER	FORCED RAPE	ROB-BERY	AGGRYTD ASSAULT	BUR-GLARY	LARCENY +$50	AUTO THEFT
70 CRIMES		3	11	1	277	340	254
RATE PER 100,000	0.0	4.7	17.1	1.6	430.1	528.0	394.4
71 CRIMES	2	1	25	3	326	516	315
RATE PER 100,000	3.1	1.6	38.8	4.7	506.2	801.3	489.2

RATIO FOR 2 YEAR PERIOD   1 CRIME PER   62.0 PEOPLE

RANKING   32

MEMPHIS,TENNESSEE

POPULATION   623,530

	MURDER	FORCED RAPE	ROB-BERY	AGGRVTD ASSAULT	BUR-GLARY	LARCENY +$50	AUTO THEFT
70 CRIMES	91	189	998	1,401	8,889	7,300	2,746
RATE PER 100,000	14.6	30.3	160.1	224.7	1425.6	1170.8	440.4
71 CRIMES	91	273	1,151	1,528	10,498	7,126	3,030
RATE PER 100,000	14.6	43.8	184.6	245.1	1683.6	1142.8	485.9

RATIO FOR 2 YEAR PERIOD   1 CRIME PER   27.5 PEOPLE

RANKING   221

MERIDEN,CONNECTICUT

POPULATION   55,959

	MURDER	FORCED RAPE	ROB-BERY	AGGRVTD ASSAULT	BUR-GLARY	LARCENY +$50	AUTO THEFT
70 CRIMES	1	5	42	35	396	587	238
RATE PER 100,000	1.8	8.9	75.1	62.5	707.7	1049.0	425.3
71 CRIMES	2	9	33	19	558	624	319
RATE PER 100,000	3.6	16.1	59.0	34.0	997.2	1115.1	570.1

RATIO FOR 2 YEAR PERIOD   1 CRIME PER   39.0 PEOPLE

RANKING   105

MESA,ARIZONA

POPULATION   62,853

	MURDER	FORCED RAPE	ROB-BERY	AGGRVTD ASSAULT	BUR-GLARY	LARCENY +$50	AUTO THEFT
70 CRIMES	2	3	35	55	660	805	269
RATE PER 100,000	3.2	4.8	55.7	87.5	1050.1	1280.8	428.0
71 CRIMES	3	6	36	48	844	968	223
RATE PER 100,000	4.8	9.5	57.3	76.4	1342.8	1540.1	354.8

RATIO FOR 2 YEAR PERIOD   1 CRIME PER   31.7 PEOPLE

RANKING   158

MESQUITE,TEXAS

POPULATION   55,131

	MURDER	FORCED RAPE	ROB- BERY	AGGRVTD ASSAULT	BUR- GLARY	LARCENY +$50	AUTO THEFT
70 CRIMES	2	3	19	51	325	573	117
RATE PER 100,000	3.6	5.4	34.5	92.5	589.5	1039.3	212.2
71 CRIMES	4	5	17	81	330	533	171
RATE PER 100,000	7.3	9.1	30.8	146.9	598.6	966.8	310.2

RATIO FOR 2 YEAR PERIOD   1 CRIME PER   49.4 PEOPLE

RANKING   71

MIAMI,FLORIDA

POPULATION   334,859

	MURDER	FORCED RAPE	ROB- BERY	AGGRVTD ASSAULT	BUR- GLARY	LARCENY +$50	AUTO THEFT
70 CRIMES	91	90	2,867	2,864	8,436	6,281	3,274
RATE PER 100,000	27.2	26.9	856.2	855.3	2519.3	1875.7	977.7
71 CRIMES	100	137	2,829	3,014	9,258	6,299	3,258
RATE PER 100,000	29.9	40.9	844.8	900.1	2764.7	1881.1	972.9

RATIO FOR 2 YEAR PERIOD   1 CRIME PER   13.7 PEOPLE

RANKING   383

MIAMI BEACH,FLORIDA

POPULATION   87,072

	MURDER	FORCED RAPE	ROB- BERY	AGGRVTD ASSAULT	BUR- GLARY	LARCENY +$50	AUTO THEFT
70 CRIMES	4	10	132	44	1,537	750	415
RATE PER 100,000	4.6	11.5	151.6	50.5	1765.2	861.4	476.6
71 CRIMES	10	4	125	58	1,754	720	314
RATE PER 100,000	11.5	4.6	143.6	66.6	2014.4	826.9	360.6

RATIO FOR 2 YEAR PERIOD   1 CRIME PER   29.6 PEOPLE

RANKING   194

MIDLAND,TEXAS

POPULATION 59,463

	MURDER	FORCED RAPE	ROB- BERY	AGGRYTD ASSAULT	BUR- GLARY	LARCENY +$50	AUTO THEFT
70 CRIMES	3	3	15	69	393	246	78
RATE PER 100,000	5.0	5.0	25.2	116.0	660.9	413.7	131.2
71 CRIMES	6	9	29	78	454	328	77
RATE PER 100,000	10.1	15.1	48.8	131.2	763.5	551.6	129.5

RATIO FOR 2 YEAR PERIOD 1 CRIME PER 66.5 PEOPLE

RANKING 24

MILFORD,CONNECTICUT

POPULATION 50,858

	MURDER	FORCED RAPE	ROB- BERY	AGGRYTD ASSAULT	BUR- GLARY	LARCENY +$50	AUTO THEFT
70 CRIMES		2	13	9	454	767	281
RATE PER 100,000	0.0	3.9	25.6	17.7	892.7	1508.1	552.5
71 CRIMES		4	19	11	766	1,040	451
RATE PER 100,000	0.0	7.9	37.4	21.6	1506.2	2044.9	886.8

RATIO FOR 2 YEAR PERIOD 1 CRIME PER 26.6 PEOPLE

RANKING 228

MILWAUKEE,WISCONSIN

POPULATION 717,099

	MURDER	FORCED RAPE	ROB- BERY	AGGRYTD ASSAULT	BUR- GLARY	LARCENY +$50	AUTO THEFT
70 CRIMES	50	93	649	720	4,303	9,355	5,018
RATE PER 100,000	7.0	13.0	90.5	100.4	600.1	1304.6	699.8
71 CRIMES	52	104	661	652	4,636	9,908	6,012
RATE PER 100,000	7.3	14.5	92.2	90.9	646.5	1381.7	838.4

RATIO FOR 2 YEAR PERIOD 1 CRIME PER 33.9 PEOPLE

RANKING 134

MINNEAPOLIS,MINNESOTA

POPULATION   434,400

	MURDER	FORCED RAPE	ROB- BERY	AGGRYTD ASSAULT	BUR- GLARY	LARCENY +$50	AUTO THEFT
70 CRIMES	28	160	1,818	760	9,723	5,731	5,200
RATE PER 100,000	6.4	36.8	418.5	175.0	2238.3	1319.3	1197.1
71 CRIMES	35	228	1,646	1,037	10,039	5,884	4,996
RATE PER 100,000	8.1	52.5	378.9	238.7	2311.0	1354.5	1150.1

RATIO FOR 2 YEAR PERIOD   1 CRIME PER   18.3 PEOPLE

RANKING   332

MOBILE,ALABAMA

POPULATION   190,026

	MURDER	FORCED RAPE	ROB- BERY	AGGRYTD ASSAULT	BUR- GLARY	LARCENY +$50	AUTO THEFT
70 CRIMES	26	77	365	473	5,282	1,734	1,230
RATE PER 100,000	13.7	40.5	192.1	248.9	2779.6	912.5	647.3
71 CRIMES	37	85	456	441	5,158	1,604	1,071
RATE PER 100,000	19.5	44.7	240.0	232.1	2714.4	844.1	563.6

RATIO FOR 2 YEAR PERIOD   1 CRIME PER   21.0 PEOPLE

RANKING   302

MODESTO,CALIFORNIA

POPULATION   61,712

	MURDER	FORCED RAPE	ROB- BERY	AGGRYTD ASSAULT	BUR- GLARY	LARCENY +$50	AUTO THEFT
70 CRIMES	1	9	79	113	1,229	1,741	321
RATE PER 100,000	1.6	14.6	128.0	183.1	1991.5	2821.2	520.2
71 CRIMES	4	21	102	162	1,275	1,913	369
RATE PER 100,000	6.5	34.0	165.3	262.5	2066.0	3099.9	597.9

RATIO FOR 2 YEAR PERIOD   1 CRIME PER   16.8 PEOPLE

RANKING   347

MONROE,LOUISIANA

POPULATION   56,374

	MURDER	FORCED RAPE	ROB-BERY	AGGRYTD ASSAULT	BUR-GLARY	LARCENY +$50	AUTO THEFT
70 CRIMES	8	1	15	215	372	228	148
RATE PER 100,000	14.2	1.8	26.6	381.4	659.9	404.4	262.5
71 CRIMES	9	8	13	220	450	281	146
RATE PER 100,000	16.0	14.2	23.1	390.3	798.2	498.5	259.0

RATIO FOR 2 YEAR PERIOD   1 CRIME PER   53.3 PEOPLE

RANKING   53

MONTGOMERY,ALABAMA

POPULATION   133,386

	MURDER	FORCED RAPE	ROB-BERY	AGGRYTD ASSAULT	BUR-GLARY	LARCENY +$50	AUTO THEFT
70 CRIMES	26	15	198	80	1,564	1,809	486
RATE PER 100,000	19.5	11.2	148.4	60.0	1172.5	1356.2	364.4
71 CRIMES	34	40	211	99	1,715	1,821	538
RATE PER 100,000	25.5	30.0	158.2	74.2	1285.7	1365.2	403.3

RATIO FOR 2 YEAR PERIOD   1 CRIME PER   30.8 PEOPLE

RANKING   175

MOUNT VERNON,NEW YORK

POPULATION   72,778

	MURDER	FORCED RAPE	ROB-BERY	AGGRYTD ASSAULT	BUR-GLARY	LARCENY +$50	AUTO THEFT
70 CRIMES	4	4	82	39	633	769	637
RATE PER 100,000	5.5	5.5	112.7	53.6	869.8	1056.6	875.3
71 CRIMES	7		82	35	425	873	788
RATE PER 100,000	9.6	0.0	112.7	48.1	584.0	1199.5	1082.7

RATIO FOR 2 YEAR PERIOD   1 CRIME PER   33.2 PEOPLE

RANKING   141

POPULATION   51,092

	MURDER	FORCED RAPE	ROB-BERY	AGGRVTD ASSAULT	BUR-GLARY	LARCENY +$50	AUTO THEFT
70 CRIMES	2	9	37	36	429	756	321
RATE PER 100,000	3.9	17.6	72.4	70.5	839.7	1479.7	628.3
71 CRIMES		10	43	48	416	757	260
RATE PER 100,000	0.0	19.6	84.2	93.9	814.2	1481.6	508.9

RATIO FOR 2 YEAR PERIOD   1 CRIME PER   32.7 PEOPLE

RANKING   149

MUNCIE,INDIANA

POPULATION   69,080

	MURDER	FORCED RAPE	ROB-BERY	AGGRVTD ASSAULT	BUR-GLARY	LARCENY +$50	AUTO THEFT
70 CRIMES	2	19	119	112	724	769	314
RATE PER 100,000	2.9	27.5	172.3	162.1	1048.1	1113.2	454.5
71 CRIMES	5	21	110	108	1,065	1,202	287
RATE PER 100,000	7.2	30.4	159.2	156.3	1541.7	1740.0	415.5

RATIO FOR 2 YEAR PERIOD   1 CRIME PER   28.4 PEOPLE

RANKING   209

NASHUA,NEW HAMPSHIRE

POPULATION   55,820

	MURDER	FORCED RAPE	ROB-BERY	AGGRVTD ASSAULT	BUR-GLARY	LARCENY +$50	AUTO THEFT
70 CRIMES	3		7	18	134	106	154
RATE PER 100,000	5.4	0.0	12.5	32.2	240.1	189.9	275.9
71 CRIMES	1	1	6	6	135	226	189
RATE PER 100,000	1.8	1.8	10.7	10.7	241.8	404.9	338.6

RATIO FOR 2 YEAR PERIOD   1 CRIME PER   113.2 PEOPLE

RANKING   5

NASHVILLE,TENNESSEE

POPULATION   447,877

	MURDER	FORCED RAPE	ROB- BERY	AGGRYTD ASSAULT	BUR- GLARY	LARCENY +$50	AUTO THEFT
70 CRIMES	64	107	1,015	1,814	6,934	4,394	3,375
RATE PER 100,000	14.3	23.9	226.6	405.0	1548.2	981.1	753.6
71 CRIMES	73	157	1,176	2,174	8,216	5,525	3,425
RATE PER 100,000	16.3	35.1	262.6	485.4	1834.4	1233.6	764.7

RATIO FOR 2 YEAR PERIOD   1 CRIME PER   23.2 PEOPLE

RANKING   271

NEW BEDFORD,MASSACHUSETTS

POPULATION   101,777

	MURDER	FORCED RAPE	ROB- BERY	AGGRYTD ASSAULT	BUR- GLARY	LARCENY +$50	AUTO THEFT
70 CRIMES	3	14	106	187	2,168	1,057	1,122
RATE PER 100,000	2.9	13.8	104.1	183.7	2130.1	1038.5	1102.4
71 CRIMES	2	12	169	119	2,566	1,488	1,247
RATE PER 100,000	2.0	11.8	166.0	116.9	2521.2	1462.0	1225.2

RATIO FOR 2 YEAR PERIOD   1 CRIME PER   19.8 PEOPLE

RANKING   316

NEW BRITAIN,CONNECTICUT

POPULATION   83,441

	MURDER	FORCED RAPE	ROB- BERY	AGGRYTD ASSAULT	BUR- GLARY	LARCENY +$50	AUTO THEFT
70 CRIMES	2	8	105	104	1,357	882	399
RATE PER 100,000	2.4	9.6	125.8	124.6	1626.3	1057.0	478.2
71 CRIMES	1	10	136	126	1,349	925	319
RATE PER 100,000	1.2	12.0	163.0	151.0	1616.7	1108.6	382.3

RATIO FOR 2 YEAR PERIOD   1 CRIME PER   29.1 PEOPLE

RANKING   201

NEW HAVEN,CONNECTICUT

POPULATION   137,707

	MURDER	FORCED RAPE	ROB- BERY	AGGRYTD ASSAULT	BUR- GLARY	LARCENY +$50	AUTO THEFT
70 CRIMES	10	42	164	341	3,783	1,910	2,223
RATE PER 100,000	7.3	30.5	119.1	247.6	2747.1	1387.0	1614.3
71 CRIMES	18	52	251	334	2,977	1,835	2,467
RATE PER 100,000	13.1	37.8	182.3	242.5	2161.8	1332.5	1791.5

RATIO FOR 2 YEAR PERIOD   1 CRIME PER   16.7 PEOPLE

RANKING   348

NEW ORLEANS,LOUISIANA

POPULATION   593,471

	MURDER	FORCED RAPE	ROB- BERY	AGGRYTD ASSAULT	BUR- GLARY	LARCENY +$50	AUTO THEFT
70 CRIMES	100	324	3,632	2,270	11,086	9,829	8,130
RATE PER 100,000	16.9	54.6	612.0	382.5	1868.0	1656.2	1369.9
71 CRIMES	116	325	3,391	2,109	10,705	10,381	8,348
RATE PER 100,000	19.5	54.8	571.4	355.4	1803.8	1749.2	1406.6

RATIO FOR 2 YEAR PERIOD   1 CRIME PER   16.7 PEOPLE

RANKING   349

NEW ROCHELLE,NEW YORK

POPULATION   75,385

	MURDER	FORCED RAPE	ROB- BERY	AGGRYTD ASSAULT	BUR- GLARY	LARCENY +$50	AUTO THEFT
70 CRIMES		2	90	77	627	972	338
RATE PER 100,000	0.0	2.7	119.4	102.1	831.7	1289.4	448.4
71 CRIMES	1	3	90	56	651	753	391
RATE PER 100,000	1.3	4.0	119.4	74.3	863.6	998.9	518.7

RATIO FOR 2 YEAR PERIOD   1 CRIME PER   37.2 PEOPLE

RANKING   114

NEW YORK CITY,NEW YORK

POPULATION   7,867,760

	MURDER	FORCED RAPE	ROB-BERY	AGGRYTD ASSAULT	BUR-GLARY	LARCENY +$50	AUTO THEFT
70 CRIMES	1,117	2,141	74,102	31,255	181,694	132,572	94,835
RATE PER 100,000	14.2	27.2	941.8	397.3	2309.3	1685.0	1205.4
71 CRIMES	1,466	2,415	88,994	33,865	181,331	124,752	96,624
RATE PER 100,000	18.6	30.7	1131.1	430.4	2304.7	1585.6	1228.1

RATIO FOR 2 YEAR PERIOD   1 CRIME PER   15.0 PEOPLE

RANKING   375

NEWARK,NEW JERSEY

POPULATION   382,417

	MURDER	FORCED RAPE	ROB-BERY	AGGRYTD ASSAULT	BUR-GLARY	LARCENY +$50	AUTO THEFT
70 CRIMES	143	253	4,666	2,170	11,375	6,105	7,069
RATE PER 100,000	37.4	66.2	1220.1	567.4	2974.5	1596.4	1848.5
71 CRIMES	131	312	5,529	2,641	13,466	5,754	6,929
RATE PER 100,000	34.3	81.6	1445.8	690.6	3521.3	1504.6	1811.9

RATIO FOR 2 YEAR PERIOD   1 CRIME PER   11.4 PEOPLE

RANKING   392

NEWPORT NEWS,VIRGINIA

POPULATION   138,177

	MURDER	FORCED RAPE	ROB-BERY	AGGRYTD ASSAULT	BUR-GLARY	LARCENY +$50	AUTO THEFT
70 CRIMES	14	37	165	317	1,841	1,618	394
RATE PER 100,000	10.1	26.8	119.4	229.4	1332.3	1171.0	285.1
71 CRIMES	12	28	216	427	1,332	1,372	306
RATE PER 100,000	8.7	20.3	156.3	309.0	964.0	992.9	221.5

RATIO FOR 2 YEAR PERIOD   1 CRIME PER   34.2 PEOPLE

RANKING   131

POPULATION   91,066

	MURDER	FORCED RAPE	ROB- BERY	AGGRYTD ASSAULT	BUR- GLARY	LARCENY +$50	AUTO THEFT
70 CRIMES		7	23	56	1,049	915	506
RATE PER 100,000	0.0	7.7	25.3	61.5	1151.9	1004.8	555.6
71 CRIMES	1	4	35	60	1,277	1,366	537
RATE PER 100,000	1.1	4.4	38.4	65.9	1402.3	1500.0	589.7

RATIO FOR 2 YEAR PERIOD   1 CRIME PER   31.2 PEOPLE

RANKING   166

NIAGARA FALLS,NEW YORK

POPULATION   85,615

	MURDER	FORCED RAPE	ROB- BERY	AGGRYTD ASSAULT	BUR- GLARY	LARCENY +$50	AUTO THEFT
70 CRIMES	2	6	177	198	1,201	1,379	293
RATE PER 100,000	2.3	7.0	206.7	231.3	1402.8	1610.7	342.2
71 CRIMES	1	11	202	231	1,561	1,650	276
RATE PER 100,000	1.2	12.8	235.9	269.8	1823.3	1927.2	322.4

RATIO FOR 2 YEAR PERIOD   1 CRIME PER   23.8 PEOPLE

RANKING   266

NORFOLK,VIRGINIA

POPULATION   307,951

	MURDER	FORCED RAPE	ROB- BERY	AGGRYTD ASSAULT	BUR- GLARY	LARCENY +$50	AUTO THEFT
70 CRIMES	38	85	857	1,149	4,351	5,371	1,551
RATE PER 100,000	12.3	27.6	278.3	373.1	1412.9	1744.1	503.7
71 CRIMES	35	122	821	1,229	4,912	5,217	1,603
RATE PER 100,000	11.4	39.6	266.6	399.1	1595.1	1694.1	520.5

RATIO FOR 2 YEAR PERIOD   1 CRIME PER   22.5 PEOPLE

RANKING   283

NORMAN, OKLAHOMA

POPULATION   52,117

	MURDER	FORCED RAPE	ROB- BERY	AGGRYTD ASSAULT	BUR- GLARY	LARCENY +$50	AUTO THEFT
70 CRIMES	4	2	7	17	452	586	76
RATE PER 100,000	7.7	3.8	13.4	32.6	867.3	1124.4	145.8
71 CRIMES	3		7	12	544	861	124
RATE PER 100,000	5.8	0.0	13.4	23.0	1043.8	1652.1	237.9

RATIO FOR 2 YEAR PERIOD   1 CRIME PER   38.6 PEOPLE

RANKING   107

NORTH LITTLE ROCK, ARKANSAS

POPULATION   60,040

	MURDER	FORCED RAPE	ROB- BERY	AGGRYTD ASSAULT	BUR- GLARY	LARCENY +$50	AUTO THEFT
70 CRIMES	14	19	70	179	723	860	171
RATE PER 100,000	23.3	31.6	116.6	298.1	1204.2	1432.4	284.8
71 CRIMES	11	17	68	163	631	715	153
RATE PER 100,000	18.3	28.3	113.3	271.5	1051.0	1190.9	254.8

RATIO FOR 2 YEAR PERIOD   1 CRIME PER   31.6 PEOPLE

RANKING   160

NORWALK, CALIFORNIA

POPULATION   91,827

	MURDER	FORCED RAPE	ROB- BERY	AGGRYTD ASSAULT	BUR- GLARY	LARCENY +$50	AUTO THEFT
70 CRIMES							
RATE PER 100,000							
71 CRIMES	1	25	119	283	1,241	1,323	583
RATE PER 100,000	1.1	27.2	129.6	308.2	1351.5	1440.8	634.9

RATIO FOR 2 YEAR PERIOD   1 CRIME PER   51.3 PEOPLE

RANKING   62

NORWALK, CONNECTICUT

POPULATION   79,113

	MURDER	FORCED RAPE	ROB- BERY	AGGRVTD ASSAULT	BUR- GLARY	LARCENY +$50	AUTO THEFT
70 CRIMES	3	12	48	88	1,252	982	297
RATE PER 100,000	3.8	15.2	60.7	111.2	1582.5	1241.3	375.4
71 CRIMES	4	11	62	108	1,035	1,052	289
RATE PER 100,000	5.1	13.9	78.4	136.5	1308.3	1329.7	365.3

RATIO FOR 2 YEAR PERIOD   1 CRIME PER   30.1 PEOPLE

RANKING   185

OAK LAWN, ILLINOIS

POPULATION   60,305

	MURDER	FORCED RAPE	ROB- BERY	AGGRVTD ASSAULT	BUR- GLARY	LARCENY +$50	AUTO THEFT
70 CRIMES	1	9	18	48	323	326	149
RATE PER 100,000	1.7	14.9	29.8	79.6	535.6	540.6	247.1
71 CRIMES	3	4	11	22	346	304	173
RATE PER 100,000	5.0	6.6	18.2	36.5	573.8	504.1	286.9

RATIO FOR 2 YEAR PERIOD   1 CRIME PER   69.4 PEOPLE

RANKING   18

OAK PARK, ILLINOIS

POPULATION   62,511

	MURDER	FORCED RAPE	ROB- BERY	AGGRVTD ASSAULT	BUR- GLARY	LARCENY +$50	AUTO THEFT
70 CRIMES		2	92	29	410	276	184
RATE PER 100,000	0.0	3.2	147.2	46.4	655.9	441.5	294.3
71 CRIMES	2	4	144	42	442	370	182
RATE PER 100,000	3.2	6.4	230.4	67.2	707.1	591.9	291.1

RATIO FOR 2 YEAR PERIOD   1 CRIME PER   57.3 PEOPLE

RANKING   43

OAKLAND,CALIFORNIA

POPULATION   361,561

70 CRIMES	MURDER	FORCED RAPE	ROB- BERY	AGGRYTD ASSAULT	BUR- GLARY	LARCENY +$50	AUTO THEFT
	69	212	2,497	1,088	13,787	6,066	4,993
RATE PER 100,000	19.1	58.6	690.6	300.9	3813.2	1677.7	1381.0
71 CRIMES	89	220	2,932	1,224	14,311	1,493	5,395
RATE PER 100,000	24.6	60.8	810.9	338.5	3958.1	412.9	1492.1

RATIO FOR 2 YEAR PERIOD   1 CRIME PER   13.2 PEOPLE

RANKING   387

ODESSA,TEXAS

POPULATION   78,380

70 CRIMES	MURDER	FORCED RAPE	ROB- BERY	AGGRYTD ASSAULT	BUR- GLARY	LARCENY +$50	AUTO THEFT
	7	3	42	75	629	241	137
RATE PER 100,000	8.9	3.8	53.6	95.7	802.5	307.5	174.8
71 CRIMES	12	7	31	58	841	289	188
RATE PER 100,000	15.3	8.9	39.6	74.0	1073.0	368.7	239.9

RATIO FOR 2 YEAR PERIOD   1 CRIME PER   61.2 PEOPLE

RANKING   33

OGDEN,UTAH

POPULATION   69,478

70 CRIMES	MURDER	FORCED RAPE	ROB- BERY	AGGRYTD ASSAULT	BUR- GLARY	LARCENY +$50	AUTO THEFT
	3	17	87	79	804	878	391
RATE PER 100,000	4.3	24.5	125.2	113.7	1157.2	1263.7	562.8
71 CRIMES	5	23	120	88	772	913	286
RATE PER 100,000	7.2	33.1	172.7	126.7	1111.1	1314.1	411.6

RATIO FOR 2 YEAR PERIOD   1 CRIME PER   31.1 PEOPLE

RANKING   169

OKLAHOMA CITY, OKLAHOMA

POPULATION 366,481

	MURDER	FORCED RAPE	ROB-BERY	AGGRVTD ASSAULT	BUR-GLARY	LARCENY +$50	AUTO THEFT
70 CRIMES	32	122	548	647	5,656	1,843	2,538
RATE PER 100,000	8.7	33.3	149.5	176.5	1543.3	502.9	692.5
71 CRIMES	45	144	521	1,142	6,314	2,136	2,657
RATE PER 100,000	12.3	39.3	142.2	311.6	1722.9	582.8	725.0

RATIO FOR 2 YEAR PERIOD   1 CRIME PER   30.1 PEOPLE

RANKING   187

OMAHA, NEBRASKA

POPULATION 347,328

	MURDER	FORCED RAPE	ROB-BERY	AGGRVTD ASSAULT	BUR-GLARY	LARCENY +$50	AUTO THEFT
70 CRIMES	33	71	753	1,137	3,739	2,889	3,340
RATE PER 100,000	9.5	20.4	216.8	327.4	1076.5	831.8	961.6
71 CRIMES	24	122	482	1,085	3,706	3,097	2,892
RATE PER 100,000	6.9	35.1	138.8	312.4	1067.0	891.7	832.6

RATIO FOR 2 YEAR PERIOD   1 CRIME PER   29.7 PEOPLE

RANKING   193

ONTARIO, CALIFORNIA

POPULATION 64,118

	MURDER	FORCED RAPE	ROB-BERY	AGGRVTD ASSAULT	BUR-GLARY	LARCENY +$50	AUTO THEFT
70 CRIMES	2	14	49	122	1,134	939	324
RATE PER 100,000	3.1	21.8	76.4	190.3	1768.6	1464.5	505.3
71 CRIMES	2	25	95	169	1,339	1,095	345
RATE PER 100,000	3.1	39.0	148.2	263.6	2088.3	1707.8	538.1

RATIO FOR 2 YEAR PERIOD   1 CRIME PER   22.6 PEOPLE

RANKING   282

ORANGE,CALIFORNIA

POPULATION   77,374

	MURDER	FORCED RAPE	ROB- BERY	AGGRYTD ASSAULT	BUR- GLARY	LARCENY +$50	AUTO THEFT
70 CRIMES		11	57	59	1,351	953	219
RATE PER 100,000	0.0	14.2	73.7	76.3	1746.1	1231.7	283.0
71 CRIMES	1	20	45	70	1,326	1,255	225
RATE PER 100,000	1.3	25.8	58.2	90.5	1713.8	1622.0	290.8

RATIO FOR 2 YEAR PERIOD   1 CRIME PER   27.6 PEOPLE

RANKING   218

ORLANDO,FLORIDA

POPULATION   99,006

	MURDER	FORCED RAPE	ROB- BERY	AGGRYTD ASSAULT	BUR- GLARY	LARCENY +$50	AUTO THEFT
70 CRIMES	10	20	267	476	2,492	1,857	344
RATE PER 100,000	10.1	20.2	269.7	480.8	2517.0	1875.6	347.5
71 CRIMES	21	30	301	989	2,389	1,941	456
RATE PER 100,000	21.2	30.3	304.0	998.9	2413.0	1960.5	460.6

RATIO FOR 2 YEAR PERIOD   1 CRIME PER   17.0 PEOPLE

RANKING   346

OSHKOSH,WISCONSIN

POPULATION   53,221

	MURDER	FORCED RAPE	ROB- BERY	AGGRYTD ASSAULT	BUR- GLARY	LARCENY +$50	AUTO THEFT
70 CRIMES		1	11	2	370	431	98
RATE PER 100,000	0.0	1.9	20.7	3.8	695.2	809.8	184.1
71 CRIMES	1	2	7		303	475	80
RATE PER 100,000	1.9	3.8	13.2	0.0	569.3	892.5	150.3

RATIO FOR 2 YEAR PERIOD   1 CRIME PER   59.7 PEOPLE

RANKING   38

OVERLAND PARK,KANSAS

POPULATION 76,623

	MURDER	FORCED RAPE	ROB- BERY	AGGRYTD ASSAULT	BUR- GLARY	LARCENY +$50	AUTO THEFT
70 CRIMES	2	5	13	55	406	805	103
RATE PER 100,000	2.6	6.5	17.0	71.8	529.9	1050.6	134.4
71 CRIMES	2	7	32	48	583	857	145
RATE PER 100,000	2.6	9.1	41.8	62.6	760.9	1118.5	189.2

RATIO FOR 2 YEAR PERIOD   1 CRIME PER   50.0 PEOPLE

RANKING   67

OWENSBORO,KENTUCKY

POPULATION 50,329

	MURDER	FORCED RAPE	ROB- BERY	AGGRYTD ASSAULT	BUR- GLARY	LARCENY +$50	AUTO THEFT
70 CRIMES	2	3	32	54	354	461	66
RATE PER 100,000	4.0	6.0	63.6	107.3	703.4	916.0	131.1
71 CRIMES	3	3	15	61	382	510	75
RATE PER 100,000	6.0	6.0	29.8	121.2	759.0	1013.3	149.0

RATIO FOR 2 YEAR PERIOD   1 CRIME PER   49.8 PEOPLE

RANKING   70

OXNARD,CALIFORNIA

POPULATION 71,225

	MURDER	FORCED RAPE	ROB- BERY	AGGRYTD ASSAULT	BUR- GLARY	LARCENY +$50	AUTO THEFT
70 CRIMES	2	18	77	122	1,643	1,064	426
RATE PER 100,000	2.8	25.3	108.1	171.3	2306.8	1493.9	598.1
71 CRIMES	3	31	170	173	1,857	1,171	511
RATE PER 100,000	4.2	43.5	238.7	242.9	2607.2	1644.1	717.4

RATIO FOR 2 YEAR PERIOD   1 CRIME PER   19.5 PEOPLE

RANKING   318

PALO ALTO,CALIFORNIA

POPULATION   55,966

	MURDER	FORCED RAPE	ROB- BERY	AGGRYTD ASSAULT	BUR- GLARY	LARCENY +$50	AUTO THEFT
70 CRIMES		11	71	60	802	1,260	258
RATE PER 100,000	0.0	19.7	126.9	107.2	1433.0	2251.4	461.0
71 CRIMES	2	9	64	43	817	1,141	275
RATE PER 100,000	3.6	16.1	114.4	76.8	1459.8	2038.7	491.4

RATIO FOR 2 YEAR PERIOD   1 CRIME PER   23.2 PEOPLE

RANKING   272

PARMA,OHIO

POPULATION   100,216

	MURDER	FORCED RAPE	ROB- BERY	AGGRYTD ASSAULT	BUR- GLARY	LARCENY +$50	AUTO THEFT
70 CRIMES	2	3	36	76	455	709	399
RATE PER 100,000	2.0	3.0	35.9	75.8	454.0	707.5	398.1
71 CRIMES	3	4	25	59	513	616	385
RATE PER 100,000	3.0	4.0	24.9	58.9	511.9	614.7	384.2

RATIO FOR 2 YEAR PERIOD   1 CRIME PER   61.0 PEOPLE

RANKING   34

PASADENA,CALIFORNIA

POPULATION   113,327

	MURDER	FORCED RAPE	ROB- BERY	AGGRYTD ASSAULT	BUR- GLARY	LARCENY +$50	AUTO THEFT
70 CRIMES	9	106	459	415	3,199	1,839	1,084
RATE PER 100,000	7.9	93.5	405.0	366.2	2822.8	1622.7	956.5
71 CRIMES	11	111	527	458	3,677	2,117	1,177
RATE PER 100,000	9.7	97.9	465.0	404.1	3244.6	1868.0	1038.6

RATIO FOR 2 YEAR PERIOD   1 CRIME PER   14.9 PEOPLE

RANKING   376

PASADENA, TEXAS

POPULATION   89,277

	MURDER	FORCED RAPE	ROBBERY	AGGRYTD ASSAULT	BURGLARY	LARCENY +$50	AUTO THEFT
70 CRIMES	2	16	34	56	557	425	378
RATE PER 100,000	2.2	17.9	38.1	62.7	623.9	476.0	423.4
71 CRIMES	2	4	43	45	756	661	429
RATE PER 100,000	2.2	4.5	48.2	50.4	846.8	740.4	480.5

RATIO FOR 2 YEAR PERIOD   1 CRIME PER   52.3 PEOPLE

RANKING   56

PASSAIC, NEW JERSEY

POPULATION   55,124

	MURDER	FORCED RAPE	ROBBERY	AGGRYTD ASSAULT	BURGLARY	LARCENY +$50	AUTO THEFT
70 CRIMES	4	11	136	207	860	663	618
RATE PER 100,000	7.3	20.0	246.7	375.5	1560.1	1202.7	1121.1
71 CRIMES	7	11	173	221	939	497	643
RATE PER 100,000	12.7	20.0	313.8	400.9	1703.4	901.6	1166.5

RATIO FOR 2 YEAR PERIOD   1 CRIME PER   22.0 PEOPLE

RANKING   290

PATERSON, NEW JERSEY

POPULATION   144,824

	MURDER	FORCED RAPE	ROBBERY	AGGRYTD ASSAULT	BURGLARY	LARCENY +$50	AUTO THEFT
70 CRIMES	20	18	652	296	2,705	683	2,533
RATE PER 100,000	13.8	12.4	450.2	204.4	1867.8	471.6	1749.0
71 CRIMES	20	41	918	977	3,177	936	2,452
RATE PER 100,000	13.8	28.3	633.9	674.6	2193.7	646.3	1693.1

RATIO FOR 2 YEAR PERIOD   1 CRIME PER   18.7 PEOPLE

RANKING   328

PAWTUCKET,RHODE ISLAND

POPULATION   76,984

	MURDER	FORCED RAPE	ROB-BERY	AGGRYTD ASSAULT	BUR-GLARY	LARCENY +$50	AUTO THEFT
70 CRIMES	3	3	35	20	612	328	560
RATE PER 100,000	3.9	3.9	45.5	26.0	795.0	426.1	727.4
71 CRIMES	4	3	27	33	440	404	613
RATE PER 100,000	5.2	3.9	35.1	42.9	571.5	524.8	796.3

RATIO FOR 2 YEAR PERIOD   1 CRIME PER   49.9 PEOPLE

RANKING   69

PENSACOLA,FLORIDA

POPULATION   59,507

	MURDER	FORCED RAPE	ROB-BERY	AGGRYTD ASSAULT	BUR-GLARY	LARCENY +$50	AUTO THEFT
70 CRIMES	9	7	119	107	870	950	181
RATE PER 100,000	15.1	11.8	200.0	179.8	1462.0	1596.5	304.2
71 CRIMES	11	15	126	196	946	899	216
RATE PER 100,000	18.5	25.2	211.7	329.4	1589.7	1510.7	363.0

RATIO FOR 2 YEAR PERIOD   1 CRIME PER   25.5 PEOPLE

RANKING   240

PEORIA,ILLINOIS

POPULATION   126,963

	MURDER	FORCED RAPE	ROB-BERY	AGGRYTD ASSAULT	BUR-GLARY	LARCENY +$50	AUTO THEFT
70 CRIMES	15	42	424	717	2,323	1,644	737
RATE PER 100,000	11.8	33.1	334.0	564.7	1829.7	1294.9	580.5
71 CRIMES	12	30	396	577	1,965	1,761	815
RATE PER 100,000	9.5	23.6	311.9	454.5	1547.7	1387.0	641.9

RATIO FOR 2 YEAR PERIOD   1 CRIME PER   22.1 PEOPLE

RANKING   288

PHILADELPHIA,PENNSYLVANIA

POPULATION   1,948,609

	MURDER	FORCED RAPE	ROB- BERY	AGGRVTD ASSAULT	BUR- GLARY	LARCENY +$50	AUTO THEFT
70 CRIMES	352	452	6,377	3,947	15,163	5,263	14,180
RATE PER 100,000	18.1	23.2	327.3	202.6	778.1	270.1	727.7
71 CRIMES	435	546	9,243	4,970	20,914	7,387	17,845
RATE PER 100,000	22.3	28.0	474.3	255.1	1073.3	379.1	915.8

RATIO FOR 2 YEAR PERIOD   1 CRIME PER   36.3 PEOPLE

RANKING   122

PHOENIX,ARIZONA

POPULATION   581,562

	MURDER	FORCED RAPE	ROB- BERY	AGGRVTD ASSAULT	BUR- GLARY	LARCENY +$50	AUTO THEFT
70 CRIMES	63	206	1,395	1,891	14,097	7,172	4,659
RATE PER 100,000	10.8	35.4	239.9	325.2	2424.0	1233.2	801.1
71 CRIMES	55	216	1,304	2,326	13,348	8,965	4,332
RATE PER 100,000	9.5	37.1	224.2	400.0	2295.2	1541.5	744.9

RATIO FOR 2 YEAR PERIOD   1 CRIME PER   19.3 PEOPLE

RANKING   323

PICO RIVERA,CALIFORNIA

POPULATION   54,170

	MURDER	FORCED RAPE	ROB- BERY	AGGRVTD ASSAULT	BUR- GLARY	LARCENY +$50	AUTO THEFT
70 CRIMES							
RATE PER 100,000							
71 CRIMES	4	12	93	248	891	596	269
RATE PER 100,000	7.4	22.2	171.7	457.8	1644.8	1100.2	496.6

RATIO FOR 2 YEAR PERIOD   1 CRIME PER   51.2 PEOPLE

RANKING   65

260

PINE BLUFF,ARKANSAS

POPULATION 57,389

	MURDER	FORCED RAPE	ROB-BERY	AGGRYTD ASSAULT	BUR-GLARY	LARCENY +$50	AUTO THEFT
70 CRIMES	6	7	52	96	1,220	608	81
RATE PER 100,000	10.5	12.2	90.6	167.3	2125.8	1059.4	141.1
71 CRIMES	5	16	54	69	953	453	88
RATE PER 100,000	8.7	27.9	94.1	120.2	1660.6	789.3	153.3

RATIO FOR 2 YEAR PERIOD   1 CRIME PER   30.9 PEOPLE

RANKING   171

PITTSBURGH,PENNSYLVANIA

POPULATION 520,117

	MURDER	FORCED RAPE	ROB-BERY	AGGRYTD ASSAULT	BUR-GLARY	LARCENY +$50	AUTO THEFT
70 CRIMES	63	246	2,690	1,646	8,432	6,571	8,748
RATE PER 100,000	12.1	47.3	517.2	316.5	1621.2	1263.4	1681.9
71 CRIMES	65	279	2,556	1,910	9,489	5,636	6,532
RATE PER 100,000	12.5	53.6	491.4	367.2	1824.4	1083.6	1255.9

RATIO FOR 2 YEAR PERIOD   1 CRIME PER   18.9 PEOPLE

RANKING   326

PITTSFIELD,MASSACHUSETTS

POPULATION 57,020

	MURDER	FORCED RAPE	ROB-BERY	AGGRYTD ASSAULT	BUR-GLARY	LARCENY +$50	AUTO THEFT
70 CRIMES		4	4	18	337	357	129
RATE PER 100,000	0.0	7.0	7.0	31.6	591.0	626.1	226.2
71 CRIMES		1	4	14	462	502	134
RATE PER 100,000	0.0	1.8	7.0	24.6	810.2	880.4	235.0

RATIO FOR 2 YEAR PERIOD   1 CRIME PER   58.0 PEOPLE

RANKING   40

POMONA,CALIFORNIA

POPULATION   87,384

	MURDER	FORCED RAPE	ROB- BERY	AGGRYTD ASSAULT	BUR- GLARY	LARCENY +$50	AUTO THEFT
70 CRIMES	3	32	196	216	1,575	1,251	568
RATE PER 100,000	3.4	36.6	224.3	247.2	1802.4	1431.6	650.0
71 CRIMES	4	28	202	236	1,819	1,128	609
RATE PER 100,000	4.6	32.0	231.2	270.1	2081.6	1290.9	696.9

RATIO FOR 2 YEAR PERIOD   1 CRIME PER   22.2 PEOPLE

RANKING   286

PONTIAC,MICHIGAN

POPULATION   85,279

	MURDER	FORCED RAPE	ROB- BERY	AGGRYTD ASSAULT	BUR- GLARY	LARCENY +$50	AUTO THEFT
70 CRIMES	14	27	691	949	2,853	1,518	581
RATE PER 100,000	16.4	31.7	810.3	1112.8	3345.5	1780.0	681.3
71 CRIMES	18	39	1,140	835	3,610	1,322	668
RATE PER 100,000	21.1	45.7	1336.8	979.1	4233.2	1550.2	783.3

RATIO FOR 2 YEAR PERIOD   1 CRIME PER   11.9 PEOPLE

RANKING   390

PORT ARTHUR,TEXAS

POPULATION   57,371

	MURDER	FORCED RAPE	ROB- BERY	AGGRYTD ASSAULT	BUR- GLARY	LARCENY +$50	AUTO THEFT
70 CRIMES	5	14	111	81	905	599	205
RATE PER 100,000	8.7	24.4	193.5	141.2	1577.5	1044.1	357.3
71 CRIMES	13	20	161	100	1,107	664	160
RATE PER 100,000	22.7	34.9	280.6	174.3	1929.5	1157.4	278.9

RATIO FOR 2 YEAR PERIOD   1 CRIME PER   27.6 PEOPLE

RANKING   217

PORTLAND,MAINE

POPULATION   65,116

	MURDER	FORCED RAPE	ROB-BERY	AGGRYTD ASSAULT	BUR-GLARY	LARCENY +$50	AUTO THEFT
70 CRIMES	1	11	38	48	492	475	380
RATE PER 100,000	1.5	16.9	58.4	73.7	755.6	729.5	583.6
71 CRIMES		6	45	29	465	617	300
RATE PER 100,000	0.0	9.2	69.1	44.5	714.1	947.5	460.7

RATIO FOR 2 YEAR PERIOD   1 CRIME PER   44.7 PEOPLE

RANKING   87

PORTLAND,OREGON

POPULATION   382,619

	MURDER	FORCED RAPE	ROB-BERY	AGGRYTD ASSAULT	BUR-GLARY	LARCENY +$50	AUTO THEFT
70 CRIMES	36	128	1,634	858	9,476	7,819	3,324
RATE PER 100,000	9.4	33.5	427.1	224.2	2476.6	2043.5	868.7
71 CRIMES	15	144	1,797	1,127	10,794	8,845	3,737
RATE PER 100,000	3.9	37.6	469.7	294.5	2821.1	2311.7	976.7

RATIO FOR 2 YEAR PERIOD   1 CRIME PER   15.3 PEOPLE

RANKING   371

PORTSMOUTH,VIRGINIA

POPULATION   110,963

	MURDER	FORCED RAPE	ROB-BERY	AGGRYTD ASSAULT	BUR-GLARY	LARCENY +$50	AUTO THEFT
70 CRIMES	11	14	357	218	1,702	1,248	570
RATE PER 100,000	9.9	12.6	321.7	196.5	1533.8	1124.7	513.7
71 CRIMES	21	52	489	269	2,276	1,329	643
RATE PER 100,000	18.9	46.9	440.7	242.4	2051.1	1197.7	579.5

RATIO FOR 2 YEAR PERIOD   1 CRIME PER   24.1 PEOPLE

RANKING   260

PROVIDENCE,RHODE ISLAND

POPULATION   179,213

	MURDER	FORCED RAPE	ROB- BERY	AGGRYTD ASSAULT	BUR- GLARY	LARCENY +$50	AUTO THEFT
70 CRIMES	16	13	524	416	3,926	1,256	4,940
RATE PER 100,000	8.9	7.3	292.4	232.1	2190.7	700.8	2756.5
71 CRIMES	12	21	625	525	4,176	894	5,724
RATE PER 100,000	6.7	11.7	348.7	292.9	2330.2	498.8	3194.0

RATIO FOR 2 YEAR PERIOD   1 CRIME PER   15.5 PEOPLE

RANKING   367

PROVO,UTAH

POPULATION   53,131

	MURDER	FORCED RAPE	ROB- BERY	AGGRYTD ASSAULT	BUR- GLARY	LARCENY +$50	AUTO THEFT
70 CRIMES			4	4	64	325	53
RATE PER 100,000	0.0	0.0	7.5	7.5	120.5	611.7	99.8
71 CRIMES		4	9	13	105	508	61
RATE PER 100,000	0.0	7.5	16.9	24.5	197.6	956.1	114.8

RATIO FOR 2 YEAR PERIOD   1 CRIME PER   92.4 PEOPLE

RANKING   7

PUEBLO,COLORADO

POPULATION   97,453

	MURDER	FORCED RAPE	ROB- BERY	AGGRYTD ASSAULT	BUR- GLARY	LARCENY +$50	AUTO THEFT
70 CRIMES	3	19	54	186	857	1,203	399
RATE PER 100,000	3.1	19.5	55.4	190.9	879.4	1234.4	409.4
71 CRIMES	2	12	56	200	1,089	1,382	391
RATE PER 100,000	2.1	12.3	57.5	205.2	1117.5	1418.1	401.2

RATIO FOR 2 YEAR PERIOD   1 CRIME PER   33.3 PEOPLE

RANKING   140

264

QUINCY,MASSACHUSETTS

POPULATION   87,966

	MURDER	FORCED RAPE	ROB- BERY	AGGRYTD ASSAULT	BUR- GLARY	LARCENY +$50	AUTO THEFT
70 CRIMES		3	57	50	1,225	1,180	835
RATE PER 100,000	0.0	3.4	64.8	56.8	1392.6	1341.4	949.2
71 CRIMES		1	71	87	1,550	941	896
RATE PER 100,000	0.0	1.1	80.7	98.9	1762.0	1069.7	1018.6

RATIO FOR 2 YEAR PERIOD   1 CRIME PER   25.5 PEOPLE

RANKING   242

RACINE,WISCONSIN

POPULATION   95,162

	MURDER	FORCED RAPE	ROB- BERY	AGGRYTD ASSAULT	BUR- GLARY	LARCENY +$50	AUTO THEFT
70 CRIMES	6	18	253	256	1,153	1,061	424
RATE PER 100,000	6.3	18.9	265.9	269.0	1211.6	1114.9	445.6
71 CRIMES	8	12	216	249	1,337	1,230	314
RATE PER 100,000	8.4	12.6	227.0	261.7	1405.0	1292.5	330.0

RATIO FOR 2 YEAR PERIOD   1 CRIME PER   29.1 PEOPLE

RANKING   202

RALEIGH,NORTH CAROLINA

POPULATION   121,577

	MURDER	FORCED RAPE	ROB- BERY	AGGRYTD ASSAULT	BUR- GLARY	LARCENY +$50	AUTO THEFT
70 CRIMES	10	19	125	518	1,135	2,304	279
RATE PER 100,000	8.2	15.6	102.8	426.1	933.6	1895.1	229.5
71 CRIMES	12	22	191	452	1,308	2,638	333
RATE PER 100,000	9.9	18.1	157.1	371.8	1075.9	2169.8	273.9

RATIO FOR 2 YEAR PERIOD   1 CRIME PER   26.0 PEOPLE

RANKING   234

READING,PENNSYLVANIA

POPULATION 87,643

	MURDER	FORCED RAPE	ROB- BERY	AGGRYTD ASSAULT	BUR- GLARY	LARCENY +$50	AUTO THEFT
70 CRIMES	2	6	81	66	639	564	244
RATE PER 100,000	2.3	6.8	92.4	75.3	729.1	643.5	278.4
71 CRIMES	7	13	103	76	483	523	302
RATE PER 100,000	8.0	14.8	117.5	86.7	551.1	596.7	344.6

RATIO FOR 2 YEAR PERIOD   1 CRIME PER   56.3 PEOPLE

RANKING   46

REDONDO BEACH,CALIFORNIA

POPULATION 56,075

	MURDER	FORCED RAPE	ROB- BERY	AGGRYTD ASSAULT	BUR- GLARY	LARCENY +$50	AUTO THEFT
70 CRIMES	5	21	95	95	980	1,477	493
RATE PER 100,000	8.9	37.4	169.4	169.4	1747.7	2634.0	879.2
71 CRIMES	4	15	85	99	1,121	1,571	497
RATE PER 100,000	7.1	26.7	151.6	176.5	1999.1	2801.6	886.3

RATIO FOR 2 YEAR PERIOD   1 CRIME PER   17.1 PEOPLE

RANKING   345

REDWOOD CITY,CALIFORNIA

POPULATION 55,686

	MURDER	FORCED RAPE	ROB- BERY	AGGRYTD ASSAULT	BUR- GLARY	LARCENY +$50	AUTO THEFT
70 CRIMES		6	56	30	692	894	417
RATE PER 100,000	0.0	10.8	100.6	53.9	1242.7	1605.4	748.8
71 CRIMES	3	6	56	33	640	967	338
RATE PER 100,000	5.4	10.8	100.6	59.3	1149.3	1736.5	607.0

RATIO FOR 2 YEAR PERIOD   1 CRIME PER   26.9 PEOPLE

RANKING   224

RENO, NEVADA

POPULATION   72,863

	MURDER	FORCED RAPE	ROB- BERY	AGGRVTD ASSAULT	BUR- GLARY	LARCENY +$50	AUTO THEFT
70 CRIMES	5	13	155	113	1,324	1,006	597
RATE PER 100,000	6.9	17.8	212.7	155.1	1817.1	1380.7	819.3
71 CRIMES	3	20	136	103	1,340	980	713
RATE PER 100,000	4.1	27.4	186.7	141.4	1839.1	1345.0	978.5

RATIO FOR 2 YEAR PERIOD   1 CRIME PER   22.3 PEOPLE

RANKING   284

RICHMOND, CALIFORNIA

POPULATION   79,043

	MURDER	FORCED RAPE	ROB- BERY	AGGRVTD ASSAULT	BUR- GLARY	LARCENY +$50	AUTO THEFT
70 CRIMES	8	66	283	439	2,331	1,277	918
RATE PER 100,000	10.1	83.5	358.0	555.4	2949.0	1615.6	1161.4
71 CRIMES	16	52	334	452	2,687	1,311	800
RATE PER 100,000	20.2	65.8	422.6	571.8	3399.4	1658.6	1012.1

RATIO FOR 2 YEAR PERIOD   1 CRIME PER   14.4 PEOPLE

RANKING   380

RICHMOND, VIRGINIA

POPULATION   249,621

	MURDER	FORCED RAPE	ROB- BERY	AGGRVTD ASSAULT	BUR- GLARY	LARCENY +$50	AUTO THEFT
70 CRIMES	65	94	921	596	6,558	4,340	2,433
RATE PER 100,000	26.0	37.7	369.0	238.8	2627.2	1738.6	974.7
71 CRIMES	72	131	1,286	786	6,191	4,143	2,697
RATE PER 100,000	28.8	52.5	515.2	314.9	2480.2	1659.7	1080.4

RATIO FOR 2 YEAR PERIOD   1 CRIME PER   16.4 PEOPLE

RANKING   352

RIVERSIDE,CALIFORNIA

POPULATION   140,089

	MURDER	FORCED RAPE	ROB- BERY	AGGRYTD ASSAULT	BUR- GLARY	LARCENY +$50	AUTO THEFT
70 CRIMES	6	48	237	390	4,069	2,529	824
RATE PER 100,000	4.3	34.3	169.2	278.4	2904.6	1805.3	588.2
71 CRIMES	14	63	255	465	4,036	3,056	824
RATE PER 100,000	10.0	45.0	182.0	331.9	2881.0	2181.5	588.2

RATIO FOR 2 YEAR PERIOD   1 CRIME PER   16.6 PEOPLE

RANKING   350

ROANOKE,VIRGINIA

POPULATION   92,115

	MURDER	FORCED RAPE	ROB- BERY	AGGRYTD ASSAULT	BUR- GLARY	LARCENY +$50	AUTO THEFT
70 CRIMES	15	28	155	277	1,549	1,056	641
RATE PER 100,000	16.3	30.4	168.3	300.7	1681.6	1146.4	695.9
71 CRIMES	13	28	127	235	1,483	1,214	540
RATE PER 100,000	14.1	30.4	137.9	255.1	1609.9	1317.9	586.2

RATIO FOR 2 YEAR PERIOD   1 CRIME PER   25.0 PEOPLE

RANKING   253

ROCHESTER,MINNESOTA

POPULATION   53,766

	MURDER	FORCED RAPE	ROB- BERY	AGGRYTD ASSAULT	BUR- GLARY	LARCENY +$50	AUTO THEFT
70 CRIMES	1	2	12	3	249	411	125
RATE PER 100,000	1.9	3.7	22.3	5.6	463.1	764.4	232.5
71 CRIMES	1	1	6	3	257	481	104
RATE PER 100,000	1.9	1.9	11.2	5.6	478.0	894.6	193.4

RATIO FOR 2 YEAR PERIOD   1 CRIME PER   64.9 PEOPLE

RANKING   29

ROCHESTER,NEW YORK

POPULATION 296,233

	MURDER	FORCED RAPE	ROB-BERY	AGGRYTD ASSAULT	BUR-GLARY	LARCENY +$50	AUTO THEFT
70 CRIMES	20	38	509	708	4,564	4,915	1,688
RATE PER 100,000	6.8	12.8	171.8	239.0	1540.7	1659.2	569.8
71 CRIMES	31	54	728	458	4,664	3,927	1,298
RATE PER 100,000	10.5	18.2	245.8	154.6	1574.4	1325.6	438.2

RATIO FOR 2 YEAR PERIOD   1 CRIME PER   25.1 PEOPLE

RANKING 252

ROCK ISLAND,ILLINOIS

POPULATION 50,166

	MURDER	FORCED RAPE	ROB-BERY	AGGRYTD ASSAULT	BUR-GLARY	LARCENY +$50	AUTO THEFT
70 CRIMES	4	10	95	100	441	787	223
RATE PER 100,000	8.0	19.9	189.4	199.3	879.1	1568.8	444.5
71 CRIMES	5	11	91	85	577	901	163
RATE PER 100,000	10.0	21.9	181.4	169.4	1150.2	1796.0	324.9

RATIO FOR 2 YEAR PERIOD   1 CRIME PER   28.7 PEOPLE

RANKING 207

ROCKFORD,ILLINOIS

POPULATION 147,370

	MURDER	FORCED RAPE	ROB-BERY	AGGRYTD ASSAULT	BUR-GLARY	LARCENY +$50	AUTO THEFT
70 CRIMES	9	16	176	194	1,473	1,711	588
RATE PER 100,000	6.1	10.9	119.4	131.6	999.5	1161.0	399.0
71 CRIMES	13	8	149	187	1,353	1,349	466
RATE PER 100,000	8.8	5.4	101.1	126.9	918.1	915.4	316.2

RATIO FOR 2 YEAR PERIOD   1 CRIME PER   38.3 PEOPLE

RANKING 109

ROME, NEW YORK

POPULATION 50,148

	MURDER	FORCED RAPE	ROB- BERY	AGGRYTD ASSAULT	BUR- GLARY	LARCENY +$50	AUTO THEFT
70 CRIMES			1	3	111	199	71
RATE PER 100,000	0.0	0.0	2.0	6.0	221.3	396.8	141.6
71 CRIMES			7	4	131	239	53
RATE PER 100,000	0.0	0.0	14.0	8.0	261.2	476.6	105.7

RATIO FOR 2 YEAR PERIOD 1 CRIME PER 122.4 PEOPLE

RANKING 2

ROSEVILLE, MICHIGAN

POPULATION 60,529

	MURDER	FORCED RAPE	ROB- BERY	AGGRYTD ASSAULT	BUR- GLARY	LARCENY +$50	AUTO THEFT
70 CRIMES	1	2	43	30	522	830	281
RATE PER 100,000	1.7	3.3	71.0	49.6	862.4	1371.2	464.2
71 CRIMES	2	6	61	36	501	965	37,7
RATE PER 100,000	3.3	9.9	100.8	59.5	827.7	1594.3	622.8

RATIO FOR 2 YEAR PERIOD 1 CRIME PER 33.1 PEOPLE

RANKING 144

ROYAL OAK, MICHIGAN

POPULATION 85,499

	MURDER	FORCED RAPE	ROB- BERY	AGGRYTD ASSAULT	BUR- GLARY	LARCENY +$50	AUTO THEFT
70 CRIMES	1	11	90	157	961	913	230
RATE PER 100,000	1.2	12.9	105.3	183.6	1124.0	1067.8	269.0
71 CRIMES	6	17	150	229	1,248	1,099	320
RATE PER 100,000	7.0	19.9	175.4	267.8	1459.7	1285.4	374.3

RATIO FOR 2 YEAR PERIOD 1 CRIME PER 31.4 PEOPLE

RANKING 163

SACRAMENTO, CALIFORNIA

POPULATION 254,413

70 CRIMES	MURDER	FORCED RAPE	ROB- BERY	AGGRYTD ASSAULT	BUR- GLARY	LARCENY +$50	AUTO THEFT
	19	68	583	432	4,518	3,933	2,155
RATE PER 100,000	7.5	26.7	229.2	169.8	1775.9	1545.9	847.0
71 CRIMES	33	84	783	565	5,509	3,745	2,691
RATE PER 100,000	13.0	33.0	307.8	222.1	2165.4	1472.0	1057.7

RATIO FOR 2 YEAR PERIOD   1 CRIME PER   20.2 PEOPLE

RANKING   309

SAGINAW, MICHIGAN

POPULATION 91,849

70 CRIMES	MURDER	FORCED RAPE	ROB- BERY	AGGRYTD ASSAULT	BUR- GLARY	LARCENY +$50	AUTO THEFT
	21	26	403	402	2,292	539	430
RATE PER 100,000	22.9	28.3	438.8	437.7	2495.4	586.8	468.2
71 CRIMES	28	37	635	554	3,356	689	428
RATE PER 100,000	30.5	40.3	691.4	603.2	3653.8	750.1	466.0

RATIO FOR 2 YEAR PERIOD   1 CRIME PER   18.6 PEOPLE

RANKING   329

SALEM, OREGON

POPULATION 68,296

70 CRIMES	MURDER	FORCED RAPE	ROB- BERY	AGGRYTD ASSAULT	BUR- GLARY	LARCENY +$50	AUTO THEFT
	2	12	43	120	890	682	220
RATE PER 100,000	2.9	17.6	63.0	175.7	1303.2	998.6	322.1
71 CRIMES	4	15	56	99	897	749	217
RATE PER 100,000	5.9	22.0	82.0	145.0	1313.4	1096.7	317.7

RATIO FOR 2 YEAR PERIOD   1 CRIME PER   34.0 PEOPLE

RANKING   133

SALINAS,CALIFORNIA

POPULATION   58,896

	MURDER	FORCED RAPE	ROB- BERY	AGGRYTD ASSAULT	BUR- GLARY	LARCENY +$50	AUTO THEFT
70 CRIMES	5	8	94	64	743	1,111	377
RATE PER 100,000	8.5	13.6	159.6	108.7	1261.5	1886.4	640.1
71 CRIMES	4	3	104	75	729	1,255	294
RATE PER 100,000	6.8	5.1	176.6	127.3	1237.8	2130.9	499.2

RATIO FOR 2 YEAR PERIOD   1 CRIME PER   24.2 PEOPLE

RANKING   259

SALT LAKE CITY,UTAH

POPULATION   175,885

	MURDER	FORCED RAPE	ROB- BERY	AGGRYTD ASSAULT	BUR- GLARY	LARCENY +$50	AUTO THEFT
70 CRIMES	9	52	358	265	4,169	3,927	1,581
RATE PER 100,000	5.1	29.6	203.5	150.7	2370.3	2232.7	898.9
71 CRIMES	16	64	409	292	4,159	4,387	1,852
RATE PER 100,000	9.1	36.4	232.5	166.0	2364.6	2494.2	1053.0

RATIO FOR 2 YEAR PERIOD   1 CRIME PER   16.3 PEOPLE

RANKING   354

SAN ANGELO,TEXAS

POPULATION   63,884

	MURDER	FORCED RAPE	ROB- BERY	AGGRYTD ASSAULT	BUR- GLARY	LARCENY +$50	AUTO THEFT
70 CRIMES	5	8	27	44	773	345	175
RATE PER 100,000	7.8	12.5	42.3	68.9	1210.0	540.0	273.9
71 CRIMES	4	9	21	50	781	371	132
RATE PER 100,000	6.3	14.1	32.9	78.3	1222.5	580.7	206.6

RATIO FOR 2 YEAR PERIOD   1 CRIME PER   46.5 PEOPLE

RANKING   81

SAN ANTONIO,TEXAS

POPULATION 654,153

70 CRIMES	MURDER	FORCED RAPE	ROB- BERY	AGGRYTD ASSAULT	BUR- GLARY	LARCENY +$50	AUTO THEFT
	73	202	1,062	1,912	11,660	7,353	4,959
RATE PER 100,000	11.2	30.9	162.3	292.3	1782.5	1124.0	758.1
71 CRIMES	96	217	911	2,091	10,579	8,008	4,801
RATE PER 100,000	14.7	33.2	139.3	319.6	1617.2	1224.2	733.9

RATIO FOR 2 YEAR PERIOD   1 CRIME PER   24.2 PEOPLE

RANKING   258

SAN BERNARINO,CALIFORNIA

POPULATION 104,251

70 CRIMES	MURDER	FORCED RAPE	ROB- BERY	AGGRYTD ASSAULT	BUR- GLARY	LARCENY +$50	AUTO THEFT
	9	20	270	239	2,569	2,285	1,055
RATE PER 100,000	8.6	19.2	259.0	229.3	2464.2	2191.8	1012.0
71 CRIMES	7	34	400	278	3,040	2,391	1,054
RATE PER 100,000	6.7	32.6	383.7	266.7	2916.0	2293.5	1011.0

RATIO FOR 2 YEAR PERIOD   1 CRIME PER   15.2 PEOPLE

RANKING   372

SAN DIEGO,CALIFORNIA

POPULATION 696,769

70 CRIMES	MURDER	FORCED RAPE	ROB- BERY	AGGRYTD ASSAULT	BUR- GLARY	LARCENY +$50	AUTO THEFT
	32	135	839	981	6,902	10,613	3,730
RATE PER 100,000	4.6	19.4	120.4	140.8	990.6	1523.2	535.3
71 CRIMES	37	142	1,106	806	8,670	11,050	3,684
RATE PER 100,000	5.3	20.4	158.7	115.7	1244.3	1585.9	528.7

RATIO FOR 2 YEAR PERIOD   1 CRIME PER   28.5 PEOPLE

RANKING   208

SAN FRANCISCO,CALIFORNIA

POPULATION   715,674

	MURDER	FORCED RAPE	ROB-BERY	AGGRYTD ASSAULT	BUR-GLARY	LARCENY +$50	AUTO THEFT
70 CRIMES	111	572	5,881	3,020	18,844	14,515	14,193
RATE PER 100,000	15.5	79.9	821.7	422.0	2633.0	2028.2	1983.2
71 CRIMES	102	512	6,584	3,101	18,264	16,130	12,845
RATE PER 100,000	14.3	71.5	920.0	433.3	2552.0	2253.8	1794.8

RATIO FOR 2 YEAR PERIOD   1 CRIME PER   12.4 PEOPLE

RANKING   389

SAN JOSE,CALIFORNIA

POPULATION   445,779

	MURDER	FORCED RAPE	ROB-BERY	AGGRYTD ASSAULT	BUR-GLARY	LARCENY +$50	AUTO THEFT
70 CRIMES	12	168	544	737	6,830	2,630	3,571
RATE PER 100,000	2.7	37.7	122.0	165.3	1532.1	590.0	801.1
71 CRIMES	16	170	497	743	8,190	4,643	3,621
RATE PER 100,000	3.6	38.1	111.5	166.7	1837.2	1041.5	812.3

RATIO FOR 2 YEAR PERIOD   1 CRIME PER   27.5 PEOPLE

RANKING   220

SAN LEANDRO,CALIFORNIA

POPULATION   68,698

	MURDER	FORCED RAPE	ROB-BERY	AGGRYTD ASSAULT	BUR-GLARY	LARCENY +$50	AUTO THEFT
70 CRIMES	4	10	84	45	1,124	1,172	292
RATE PER 100,000	5.8	14.6	122.3	65.5	1636.1	1706.0	425.0
71 CRIMES	2	9	111	42	1,113	1,156	273
RATE PER 100,000	2.9	13.1	161.6	61.1	1620.1	1682.7	397.4

RATIO FOR 2 YEAR PERIOD   1 CRIME PER   25.2 PEOPLE

RANKING   249

SAN MATEO,CALIFORNIA

POPULATION   78,991

	MURDER	FORCED RAPE	ROB- BERY	AGGRYTD ASSAULT	BUR- GLARY	LARCENY +$50	AUTO THEFT
70 CRIMES	2	15	115	106	1,377	984	496
RATE PER 100,000	2.5	19.0	145.6	134.2	1743.2	1245.7	627.9
71 CRIMES	3	10	140	110	1,365	1,025	425
RATE PER 100,000	3.8	12.7	177.2	139.3	1728.0	1297.6	538.0

RATIO FOR 2 YEAR PERIOD   1 CRIME PER   25.5 PEOPLE

RANKING   239

SANTA ANA,CALIFORNIA

POPULATION   156,601

	MURDER	FORCED RAPE	ROB- BERY	AGGRYTD ASSAULT	BUR- GLARY	LARCENY +$50	AUTO THEFT
70 CRIMES	7	52	225	260	3,293	976	806
RATE PER 100,000	4.5	33.2	143.7	166.0	2102.8	623.2	514.7
71 CRIMES	4	83	276	282	3,719	1,508	844
RATE PER 100,000	2.6	53.0	176.2	180.1	2374.8	963.0	538.9

RATIO FOR 2 YEAR PERIOD   1 CRIME PER   25.3 PEOPLE

RANKING   247

SANTA BARBARA,CALIFORNIA

POPULATION   70,215

	MURDER	FORCED RAPE	ROB- BERY	AGGRYTD ASSAULT	BUR- GLARY	LARCENY +$50	AUTO THEFT
70 CRIMES	7	13	63	77	1,025	937	290
RATE PER 100,000	10.0	18.5	89.7	109.7	1459.8	1334.5	413.0
71 CRIMES	8	8	75	84	1,000	878	285
RATE PER 100,000	11.4	11.4	106.8	119.6	1424.2	1250.4	405.9

RATIO FOR 2 YEAR PERIOD   1 CRIME PER   29.5 PEOPLE

RANKING   196

SANTA CLARA,CALIFORNIA

POPULATION   87,717

	MURDER	FORCED RAPE	ROB-BERY	AGGRYTD ASSAULT	BUR-GLARY	LARCENY +$50	AUTO THEFT
70 CRIMES	4	34	31	90	1,038	1,061	385
RATE PER 100,000	4.6	38.8	35.3	102.6	1183.4	1209.6	438.9
71 CRIMES	3	23	67	56	1,118	952	453
RATE PER 100,000	3.4	26.2	76.4	63.8	1274.6	1085.3	516.4

RATIO FOR 2 YEAR PERIOD   1 CRIME PER   33.0 PEOPLE

RANKING   145

SANTA MONICA,CALIFORNIA

POPULATION   88,289

	MURDER	FORCED RAPE	ROB-BERY	AGGRYTD ASSAULT	BUR-GLARY	LARCENY +$50	AUTO THEFT
70 CRIMES	6	73	299	281	1,758	2,380	791
RATE PER 100,000	6.8	82.7	338.7	318.3	1991.2	2695.7	895.9
71 CRIMES	5	69	281	268	1,868	2,459	818
RATE PER 100,000	5.7	78.2	318.3	303.5	2115.8	2785.2	926.5

RATIO FOR 2 YEAR PERIOD   1 CRIME PER   15.5 PEOPLE

RANKING   366

SANTA ROSA,CALIFORNIA

POPULATION   50,006

	MURDER	FORCED RAPE	ROB-BERY	AGGRYTD ASSAULT	BUR-GLARY	LARCENY +$50	AUTO THEFT
70 CRIMES	2	3	35	44	692	1,172	219
RATE PER 100,000	4.0	6.0	70.0	88.0	1383.8	2343.7	437.9
71 CRIMES	2	4	44	47	977	1,385	378
RATE PER 100,000	4.0	8.0	88.0	94.0	1953.8	2769.7	755.9

RATIO FOR 2 YEAR PERIOD   1 CRIME PER   19.9 PEOPLE

RANKING   312

SAVANNAH,GEORGIA

POPULATION   118,349

	MURDER	FORCED RAPE	ROB- BERY	AGGRYTD ASSAULT	BUR- GLARY	LARCENY +$50	AUTO THEFT
70 CRIMES	29	48	310	248	2,022	2,158	554
RATE PER 100,000	24.5	40.6	261.9	209.5	1708.5	1823.4	468.1
71 CRIMES	22	86	393	414	3,372	2,106	716
RATE PER 100,000	18.6	72.7	332.1	349.8	2849.2	1779.5	605.0

RATIO FOR 2 YEAR PERIOD   1 CRIME PER   18.9 PEOPLE

RANKING   327

SCHENECTADY,NEW YORK

POPULATION   77,859

	MURDER	FORCED RAPE	ROB- BERY	AGGRYTD ASSAULT	BUR- GLARY	LARCENY +$50	AUTO THEFT
70 CRIMES	1	2	86	36	445	318	287
RATE PER 100,000	1.3	2.6	110.5	46.2	571.5	408.4	368.6
71 CRIMES	5	7	52	48	553	497	408
RATE PER 100,000	6.4	9.0	66.8	61.6	710.3	638.3	524.0

RATIO FOR 2 YEAR PERIOD   1 CRIME PER   56.7 PEOPLE

RANKING   44

SCOTTSDALE,ARIZONA

POPULATION   67,823

	MURDER	FORCED RAPE	ROB- BERY	AGGRYTD ASSAULT	BUR- GLARY	LARCENY +$50	AUTO THEFT
70 CRIMES	4	8	30	72	713	988	275
RATE PER 100,000	5.9	11.8	44.2	106.2	1051.3	1456.7	405.5
71 CRIMES		11	22	75	929	1,208	511
RATE PER 100,000	0.0	16.2	32.4	110.6	1369.7	1781.1	458.5

RATIO FOR 2 YEAR PERIOD   1 CRIME PER   29.1 PEOPLE

RANKING   200

SCRANTON,PENNSYLVANIA

POPULATION   103,564

	MURDER	FORCED RAPE	ROB- BERY	AGGRYTD ASSAULT	BUR- GLARY	LARCENY +$50	AUTO THEFT
70 CRIMES	5	6	25	129	604	595	361
RATE PER 100,000	4.8	5.8	24.1	124.6	583.2	574.5	367.9
71 CRIMES	1	7	68	144	795	770	452
RATE PER 100,000	1.0	6.8	65.7	139.0	767.6	743.5	436.4

RATIO FOR 2 YEAR PERIOD   1 CRIME PER   52.0 PEOPLE

RANKING   60

SEATTLE,WASHINGTON

POPULATION   530,831

	MURDER	FORCED RAPE	ROB- BERY	AGGRYTD ASSAULT	BUR- GLARY	LARCENY +$50	AUTO THEFT
70 CRIMES	42	184	1,984	954	14,770	8,942	4,300
RATE PER 100,000	7.9	34.7	373.8	179.7	2782.4	1684.5	810.1
71 CRIMES	42	208	1,801	1,093	12,455	7,858	3,510
RATE PER 100,000	7.9	39.2	339.3	205.9	2346.3	1480.3	661.2

RATIO FOR 2 YEAR PERIOD   1 CRIME PER   18.2 PEOPLE

RANKING   333

SHREVEPORT,LOUISIANA

POPULATION   182,064

	MURDER	FORCED RAPE	ROB- BERY	AGGRYTD ASSAULT	BUR- GLARY	LARCENY +$50	AUTO THEFT
70 CRIMES	34	13	142	659	2,007	1,110	702
RATE PER 100,000	18.7	7.1	78.0	362.0	1102.4	609.7	385.6
71 CRIMES	40	25	186	585	2,595	1,272	769
RATE PER 100,000	22.0	13.7	102.2	321.3	1425.3	698.7	422.4

RATIO FOR 2 YEAR PERIOD   1 CRIME PER   35.9 PEOPLE

RANKING   125

SIOUX CITY,IOWA

POPULATION   85,925

	MURDER	FORCED RAPE	ROB-BERY	AGGRYTD ASSAULT	BUR-GLARY	LARCENY +$50	AUTO THEFT
70 CRIMES	4	4	12	94	491	840	602
RATE PER 100,000	4.7	4.7	14.0	109.4	571.4	977.6	700.6
71 CRIMES	4	4	13	73	660	921	491
RATE PER 100,000	4.7	4.7	15.1	85.0	768.1	1071.9	571.4

RATIO FOR 2 YEAR PERIOD   1 CRIME PER   40.7 PEOPLE

RANKING   100

SIOUX FALLS,SOUTH DAKOTA

POPULATION   72,488

	MURDER	FORCED RAPE	ROB-BERY	AGGRYTD ASSAULT	BUR-GLARY	LARCENY +$50	AUTO THEFT
70 CRIMES	5	21	20	33	398	498	121
RATE PER 100,000	6.9	29.0	27.6	45.5	549.1	687.0	166.9
71 CRIMES		13	23	13	391	618	77
RATE PER 100,000	0.0	17.9	31.7	17.9	539.4	852.6	106.2

RATIO FOR 2 YEAR PERIOD   1 CRIME PER   64.9 PEOPLE

RANKING   28

SKOKIE,ILLINOIS

POPULATION   68,627

	MURDER	FORCED RAPE	ROB-BERY	AGGRYTD ASSAULT	BUR-GLARY	LARCENY +$50	AUTO THEFT
70 CRIMES		4	14	45	600	996	156
RATE PER 100,000	0.0	5.8	20.4	65.6	874.3	1451.3	227.3
71 CRIMES		3	24	77	555	989	154
RATE PER 100,000	0.0	4.4	35.0	112.2	808.7	1441.1	224.4

RATIO FOR 2 YEAR PERIOD   1 CRIME PER   37.9 PEOPLE

RANKING   110

SOMERVILLE, MASSACHUSETTS

POPULATION   88,779

	MURDER	FORCED RAPE	ROB- BERY	AGGRYTD ASSAULT	BUR- GLARY	LARCENY +$50	AUTO THEFT
70 CRIMES	7	7	60	54	1,203	585	991
RATE PER 100,000	7.9	7.9	67.6	60.8	1355.1	658.9	1037.4
71 CRIMES	5	9	65	53	1,004	240	1,208
RATE PER 100,000	5.6	10.1	73.2	59.7	1130.9	270.3	1360.7

RATIO FOR 2 YEAR PERIOD   1 CRIME PER   32.7 PEOPLE

RANKING   148

SOUTH BEND, INDIANA

POPULATION   125,580

	MURDER	FORCED RAPE	ROB- BERY	AGGRYTD ASSAULT	BUR- GLARY	LARCENY +$50	AUTO THEFT
70 CRIMES	9	17	430	134	2,195	1,847	874
RATE PER 100,000	7.2	13.5	342.4	106.7	1747.9	1470.8	696.0
71 CRIMES	17	26	463	132	1,843	1,466	846
RATE PER 100,000	13.5	20.7	368.7	105.1	1467.6	1167.4	673.7

RATIO FOR 2 YEAR PERIOD   1 CRIME PER   24.3 PEOPLE

RANKING   257

SOUTH GATE, CALIFORNIA

POPULATION   56,909

	MURDER	FORCED RAPE	ROB- BERY	AGGRYTD ASSAULT	BUR- GLARY	LARCENY +$50	AUTO THEFT
70 CRIMES	6	19	150	55	1,018	777	591
RATE PER 100,000	10.5	33.4	263.6	96.6	1788.8	1365.3	1038.5
71 CRIMES	4	8	170	74	972	695	586
RATE PER 100,000	7.0	14.1	298.7	130.0	1708.0	1221.2	1029.7

RATIO FOR 2 YEAR PERIOD   1 CRIME PER   22.2 PEOPLE

RANKING   287

SOUTHFIELD,MICHIGAN

POPULATION   69,285

70 CRIMES	MURDER	FORCED RAPE	ROB- BERY	AGGRYTD ASSAULT	BUR- GLARY	LARCENY +$50	AUTO THEFT
		5	58	49	909	1,335	364
RATE PER 100,000	0.0	7.2	83.7	70.7	1312.0	1926.8	525.4
71 CRIMES	5	11	86	42	880	1,522	490
RATE PER 100,000	7.2	15.9	124.1	60.6	1270.1	2196.7	707.2

RATIO FOR 2 YEAR PERIOD   1 CRIME PER   24.0 PEOPLE

RANKING   262

SPOKANE,WASHINGTON

POPULATION   170,516

70 CRIMES	MURDER	FORCED RAPE	ROB- BERY	AGGRYTD ASSAULT	BUR- GLARY	LARCENY +$50	AUTO THEFT
	4	30	181	110	2,432	2,143	660
RATE PER 100,000	2.3	17.6	106.1	64.5	1426.3	1256.8	387.1
71 CRIMES	9	18	181	168	2,645	2,208	748
RATE PER 100,000	5.3	10.6	106.1	98.5	1551.2	1294.9	438.7

RATIO FOR 2 YEAR PERIOD   1 CRIME PER   29.5 PEOPLE

RANKING   197

SPRINGFIELD,ILLINOIS

POPULATION   91,753

70 CRIMES	MURDER	FORCED RAPE	ROB- BERY	AGGRYTD ASSAULT	BUR- GLARY	LARCENY +$50	AUTO THEFT
	3	6	132	88	1,171	702	451
RATE PER 100,000	3.3	6.5	143.9	95.9	1276.3	765.1	491.5
71 CRIMES	6	4	111	136	1,024	583	439
RATE PER 100,000	6.5	4.4	121.0	148.2	1116.0	635.4	478.5

RATIO FOR 2 YEAR PERIOD   1 CRIME PER   37.7 PEOPLE

RANKING   111

SPRINGFIELD, MASSACHUSETTS

POPULATION   163,905

	MURDER	FORCED RAPE	ROB-BERY	AGGRYTD ASSAULT	BUR-GLARY	LARCENY +$50	AUTO THEFT
70 CRIMES	12	17	70	272	3,117	1,402	2,944
RATE PER 100,000	7.3	10.4	42.7	165.9	1901.7	855.4	1796.2
71 CRIMES	12	10	407	325	4,358	2,011	3,150
RATE PER 100,000	7.3	6.1	248.3	198.3	2658.9	1226.9	1921.8

RATIO FOR 2 YEAR PERIOD   1 CRIME PER   18.1 PEOPLE

RANKING   335

SPRINGFIELD, MISSOURI

POPULATION   120,096

	MURDER	FORCED RAPE	ROB-BERY	AGGRYTD ASSAULT	BUR-GLARY	LARCENY +$50	AUTO THEFT
70 CRIMES	4	4	74	50	1,732	1,544	260
RATE PER 100,000	3.3	3.3	61.6	41.6	1442.2	1285.6	216.5
71 CRIMES	4	5	64	77	1,831	1,665	317
RATE PER 100,000	3.3	4.2	53.3	64.1	1524.6	1386.4	264.0

RATIO FOR 2 YEAR PERIOD   1 CRIME PER   31.4 PEOPLE

RANKING   162

SPRINGFIELD, OHIO

POPULATION   81,926

	MURDER	FORCED RAPE	ROB-BERY	AGGRYTD ASSAULT	BUR-GLARY	LARCENY +$50	AUTO THEFT
70 CRIMES	6	12	170	28	775	382	219
RATE PER 100,000	7.3	14.6	207.5	34.2	946.0	466.3	267.3
71 CRIMES	4	10	191	28	877	338	239
RATE PER 100,000	4.9	12.2	233.1	34.2	1070.5	412.6	291.7

RATIO FOR 2 YEAR PERIOD   1 CRIME PER   49.9 PEOPLE

RANKING   68

282

ST. CLAIR SHORES, MICHIGAN

POPULATION   88,093

70 CRIMES	MURDER	FORCED RAPE	ROB-BERY	AGGRVTD ASSAULT	BUR-GLARY	LARCENY +$50	AUTO THEFT
70 CRIMES	3	14	40	80	752	939	117
RATE PER 100,000	3.4	15.9	45.4	90.8	853.6	1065.9	132.8
71 CRIMES	1	9	46	94	1,022	1,434	265
RATE PER 100,000	1.1	10.2	52.2	106.7	1160.1	1627.8	300.8

RATIO FOR 2 YEAR PERIOD   1 CRIME PER   36.5 PEOPLE

RANKING   120

ST. JOSEPH, MISSOURI

POPULATION   72,691

70 CRIMES	MURDER	FORCED RAPE	ROB-BERY	AGGRVTD ASSAULT	BUR-GLARY	LARCENY +$50	AUTO THEFT
70 CRIMES	1	1	25	65	676	946	269
RATE PER 100,000	1.4	1.4	34.4	89.4	930.0	1301.4	370.1
71 CRIMES	2	4	23	104	858	989	187
RATE PER 100,000	2.8	5.5	31.6	143.1	1180.3	1360.6	257.3

RATIO FOR 2 YEAR PERIOD   1 CRIME PER   35.0 PEOPLE

RANKING   128

ST. LOUIS, MISSOURI

POPULATION   622,236

70 CRIMES	MURDER	FORCED RAPE	ROB-BERY	AGGRVTD ASSAULT	BUR-GLARY	LARCENY +$50	AUTO THEFT
70 CRIMES	266	546	5,296	3,239	19,011	4,532	13,025
RATE PER 100,000	42.7	87.7	851.1	520.5	3055.3	728.3	2093.3
71 CRIMES	220	498	4,956	3,231	18,876	4,763	11,865
RATE PER 100,000	35.4	80.0	796.5	519.3	3033.6	765.5	1906.8

RATIO FOR 2 YEAR PERIOD   1 CRIME PER   13.7 PEOPLE

RANKING   381

ST. PAUL, MINNESOTA

POPULATION   309,980

	MURDER	FORCED RAPE	ROB-BERY	AGGRYTD ASSAULT	BUR-GLARY	LARCENY +$50	AUTO THEFT
70 CRIMES	14	65	1,160	562	5,927	3,929	3,393
RATE PER 100,000	4.5	21.0	374.2	181.3	1912.1	1267.5	1094.6
71 CRIMES	20	79	892	498	5,919	3,998	3,011
RATE PER 100,000	6.5	25.5	287.8	160.7	1909.5	1289.8	971.4

RATIO FOR 2 YEAR PERIOD   1 CRIME PER   21.0 PEOPLE

RANKING   303

ST. PETERSBURG, FLORIDA

POPULATION   216,232

	MURDER	FORCED RAPE	ROB-BERY	AGGRYTD ASSAULT	BUR-GLARY	LARCENY +$50	AUTO THEFT
70 CRIMES	20	51	632	667	4,003	2,009	504
RATE PER 100,000	9.2	23.6	292.3	308.5	1851.3	929.1	233.1
71 CRIMES	29	52	633	671	4,487	2,337	452
RATE PER 100,000	13.4	24.0	292.7	310.3	2075.1	1080.8	209.0

RATIO FOR 2 YEAR PERIOD   1 CRIME PER   26.1 PEOPLE

RANKING   233

STAMFORD, CONNECTICUT

POPULATION   108,798

	MURDER	FORCED RAPE	ROB-BERY	AGGRYTD ASSAULT	BUR-GLARY	LARCENY +$50	AUTO THEFT
70 CRIMES	6	15	138	71	2,206	426	703
RATE PER 100,000	5.5	13.8	126.8	65.3	2027.6	391.6	646.2
71 CRIMES	1	16	150	91	2,331	522	704
RATE PER 100,000	0.9	14.7	137.9	83.6	2142.5	479.8	647.1

RATIO FOR 2 YEAR PERIOD   1 CRIME PER   29.4 PEOPLE

RANKING   199

STERLING HEIGHTS,MICHIGAN

POPULATION   61,365

70 CRIMES	MURDER	FORCED RAPE	ROB- BERY	AGGRYTD ASSAULT	BUR- GLARY	LARCENY +$50	AUTO THEFT
		18	20	83	646	762	201
RATE PER 100,000	0.0	29.3	32.6	135.3	1052.7	1241.8	327.5
71 CRIMES	2	12	29	112	724	895	232
RATE PER 100,000	3.3	19.6	47.3	182.5	1179.8	1458.5	378.1

RATIO FOR 2 YEAR PERIOD   1 CRIME PER   32.8 PEOPLE

RANKING   146

STOCKTON,CALIFORNIA

POPULATION   107,644

70 CRIMES	MURDER	FORCED RAPE	ROB- BERY	AGGRYTD ASSAULT	BUR- GLARY	LARCENY +$50	AUTO THEFT
	9	17	411	213	2,461	1,806	1,230
RATE PER 100,000	8.4	15.8	381.8	197.9	2286.2	1677.8	1142.7
71 CRIMES	20	34	474	256	3,452	1,973	1,337
RATE PER 100,000	18.6	31.6	440.3	237.8	3206.9	1832.9	1242.1

RATIO FOR 2 YEAR PERIOD   1 CRIME PER   15.7 PEOPLE

RANKING   363

SUNNYVALE,CALIFORNIA

POPULATION   95,408

70 CRIMES	MURDER	FORCED RAPE	ROB- BERY	AGGRYTD ASSAULT	BUR- GLARY	LARCENY +$50	AUTO THEFT
	2	14	35	62	655	614	364
RATE PER 100,000	2.1	14.7	36.7	65.0	686.5	643.6	381.5
71 CRIMES	1	10	41	65	752	587	363
RATE PER 100,000	1.0	10.5	43.0	68.1	788.2	615.3	380.5

RATIO FOR 2 YEAR PERIOD   1 CRIME PER   53.5 PEOPLE

RANKING   52

SYRACUSE,NEW YORK

POPULATION   197,208

	MURDER	FORCED RAPE	ROB- BERY	AGGRYTD ASSAULT	BUR- GLARY	LARCENY +$50	AUTO THEFT
70 CRIMES	12	36	444	212	2,671	2,566	539
RATE PER 100,000	6.1	18.3	225.1	107.5	1354.4	1301.2	273.3
71 CRIMES	5	38	528	284	2,968	2,382	664
RATE PER 100,000	2.5	19.3	267.7	144.0	1505.0	1207.9	336.7

RATIO FOR 2 YEAR PERIOD   1 CRIME PER   29.5 PEOPLE

RANKING   198

TACOMA,WASHINGTON

POPULATION   154,581

	MURDER	FORCED RAPE	ROB- BERY	AGGRYTD ASSAULT	BUR- GLARY	LARCENY +$50	AUTO THEFT
70 CRIMES	14	38	221	343	2,611	1,903	966
RATE PER 100,000	9.1	24.6	143.0	221.9	1689.1	1231.1	624.9
71 CRIMES	10	44	310	297	2,493	1,930	921
RATE PER 100,000	6.5	28.5	200.5	192.1	1612.7	1248.5	595.8

RATIO FOR 2 YEAR PERIOD   1 CRIME PER   25.5 PEOPLE

RANKING   241

TALLAHASSEE,FLORIDA

POPULATION   71,897

	MURDER	FORCED RAPE	ROB- BERY	AGGRYTD ASSAULT	BUR- GLARY	LARCENY +$50	AUTO THEFT
70 CRIMES	4	11	63	123	1,119	744	167
RATE PER 100,000	5.6	15.3	87.6	171.1	1556.4	1034.8	232.3
71 CRIMES	11	22	112	236	808	1,050	263
RATE PER 100,000	15.3	30.6	155.8	328.2	1123.8	1460.4	365.8

RATIO FOR 2 YEAR PERIOD   1 CRIME PER   30.3 PEOPLE

RANKING   180

TAMPA,FLORIDA

POPULATION   277,767

70 CRIMES	MURDER	FORCED RAPE	ROB- BERY	AGGRYTD ASSAULT	BUR- GLARY	LARCENY +$50	AUTO THEFT
70 CRIMES	52	62	812	999	6,216	4,404	1,441
RATE PER 100,000	18.7	22.3	292.3	359.7	2237.8	1585.5	518.8
71 CRIMES	54	68	951	1,143	6,346	3,893	1,369
RATE PER 100,000	19.4	24.5	342.4	411.5	2284.6	1401.5	492.9

RATIO FOR 2 YEAR PERIOD   1 CRIME PER   19.9 PEOPLE

RANKING   313

TAYLOR,MICHIGAN

POPULATION   70,020

70 CRIMES	MURDER	FORCED RAPE	ROB- BERY	AGGRYTD ASSAULT	BUR- GLARY	LARCENY +$50	AUTO THEFT
70 CRIMES	1	15	75	103	1,002	1,104	327
RATE PER 100,000	1.4	21.4	107.1	147.1	1431.0	1576.7	467.0
71 CRIMES							
RATE PER 100,000							

RATIO FOR 2 YEAR PERIOD   1 CRIME PER   53.3 PEOPLE

RANKING   54

TEMPE,ARIZONA

POPULATION   62,907

70 CRIMES	MURDER	FORCED RAPE	ROB- BERY	AGGRYTD ASSAULT	BUR- GLARY	LARCENY +$50	AUTO THEFT
70 CRIMES	4	25	38	103	732	1,526	283
RATE PER 100,000	6.4	39.7	60.4	163.7	1163.6	2425.8	449.9
71 CRIMES	4	18	44	63	747	1,493	267
RATE PER 100,000	6.4	28.6	69.9	100.1	1187.5	2373.3	424.4

RATIO FOR 2 YEAR PERIOD   1 CRIME PER   23.5 PEOPLE

RANKING   269

TERRE HAUTE,INDIANA

POPULATION   70,286

	MURDER	FORCED RAPE	ROB- BERY	AGGRYTD ASSAULT	BUR- GLARY	LARCENY +$50	AUTO THEFT
70 CRIMES	2	7	54	57	831	966	272
RATE PER 100,000	2.8	10.0	76.8	81.1	1182.3	1374.4	387.0
71 CRIMES	4	9	48	57	889	871	296
RATE PER 100,000	5.7	12.8	68.3	81.1	1264.8	1239.2	421.1

RATIO FOR 2 YEAR PERIOD   1 CRIME PER   32.2 PEOPLE

RANKING   156

TOLEDO,OHIO

POPULATION   383,818

	MURDER	FORCED RAPE	ROB- BERY	AGGRYTD ASSAULT	BUR- GLARY	LARCENY +$50	AUTO THEFT
70 CRIMES	30	94	1,003	379	5,742	4,482	1,677
RATE PER 100,000	7.8	24.5	261.3	98.7	1496.0	1167.7	436.9
71 CRIMES	29	118	1,081	457	5,227	5,149	1,760
RATE PER 100,000	7.6	30.7	281.6	119.1	1361.8	1341.5	458.6

RATIO FOR 2 YEAR PERIOD   1 CRIME PER   28.1 PEOPLE

RANKING   210

TOPEKA,KANSAS

POPULATION   125,011

	MURDER	FORCED RAPE	ROB- BERY	AGGRYTD ASSAULT	BUR- GLARY	LARCENY +$50	AUTO THEFT
70 CRIMES	3	29	188	306	1,582	2,210	383
RATE PER 100,000	2.4	23.2	150.4	244.8	1265.5	1767.8	306.4
71 CRIMES	7	40	202	442	1,583	1,956	356
RATE PER 100,000	5.6	32.0	161.6	353.6	1266.3	1564.7	284.8

RATIO FOR 2 YEAR PERIOD   1 CRIME PER   26.9 PEOPLE

RANKING   223

TORRANCE,CALIFORNIA

POPULATION   134,584

70 CRIMES	MURDER	FORCED RAPE	ROB- BERY	AGGRVTD ASSAULT	BUR- GLARY	LARCENY +$50	AUTO THEFT
70 CRIMES	3	22	129	99	1,992	2,245	815
RATE PER 100,000	2.2	16.3	95.9	73.6	1480.1	1668.1	605.6
71 CRIMES	6	39	155	121	2,459	2,372	907
RATE PER 100,000	4.5	29.0	115.2	89.9	1827.1	1762.5	673.9

RATIO FOR 2 YEAR PERIOD   1 CRIME PER   23.6 PEOPLE

RANKING   268

TRENTON,NEW JERSEY

POPULATION   104,638

70 CRIMES	MURDER	FORCED RAPE	ROB- BERY	AGGRVTD ASSAULT	BUR- GLARY	LARCENY +$50	AUTO THEFT
70 CRIMES	27	38	657	239	3,333	1,785	1,345
RATE PER 100,000	25.8	36.3	627.9	228.4	3185.3	1705.9	1285.4
71 CRIMES	16	22	913	300	3,378	1,816	1,360
RATE PER 100,000	15.3	21.0	872.5	286.7	3228.3	1735.5	1299.7

RATIO FOR 2 YEAR PERIOD   1 CRIME PER   13.7 PEOPLE

RANKING   382

TROY,NEW YORK

POPULATION   62,918

70 CRIMES	MURDER	FORCED RAPE	ROB- BERY	AGGRVTD ASSAULT	BUR- GLARY	LARCENY +$50	AUTO THEFT
70 CRIMES	3	8	45	76	567	404	275
RATE PER 100,000	4.8	12.7	71.5	120.8	901.2	642.1	437.1
71 CRIMES		7	55	95	549	296	248
RATE PER 100,000	0.0	11.1	87.4	151.0	872.6	470.5	394.2

RATIO FOR 2 YEAR PERIOD   1 CRIME PER   47.8 PEOPLE

RANKING   77

TUCSON, ARIZONA

POPULATION   262,933

	MURDER	FORCED RAPE	ROB- BERY	AGGRYTD ASSAULT	BUR- GLARY	LARCENY +$50	AUTO THEFT
70 CRIMES	53	72	347	387	3,782	2,175	1,713
RATE PER 100,000	20.2	27.4	132.0	147.2	1438.4	827.2	651.5
71 CRIMES	19	91	383	465	3,704	2,450	1,353
RATE PER 100,000	7.2	34.6	145.7	176.9	1408.7	931.8	514.6

RATIO FOR 2 YEAR PERIOD   1 CRIME PER   30.9 PEOPLE

RANKING   173

TULSA, OKLAHOMA

POPULATION   331,638

	MURDER	FORCED RAPE	ROB- BERY	AGGRYTD ASSAULT	BUR- GLARY	LARCENY +$50	AUTO THEFT
70 CRIMES	31	74	384	546	4,682	4,781	2,169
RATE PER 100,000	9.3	22.3	115.8	164.6	1411.8	1441.6	654.0
71 CRIMES	33	73	459	838	5,113	3,922	1,994
RATE PER 100,000	10.0	22.0	138.4	252.7	1541.7	1182.6	601.3

RATIO FOR 2 YEAR PERIOD   1 CRIME PER   26.4 PEOPLE

RANKING   230

TUSCALOOSA, ALABAMA

POPULATION   65,773

	MURDER	FORCED RAPE	ROB- BERY	AGGRYTD ASSAULT	BUR- GLARY	LARCENY +$50	AUTO THEFT
70 CRIMES	7	8	40	238	977	612	226
RATE PER 100,000	10.6	12.2	60.8	361.9	1485.4	930.5	343.6
71 CRIMES	10	21	38	185	868	534	241
RATE PER 100,000	15.2	31.9	57.8	281.3	1319.7	811.9	366.4

RATIO FOR 2 YEAR PERIOD   1 CRIME PER   32.8 PEOPLE

RANKING   147

TYLER, TEXAS

POPULATION   57,770

	MURDER	FORCED RAPE	ROB- BERY	AGGRVTD ASSAULT	BUR- GLARY	LARCENY +$50	AUTO THEFT
70 CRIMES	6	28	20	179	722	630	173
RATE PER 100,000	10.4	48.5	34.6	309.8	1249.8	1090.5	299.5
71 CRIMES	8	19	22	202	669	584	154
RATE PER 100,000	13.8	32.9	38.1	349.7	1158.0	1010.9	266.6

RATIO FOR 2 YEAR PERIOD   1 CRIME PER   33.8 PEOPLE

RANKING   137

UNION CITY, NEW JERSEY

POPULATION   58,537

	MURDER	FORCED RAPE	ROB- BERY	AGGRYTD ASSAULT	BUR- GLARY	LARCENY +$50	AUTO THEFT
70 CRIMES	2	5	35	38	742	228	532
RATE PER 100,000	3.4	8.5	59.8	64.9	1267.6	389.5	908.8
71 CRIMES	5	5	50	31	769	364	542
RATE PER 100,000	8.5	8.5	85.4	53.0	1313.7	621.8	925.9

RATIO FOR 2 YEAR PERIOD   1 CRIME PER   34.9 PEOPLE

RANKING   130

UTICA, NEW YORK

POPULATION   91,611

	MURDER	FORCED RAPE	ROB- BERY	AGGRYTD ASSAULT	BUR- GLARY	LARCENY +$50	AUTO THEFT
70 CRIMES	2	3	64	21	356	162	135
RATE PER 100,000	2.2	3.3	69.9	22.9	388.6	176.8	147.4
71 CRIMES	2	11	72	26	419	182	121
RATE PER 100,000	2.2	12.0	78.6	28.4	457.4	198.7	132.1

RATIO FOR 2 YEAR PERIOD   1 CRIME PER   116.2 PEOPLE

RANKING   4

VALLEJO,CALIFORNIA

POPULATION   66,733

	MURDER	FORCED RAPE	ROB- BERY	AGGRYTD ASSAULT	BUR- GLARY	LARCENY +$50	AUTO THEFT
70 CRIMES	3	10	114	80	1,391	1,174	409
RATE PER 100,000	4.5	15.0	170.8	119.9	2084.4	1759.2	612.9
71 CRIMES	8	15	173	95	1,385	1,480	498
RATE PER 100,000	12.0	22.5	259.2	142.4	2075.4	2217.8	746.3

RATIO FOR 2 YEAR PERIOD   1 CRIME PER   19.5 PEOPLE

RANKING   320

VENTURA(SAN BUENAVENTURA),CALIFORNIA

POPULATION   55,797

	MURDER	FORCED RAPE	ROB- BERY	AGGRYTD ASSAULT	BUR- GLARY	LARCENY +$50	AUTO THEFT
70 CRIMES	1	10	28	42	813	1,125	197
RATE PER 100,000	1.8	17.9	50.2	75.3	1457.1	2016.2	353.1
71 CRIMES	1	20	42	50	1,011	1,389	277
RATE PER 100,000	1.8	35.8	75.3	89.6	1811.9	2489.4	496.4

RATIO FOR 2 YEAR PERIOD   1 CRIME PER   22.2 PEOPLE

RANKING   285

VIRGINIA BEACH,VIRGINIA

POPULATION   172,106

	MURDER	FORCED RAPE	ROB- BERY	AGGRYTD ASSAULT	BUR- GLARY	LARCENY +$50	AUTO THEFT
70 CRIMES	11	24	47	191	946	2,902	297
RATE PER 100,000	6.4	13.9	27.3	111.0	549.7	1686.2	172.6
71 CRIMES	5	28	63	192	1,205	2,495	206
RATE PER 100,000	2.9	16.3	36.6	111.6	700.1	1449.7	119.7

RATIO FOR 2 YEAR PERIOD   1 CRIME PER   39.9 PEOPLE

RANKING   102

WACO,TEXAS

POPULATION   95,326

	MURDER	FORCED RAPE	ROB- BERY	AGGRYTD ASSAULT	BUR- GLARY	LARCENY +$50	AUTO THEFT
70 CRIMES	9	23	155	277	1,815	1,171	322
RATE PER 100,000	9.4	24.1	162.6	290.6	1904.0	1228.4	337.8
71 CRIMES	21	37	122	449	1,932	1,247	324
RATE PER 100,000	22.0	38.8	128.0	471.0	2026.7	1308.1	339.9

RATIO FOR 2 YEAR PERIOD   1 CRIME   PER   24.1 PEOPLE

RANKING   261

WALTHAM,MASSACHUSETTS

POPULATION   61,582

	MURDER	FORCED RAPE	ROB- BERY	AGGRYTD ASSAULT	BUR- GLARY	LARCENY +$50	AUTO THEFT
70 CRIMES	1	1	6	38	593	328	302
RATE PER 100,000	1.6	1.6	9.7	61.7	962.9	532.6	490.4
71 CRIMES	2	1	32	68	503	334	304
RATE PER 100,000	3.2	1.6	52.0	110.4	816.8	542.4	493.7

RATIO FOR 2 YEAR PERIOD   1 CRIME   PER   49.0 PEOPLE

RANKING   74

WARREN,MICHIGAN

POPULATION   179,260

	MURDER	FORCED RAPE	ROB- BERY	AGGRYTD ASSAULT	BUR- GLARY	LARCENY +$50	AUTO THEFT
70 CRIMES	3	23	201	231	1,670	2,356	773
RATE PER 100,000	1.7	12.8	112.1	128.9	931.6	1314.3	431.2
71 CRIMES	2	37	241	199	1,902	2,644	849
RATE PER 100,000	1.1	20.6	134.4	111.0	1061.0	1475.0	473.6

RATIO FOR 2 YEAR PERIOD   1 CRIME   PER   32.2 PEOPLE

RANKING   157

WARREN,OHIO

POPULATION 63,494

70 CRIMES	MURDER	FORCED RAPE	ROB- BERY	AGGRYTD ASSAULT	BUR- GLARY	LARCENY +$50	AUTO THEFT
	4	7	114	129	770	850	248
RATE PER 100,000	6.3	11.0	179.5	203.2	1212.7	1338.7	390.6
71 CRIMES	6	11	92	67	690	851	233
RATE PER 100,000	9.4	17.3	144.9	105.5	1086.7	1340.3	367.0

RATIO FOR 2 YEAR PERIOD 1 CRIME PER 31.1 PEOPLE

RANKING 167

WARWICK,RHODE ISLAND

POPULATION 83,694

70 CRIMES	MURDER	FORCED RAPE	ROB- BERY	AGGRYTD ASSAULT	BUR- GLARY	LARCENY +$50	AUTO THEFT
		3	8	53	517	1,333	447
RATE PER 100,000	0.0	3.6	9.6	63.3	617.7	1592.7	534.1
71 CRIMES	2	2	11	53	866	1,663	668
RATE PER 100,000	2.4	2.4	13.1	63.3	1034.7	1987.0	798.1

RATIO FOR 2 YEAR PERIOD 1 CRIME PER 29.7 PEOPLE

RANKING 192

WASHINGTON,D.C.

POPULATION 756,510

70 CRIMES	MURDER	FORCED RAPE	ROB- BERY	AGGRYTD ASSAULT	BUR- GLARY	LARCENY +$50	AUTO THEFT
	221	313	11,816	4,089	22,348	9,414	11,110
RATE PER 100,000	29.2	41.4	1561.9	540.5	2954.1	1244.4	1468.6
71 CRIMES	275	615	11,222	3,972	18,818	7,622	8,732
RATE PER 100,000	36.4	81.3	1483.4	525.0	2487.5	1007.5	1154.2

RATIO FOR 2 YEAR PERIOD 1 CRIME PER 13.6 PEOPLE

RANKING 384

WATERBURY,CONNECTICUT

POPULATION   108,033

	MURDER	FORCED RAPE	ROB- BERY	AGGRYTD ASSAULT	BUR- GLARY	LARCENY +$50	AUTO THEFT
70 CRIMES	5	5	125	111	1,390	890	810
RATE PER 100,000	4.6	4.6	115.7	102.7	1286.6	823.8	749.8
71 CRIMES	5	10	175	128	1,499	960	1,110
RATE PER 100,000	4.6	9.3	162.0	118.5	1387.5	888.6	1027.5

RATIO FOR 2 YEAR PERIOD   1 CRIME PER   29.9 PEOPLE

RANKING   190

WATERLOO,IOWA

POPULATION   75,533

	MURDER	FORCED RAPE	ROB- BERY	AGGRYTD ASSAULT	BUR- GLARY	LARCENY +$50	AUTO THEFT
70 CRIMES	4	14	84	157	553	759	159
RATE PER 100,000	5.3	18.5	111.2	207.9	732.1	1004.9	210.5
71 CRIMES	4	14	80	78	512	825	152
RATE PER 100,000	5.3	18.5	105.9	103.3	677.8	1092.2	201.2

RATIO FOR 2 YEAR PERIOD   1 CRIME PER   44.4 PEOPLE

RANKING   89

WAUKEGAN,ILLINOIS

POPULATION   65,269

	MURDER	FORCED RAPE	ROB- BERY	AGGRYTD ASSAULT	BUR- GLARY	LARCENY +$50	AUTO THEFT
70 CRIMES	7	13	160	96	746	863	341
RATE PER 100,000	10.7	19.9	245.1	147.1	1143.0	1322.2	522.5
71 CRIMES	2	15	148	160	827	1,497	265
RATE PER 100,000	3.1	23.0	226.8	245.1	1267.1	2293.6	406.0

RATIO FOR 2 YEAR PERIOD   1 CRIME PER   25.3 PEOPLE

RANKING   246

WAUWATOSA,WISCONSIN

POPULATION   58,676

	MURDER	FORCED RAPE	ROB- BERY	AGGRYTD ASSAULT	BUR- GLARY	LARCENY +$50	AUTO THEFT
70 CRIMES		3	17	13	318	552	88
RATE PER 100,000	0.0	5.1	29.0	22.2	542.0	940.8	150.0
71 CRIMES		1	19	14	290	673	106
RATE PER 100,000	0.0	1.7	32.4	23.9	494.2	1147.0	180.7

RATIO FOR 2 YEAR PERIOD   1 CRIME PER   56.0 PEOPLE

RANKING   49

WEST ALLIS,WISCONSIN

POPULATION   71,723

	MURDER	FORCED RAPE	ROB- BERY	AGGRYTD ASSAULT	BUR- GLARY	LARCENY +$50	AUTO THEFT
70 CRIMES		4	15	11	274	598	95
RATE PER 100,000	0.0	5.6	20.9	15.3	382.0	833.8	132.5
71 CRIMES		4	30	16	294	646	174
RATE PER 100,000	0.0	5.6	41.8	22.3	409.9	900.7	242.6

RATIO FOR 2 YEAR PERIOD   1 CRIME PER   66.3 PEOPLE

RANKING   25

WEST COVINA,CALIFORNIA

POPULATION   68,034

	MURDER	FORCED RAPE	ROB- BERY	AGGRYTD ASSAULT	BUR- GLARY	LARCENY +$50	AUTO THEFT
70 CRIMES	1	9	57	63	853	1,147	280
RATE PER 100,000	1.5	13.2	83.8	92.6	1253.8	1685.9	411.6
71 CRIMES	2	9	64	87	1,021	1,356	323
RATE PER 100,000	2.9	13.2	94.1	127.9	1500.7	1993.1	474.8

RATIO FOR 2 YEAR PERIOD   1 CRIME PER   25.8 PEOPLE

RANKING   237

WEST HARTFORD,CONNECTICUT

POPULATION   68,031

	MURDER	FORCED RAPE	ROB- BERY	AGGRYTD ASSAULT	BUR- GLARY	LARCENY +$50	AUTO THEFT
70 CRIMES		2	12	22	514	333	170
RATE PER 100,000	0.0	2.9	17.6	32.3	755.5	489.5	249.9
71 CRIMES	1	3	9	34	370	179	145
RATE PER 100,000	1.5	4.4	13.2	50.0	543.9	263.1	213.1

RATIO FOR 2 YEAR PERIOD   1 CRIME PER   75.8 PEOPLE

RANKING   12

WEST HAVEN,CONNECTICUT

POPULATION   52,851

	MURDER	FORCED RAPE	ROB- BERY	AGGRYTD ASSAULT	BUR- GLARY	LARCENY +$50	AUTO THEFT
70 CRIMES		6	12	13	394	387	237
RATE PER 100,000	0.0	11.4	22.7	24.6	745.5	732.2	448.4
71 CRIMES	1	1	9	24	343	364	270
RATE PER 100,000	1.9	1.9	17.0	45.4	649.0	688.7	510.9

RATIO FOR 2 YEAR PERIOD   1 CRIME PER   51.2 PEOPLE

RANKING   64

WEST PALM BEACH,FLORIDA

POPULATION   57,375

	MURDER	FORCED RAPE	ROB- BERY	AGGRYTD ASSAULT	BUR- GLARY	LARCENY +$50	AUTO THEFT
70 CRIMES	12	10	146	159	1,160	934	258
RATE PER 100,000	20.9	17.4	254.5	277.1	2021.8	1627.9	449.7
71 CRIMES	17	15	173	152	1,585	1,053	245
RATE PER 100,000	29.6	26.1	301.5	264.9	2762.5	1835.3	427.0

RATIO FOR 2 YEAR PERIOD   1 CRIME PER   19.3 PEOPLE

RANKING   322

WESTLAND,MICHIGAN

POPULATION   86,749

	MURDER	FORCED RAPE	ROB-BERY	AGGRYTD ASSAULT	BUR-GLARY	LARCENY +$50	AUTO THEFT
70 CRIMES							
RATE PER 100,000							
71 CRIMES	3	12	54	99	747	919	365
RATE PER 100,000	3.5	13.8	62.2	114.1	861.1	1059.4	420.8

RATIO FOR 2 YEAR PERIOD   1 CRIME PER   78.8 PEOPLE

RANKING   10

WESTMINSTER,CALIFORNIA

POPULATION   59,865

	MURDER	FORCED RAPE	ROB-BERY	AGGRYTD ASSAULT	BUR-GLARY	LARCENY +$50	AUTO THEFT
70 CRIMES		16	56	48	1,044	667	258
RATE PER 100,000	0.0	26.7	93.5	80.2	1743.9	1114.2	431.0
71 CRIMES	1	9	85	68	1,259	898	222
RATE PER 100,000	1.7	15.0	142.0	113.6	2103.1	1500.0	370.8

RATIO FOR 2 YEAR PERIOD   1 CRIME PER   25.8 PEOPLE

RANKING   236

WEYMOUTH,MASSACHUSETTS

POPULATION   54,610

	MURDER	FORCED RAPE	ROB-BERY	AGGRYTD ASSAULT	BUR-GLARY	LARCENY +$50	AUTO THEFT
70 CRIMES			8	10	131	84	86
RATE PER 100,000	0.0	0.0	14.6	18.3	239.9	153.8	157.5
71 CRIMES		1	19	20	273	144	148
RATE PER 100,000	0.0	1.8	34.8	36.6	499.9	263.7	271.0

RATIO FOR 2 YEAR PERIOD   1 CRIME PER   118.2 PEOPLE

RANKING   3

298

WHITE PLAINS, NEW YORK

POPULATION 50,220

	MURDER	FORCED RAPE	ROB-BERY	AGGRYTD ASSAULT	BUR-GLARY	LARCENY +$50	AUTO THEFT
70 CRIMES	2	2	99	114	430	839	170
RATE PER 100,000	4.0	4.0	197.1	227.0	856.2	1670.6	338.5
71 CRIMES	2	7	80	129	443	974	175
RATE PER 100,000	4.0	13.9	159.3	256.9	882.1	1939.5	348.5

RATIO FOR 2 YEAR PERIOD   1 CRIME PER   28.9 PEOPLE

RANKING   203

WHITTIER, CALIFORNIA

POPULATION 72,863

	MURDER	FORCED RAPE	ROB-BERY	AGGRYTD ASSAULT	BUR-GLARY	LARCENY +$50	AUTO THEFT
70 CRIMES	2	11	70	73	948	831	251
RATE PER 100,000	2.7	15.1	96.1	100.2	1301.1	1140.5	344.5
71 CRIMES	1	16	63	85	1,108	997	276
RATE PER 100,000	1.4	22.0	86.5	116.7	1520.7	1368.3	378.8

RATIO FOR 2 YEAR PERIOD   1 CRIME PER   30.7 PEOPLE

RANKING   176

WICHITA, KANSAS

POPULATION 276,554

	MURDER	FORCED RAPE	ROB-BERY	AGGRYTD ASSAULT	BUR-GLARY	LARCENY +$50	AUTO THEFT
70 CRIMES	18	51	484	417	4,444	4,011	1,672
RATE PER 100,000	6.5	18.4	175.0	150.8	1606.9	1450.3	604.6
71 CRIMES	14	57	374	400	4,388	3,829	1,627
RATE PER 100,000	5.1	20.6	135.2	144.6	1586.7	1384.5	588.3

RATIO FOR 2 YEAR PERIOD   1 CRIME PER   25.3 PEOPLE

RANKING   248

WICHITA FALLS,TEXAS

POPULATION   97,564

	MURDER	FORCED RAPE	ROB- BERY	AGGRYTD ASSAULT	BUR- GLARY	LARCENY +$50	AUTO THEFT
70 CRIMES	6	5	55	119	686	453	234
RATE PER 100,000	6.1	5.1	56.4	122.0	703.1	464.3	239.8
71 CRIMES	7	11	78	135	621	579	232
RATE PER 100,000	7.2	11.3	79.9	138.4	636.5	593.5	237.8

RATIO FOR 2 YEAR PERIOD   1 CRIME PER   60.5 PEOPLE

RANKING   36

WILKES-BARRE,PENNSYLVANIA

POPULATION   58,856

	MURDER	FORCED RAPE	ROB- BERY	AGGRYTD ASSAULT	BUR- GLARY	LARCENY +$50	AUTO THEFT
70 CRIMES		2	6	19	229	350	179
RATE PER 100,000	0.0	3.4	10.2	32.3	389.1	594.7	304.1
71 CRIMES	1	3	19	2	246	532	193
RATE PER 100,000	1.7	5.1	32.3	3.4	418.0	903.9	327.9

RATIO FOR 2 YEAR PERIOD   1 CRIME PER   66.0 PEOPLE

RANKING   26

WILMINGTON,DELAWARE

POPULATION   80,386

	MURDER	FORCED RAPE	ROB- BERY	AGGRYTD ASSAULT	BUR- GLARY	LARCENY +$50	AUTO THEFT
70 CRIMES	18	17	393	90	2,033	1,601	1,838
RATE PER 100,000	22.4	21.1	488.9	112.0	2529.0	1991.6	2286.5
71 CRIMES	15	24	458	118	2,982	1,590	1,651
RATE PER 100,000	18.7	29.9	569.8	146.8	3709.6	1978.0	2053.8

RATIO FOR 2 YEAR PERIOD   1 CRIME PER   12.5 PEOPLE

RANKING   388

WINSTON-SALEM, NORTH CAROLINA

POPULATION   132,913

	MURDER	FORCED RAPE	ROB-BERY	AGGRYTD ASSAULT	BUR-GLARY	LARCENY +$50	AUTO THEFT
70 CRIMES	26	35	204	863	2,012	1,722	399
RATE PER 100,000	19.6	26.3	153.5	649.3	1513.8	1295.6	300.2
71 CRIMES	33	43	199	1,019	2,242	1,459	408
RATE PER 100,000	24.8	32.4	149.7	766.7	1686.8	1097.7	307.0

RATIO FOR 2 YEAR PERIOD   1 CRIME PER   24.9 PEOPLE

RANKING   254

WORCESTER, MASSACHUSETTS

POPULATION   176,572

	MURDER	FORCED RAPE	ROB-BERY	AGGRYTD ASSAULT	BUR-GLARY	LARCENY +$50	AUTO THEFT
70 CRIMES	7	16	369	131	4,612	2,250	4,011
RATE PER 100,000	4.0	9.1	209.0	74.2	2612.0	1274.3	2271.6
71 CRIMES	12	33	452	207	5,110	2,356	4,389
RATE PER 100,000	6.8	18.7	256.0	117.2	2894.0	1334.3	2485.7

RATIO FOR 2 YEAR PERIOD   1 CRIME PER   14.7 PEOPLE

RANKING   378

WYOMING, MICHIGAN

POPULATION   56,560

	MURDER	FORCED RAPE	ROB-BERY	AGGRYTD ASSAULT	BUR-GLARY	LARCENY +$50	AUTO THEFT
70 CRIMES	1	4	18	27	363	648	109
RATE PER 100,000	1.8	7.1	31.8	47.7	641.8	1145.7	192.7
71 CRIMES	1	12	18	39	389	579	97
RATE PER 100,000	1.8	21.2	31.8	69.0	687.8	1023.7	171.5

RATIO FOR 2 YEAR PERIOD   1 CRIME PER   49.0 PEOPLE

RANKING   73

YONKERS,NEW YORK

POPULATION   204,370

	MURDER	FORCED RAPE	ROB-BERY	AGGRYTD ASSAULT	BUR-GLARY	LARCENY +$50	AUTO THEFT
70 CRIMES	6	4	364	148	2,089	2,314	1,552
RATE PER 100,000	2.9	2.0	178.1	72.4	1022.2	1132.3	759.4
71 CRIMES	11	9	485	196	2,507	2,287	1,757
RATE PER 100,000	5.4	4.4	237.3	95.9	1226.7	1119.0	859.7

RATIO FOR 2 YEAR PERIOD   1 CRIME   PER   29.7 PEOPLE

RANKING   191

YORK,PENNSYLVANIA

POPULATION   50,335

	MURDER	FORCED RAPE	ROB-BERY	AGGRYTD ASSAULT	BUR-GLARY	LARCENY +$50	AUTO THEFT
70 CRIMES	3	14	219	113	644	419	246
RATE PER 100,000	6.0	27.8	435.1	224.5	1279.4	832.4	488.7
71 CRIMES	9	16	168	49	622	463	194
RATE PER 100,000	17.9	31.8	333.8	97.3	1235.7	919.8	385.4

RATIO FOR 2 YEAR PERIOD   1 CRIME   PER   31.6 PEOPLE

RANKING   159

YOUNGSTOWN,OHIO

POPULATION   139,788

	MURDER	FORCED RAPE	ROB-BERY	AGGRYTD ASSAULT	BUR-GLARY	LARCENY +$50	AUTO THEFT
70 CRIMES	25	31	440	223	2,575	935	1,671
RATE PER 100,000	17.9	22.2	314.8	159.5	1842.1	668.9	1195.4
71 CRIMES	23	36	354	300	2,700	691	1,001
RATE PER 100,000	16.5	25.8	253.2	214.6	1931.5	494.3	716.1

RATIO FOR 2 YEAR PERIOD   1 CRIME   PER   25.4 PEOPLE

RANKING   245